The Rules of Sociological Method

The Rules of Sociological Method

And Selected Texts on Sociology and Its Method

EMILE DURKHEIM

Edited and with a new introduction by Steven Lukes

Translation by W. D. Halls

FREE PRESS

New York   London   Toronto   Sydney   New Delhi

*f*P

Free Press
An Imprint of Simon & Schuster, Inc.
1230 Avenue of the Americas
New York, NY 10020

This Free Press trade paperback edition February 2014

FREE PRESS and colophon are trademarks of Simon & Schuster, Inc.

For information about special discounts for bulk purchases,
please contact Simon & Schuster Special Sales at 1-866-506-1949
or business@simonandschuster.com.

The Simon & Schuster Speakers Bureau can bring authors to your
live event. For more information or to book an event contact the
Simon & Schuster Speakers Bureau at 1-866-248-3049 or visit our
website at www.simonspeakers.com.

Cover design by Jason Heuer

Manufactured in the United States of America

10 9 8 7 6 5 4 3 2 1

ISBN 978-1-4767-4972-3
ISBN 978-1-4391-1837-5 (ebook)

Contents

Preface to This Edition

The story of English translations of Durkheim's major works has not been an especially happy one. The earliest translations—of *Elementary Forms of Religious Life* (Durkheim 1915), *The Division of Labor in Society* (Durkheim 1933) and *The Rules of Sociological Method* (Durkheim 1938)—were defective, sometimes seriously so.[1] Of course there is always room for dispute over what constitutes success in translation, but these translations contained just too many straightforward errors, slips and misunderstandings to be counted as reliable (which did not prevent their being influential upon, and sometimes misleading, generations of Anglophone students and scholars). The situation in all three cases has much improved, with Karen Fields's excellent rendering of *Elementary Forms* in 1995, together with a wonderfully insightful and reflective introduction to that great work, and with the publication, in 1982 and 1984 respectively, of W. D. Halls's translations of *The Rules* and *The Division*. But perfection in translation is an inherently elusive goal, in part because of the need for innumerable contestable decisions[2] (should one, for instance, respect the author's unclarities and ambiguities or help the reader by plumping for precision?) and in part because the barriers separating a past author from present readers tend to rise up with time and generational change (so should the translator try to lower them?).

The present edition of *The Rules* offers the reader a revised version of that published in 1982. It includes a chronology of Durkheim's life and works and suggestions for further reading. The revisions to the translation are intended to attain maximum precision, both linguistic and conceptual, where the English can be rendered closer to the French, which sometimes means strengthening and sometimes weakening the earlier renderings of what Durkheim wrote. They also aim at consistency of usage of key terms within the text. And they seek fidelity to Durkheim's intentions—what he was meaning to say, insofar as this is ascertainable—which sometimes means opting for vagueness and ambiguity and even for anachronism where implicit reference is made to a past thinker or school of thought. I want here to acknowledge the invaluable assistance of Raphaelle Thery, who meticulously checked the entire translation. The original French volume of *Les règles de la méthode sociologique* (second edition), published in 1901, which is translated here, contained, according to the convention of the time, an extended table of contents. This is included

vii

here, following the text of the book, in order further to aid readers in navigating the text.

Durkheim's intentions were in the process of development and it is important to note that *The Rules* is a transitional work. As Durkheim himself notes, in his letter to the *Revue néo-scolastique* responding to Simon Deploige, included here, it was precisely in 1895, when *The Rules* was published as a book, that he found "a means of tackling sociologically the study of religion" (199). That year, he wrote, "marked a watershed in my thinking," so much so that "all my previous research had to be started all over again so as to be harmonized with these new views." That is one reason for the inclusion of Durkheim's subsequent methodological reflections, in the form of debates with fellow scholars from neighboring disciplines, short notes and letters, so that the enterprising reader can trace continuities and changes in relation to the positions taken in the text of *The Rules*. For guidance in this such a reader should find helpful Durkheim's Preface to the second edition of the book, published in 1901, in which he seeks to defend those positions—or better, perhaps, reformulate them in order to render them, or so at least he thought, more defensible.

What should be evident from these texts—from Durkheim's combative manifesto for sociology, from the objections of his numerous critics and from his energetic responses to these over time—is that they center on issues that are still very much alive within sociology and, more widely, in the social sciences at large. Here the reader will find debated a range of questions to which there are still today no settled, agreed-upon answers. Is the doctrine of "methodological individualism" successfully refuted by what is now called the concept of "emergence"?[3] What kind and degree of objectivity should social scientists seek to obtain (see Daston and Galison 2008)? How are theoretical concepts to be "operationalized" and thereby linked to observation? What scientific sense, if any, can be made of the distinction between "the normal" and "the pathological" (see Canguilhem 1991)? Does the concept of pathology have a place in social science and social theory and how does it relate to "critique" and the practice of social and political criticism (see Honneth 2009)? In what ways are biological accounts of evolution relevant to the understanding of social and cultural evolution (see Runciman 2000 and 2009)? How are we to construct typologies of, and classify, societies, groups, movements, institutions and organizations? How should social scientists think about causation and what counts as explanation (see Reed 2011)? Is Durkheim right to find fruitful what he takes to be the Marxist idea that "social life must be explained not by the conception formed of it by those who participate in it, but by the profound causes which escape their consciousness" (126)?[4] And how are we to decide when the evidence confirms and when it decisively refutes theories in the social sciences?

Notes

1. The worst example is the omission from the Solovay and Mueller translation of *The Rules* (Durkheim 1938) of an entire paragraph, about structural or "morphological" facts forming "the substratum of collective life," that is essential to the argument of the first chapter of *The Rules* and indeed, as I argue here in the Introduction, to understanding the development of Durkheim's thought. For a list of the more egregious mistranslations in *The Rules* and *The Division*, see appendix to Lukes 1968. For discussions of Swain's translation of *Elementary Forms* see Fields's introduction to Durkheim 1995 and Fields 2005. For a general discussion of these issues see Lukes 2012.

2. The situation regarding Durkheim's *Suicide* differs from that of the other three works cited. Here the earlier translation (Durkheim 1951) is adequate and serviceable, whereas the new translation, though generally accurate and easy to read, makes bad decisions, translating *égoisme* throughout as "egotism," which suggests selfishness, whereas Durkheim intended isolation and detachment, which "egoism" (used in the earlier translation) allows. It also specifies the meaning of Durkheim's *société* –a term he notoriously left undefined—in different ways at different points, thereby masking Durkheim's uncertainty and unclarity as to the meaning of this crucial word.

3. For a forceful present-day defense of the concept of emergence, advancing a relational theory of emergent properties as applicable to the analysis of the social world, see Elder-Vass 2010.

4. See the remarkable book by John Levi Martin (2011), which sharply disputes this idea (citing Durkheim's endorsement of it on p. 143), in the service of a broader argument which contests the very idea, prevalent in the social sciences, that "the most important sort of explanation is one that comes in the form of a third-person answer to a why question" (p. 24). For Levi Martin the social sciences have gone seriously astray by inheriting from Freud and from Durkheim inappropriate and untenable conceptions of causation and explanation.

References

Canguilhem, Georges 1991. *The Normal and the Pathological*. Translated by Catherine R. Fawcett with an Introduction by Michel Foucault. Brooklyn, NY: Zone Books (first published in French in 1943 and a fuller version in 1966).

Daston, Lorraine and Galison, Peter 2008. *Objectivity*. Brooklyn, NY: Zone Books.

Durkheim, Emile 1915. *Elementary Forms of the Religious Life: A Study in Religious Sociology*. Translated by J. W. Swain. London: Allen and Unwin; New York: Macmillan.

Durkheim, Emile 1933. *The Division of Labor in Society*. Translated by G. Simpson. New York: Macmillan.

Durkheim, Emile 1938. *The Rules of Sociological Method*. Translated by S. A. Solovay and J. H. Mueller and edited with an introduction by G. E. G. Caitlin. Chicago: Chicago University Press, republished 1950 by Glencoe, IL: Free Press of Glencoe.

Durkheim, Emile 1951. *Suicide: A Study in Sociology*. Translated by J. A. Spaulding and G. Simpson. Glencoe, IL: Free Press of Glencoe and London: Routledge & Kegan Paul.

Durkheim, Emile 1995. *Elementary Forms of Religious Life*. Translated with an Introduction by Karen Fields. New York: The Free Press.

Durkheim, Emile 2006. *On Suicide*. Translated by Robin Buss with an Introduction by Richard Sennett and Notes by Alexander Riley. Harmondsworth and New York: Penguin Books.

Elder-Vass, Dave 2010. *The Causal Power of Social Structures: Emergence, Structure and Agency*. Cambridge and New York: Cambridge University Press.

Fields, Karen E. 2005. "What difference does translation make? *Les formes élémentaires de la vie religieuse* in French and English" in Jeffrey C. Alexander and Philip Smith (eds.), *The Cambridge Companion to Durkheim*. Cambridge and New York: Cambridge University Press: 160–180.

Honneth, Axel 2009. *Pathologies of Reason: On the Legacy of Critical Theory*. Translated by James Ingram. New York: Columbia University Press.

Lukes, Steven 1968. *Emile Durkheim: An Intellectual Biography*. Thesis presented for the Degree of Doctor of Philosophy deposited at the Bodleian Library, Oxford, 2 vols.

Lukes, Steven 2012. "On Translating Durkheim" in Martin J. Burke and Melvin Richter (eds.), *Why Concepts Matter: Translating Social and Political Thought*, Leiden and Boston: Brill.

Martin, John Levi 2011. *The Explanation of Social Action*. New York: Oxford University Press.

Reed, Isaac Ariail 2011. *Interpretation and Social Knowledge: On the Use of Theory in the Human Sciences*. Chicago, IL: University of Chicago Press.

Runciman, W. G. 2000. *The Social Animal*. Ann Arbor, MI: University of Michigan Press.

Runciman, W. G. 2009. *The Theory of Cultural and Social Selection*. Cambridge and New York: Cambridge University Press.

Introduction to This Edition

Steven Lukes

Emile Durkheim first published *The Rules of Sociological Method* as a series of articles in a philosophical journal and then as a book in 1895. This then appeared in a second edition in 1901 with a new preface in which Durkheim robustly responded to critics. The present volume is a newly revised translation of that edition, together with various later texts in which he clarified some of his views, modified others, and defended his conception of sociology's relations to other disciplines. In what follows we shall first place *The Rules* in its historical context—intellectual and academic, moral and political—and within the trajectory of Durkheim's thought, giving some indications of its relation to his other major works. We shall then comment on the arguments set out in its six short chapters, identifying key features of present-day interest. Along the way we shall indicate potential conceptual and linguistic blocks, deriving from their context, that stand in the way of contemporary readers understanding the import of Durkheim's arguments and thus the many ways in which they continue to contribute to the understanding of live issues and debates among social scientists today.

The text in context

Most obviously, this is a manifesto for sociology, intended to establish its credentials as a natural science, to provide a rationale and guiding principles for future research. It was partly directed at fellow scholars and future collaborators.[1] Durkheim had been appointed to teach sociology at Bordeaux and had recently published *The Division of Labor in Society* (1893). He was soon to publish *Suicide* (1897) and in the following year began the editorship of *L'Année sociologique*. The twelve volumes (1898–1913) of *L'Année* contain a rich store of reviews of world social science literature, as well as monographs by himself and the young scholars he grouped around that remarkable journal. The goal was that they would engage in specialized studies that would ultimately transform the various social sciences into systematically organized branches of a unified social science. These would be ever more deeply penetrated by "the sociological idea," which implied that "social facts are solidly linked to each other and above all must be treated as natural phenomena, subject to necessary laws" (146). Social phenomena were natural and "only distinguishable from other phenomena by virtue of their greater complexity" (102); and yet sociology was to be "a distinct and autonomous science" (113), with its own field of study, namely "social facts." This field was not to be "confused with that of biology and psychology" (20), though he also claimed that sociology was "a *special* psychology, having its own subject matter and a distinctive method" (195). It was also "independent of all philosophy"(111). The point was not to provide a philosophical view of "the nature of social reality" but to "indicate how, by outward signs, it is possible to identify the facts that the science must deal with, so that the social scientist may learn how to pick out their location and not to confuse them with other facts" (13). It should also indicate how social phenomena are classified, or sorted into types, what should constitute a sociological explanation and how proposed explanations were to be confirmed and disconfirmed.

But *The Rules* was also forthrightly addressed to a wider audience, offering a radically new vision of social science suitable for the times. Here it met with scepticism and hostility. It made almost no reference to alternative and rival contemporary practitioners of sociology and related social sciences, with the exception of Durkheim's *bêtes noires,* Herbert Spencer and Gabriel Tarde,[2] whom he saw as perfectly exemplifying misconceptions to be eradicated because they failed to grant the shaping and constraining nature of social facts. A close reading of the text, however, shows it to contain a sharp critique of biological, and in particular racially based, determinism (88–9), a sustained attack on the individual-focused psychology of the time and a rejection of contemporary criminology's focus on the pathological criminal and on crime as a sickness for which punishment is the cure (64).

Its polemical strategy was, indeed, to challenge his readers at a fundamental level. The book's very title echoes Descartes' *Discourse on Method* and in its Preface Durkheim accepted the label of "rationalist." There is, he wrote, "nothing in reality that one may be justified in considering as radically refractory to human reason" (Durkheim 1961: 4, 291; see Schmaus 1994: 62). But, he insisted, his rationalism was *scientific*, its aim being to render human behavior intelligible though causal explanations that, in turn, yield "rules of action for the future." But this implied a firm rejection of the reliance of traditional French rationalism on introspection and deduction. The Cartesian insistence on clarity of thought was invaluable, especially "in this time of resurgent mysticism" (4), but, as he wrote elsewhere, "it will not be enough to turn oneself inward, to meditate internally and to make deductions." To discover the laws of human reality "one must observe it in the same way as we observe things in the external world, that is to say from outside; we must experiment, engage in induction, or if experimentation in the strict sense is practically impossible, we must find a way of setting up objective comparisons which can fulfill the same logical functions" (Durkheim 1977: 342 amended trs).

Hence his invocation of Copernicus, Galileo and Bacon and his injunction to discard "prenotions"—"what Bacon called *notions vulgares*, or *praenotiones*," or "*idola*"—which "distort the true appearance of things, but which we nevertheless mistake for the things themselves" (31). Hence his distrust of common sense, of people's self-understandings and interpretations of their world, and his readiness to embrace paradox. Hence too his acceptance, expressed in his only engagement with Marxist thought, of the "fruitful idea that social life must be explained not by the conception of it formed by those who participate in it, but by the profound causes which escape their consciousness" (126) (while firmly denying that they can be traced, "in the last resort, to the state of industrial technology" and that "the economic factor" is "the mainspring of progress" (127)). He also insisted on this idea in his rather fierce debate with the historian Charles Seignobos (160–173). And hence his repeated insistence on replacing what he called "ideological analysis," by which he meant speculation based on our ideas about realities, with "a science which deals with realities" through systematic observation and explanations subjected to testing by confrontation with evidence. To philosophize, he once told a doctoral candidate, "is to think what one wants" (cited in Lukes 1972: 644).

It was Durkheim's account of these realities—his "basic principle, that of the objective reality of social facts" upon which "everything rests, and everything comes back to it" (15)—that evoked the considerable hostility that greeted the text's publication, both in France and abroad. The general complaint was that Durkheim was engaging in bad social ontology. Thus Tarde denounced "the ontological illusion of M. Durkheim" ("Are we going," he asked, "to return to the realism of the Middle Ages?'), Lucien Herr similarly accused him of resurrecting "the phantom of the old realist metaphysics," Simon Deploige accused Durkheim of importing German metaphysical ideas into French thought and James Tufts in the United States enlisted against him John Stuart Mill's observation that "Men are not, when brought together, converted into another kind of substance" (all cited in Lukes 1972: 306, 315, 314). Most reviews of the book were unfavorable, denouncing it for both its "social realism" and its "*chosisme*," and in the 1901 Preface Durkheim sought to address these "misunderstandings and confusion." Yet they have never gone away. In 1946 Jules Monnerot published a book entitled *Les faits sociaux ne sont pas des choses* (Monnerot 1946)[3] and, as we shall see, these issues have remained alive and controversial to this day.

But there was also a further and wider message conveyed by *The Rules* and its injunction to "treat social facts as things." At the center of

Durkheim's concerns was contributing to the educational reform program of the Third French Republic that sought to promote national solidarity through a curriculum based on science and secular ethics. That program would instruct future leaders and citizens, as the saying went, "*à l'école des choses*" (see Jones 1999, especially Ch. 4). He was also a Professor of Education, first in Bordeaux, then in Paris, teaching future schoolteachers, and he lectured on moral education and professional and civic ethics. His ideas came to exercise considerable influence over the French school system. He had visited Germany in the mid-1880s on a publicly funded mission to observe and draw lessons from the latest advances in social science there in the wake of France's defeat in the Franco-Prussian War. He returned impressed by what he saw as German scholars' "pronounced feeling for the collective life, for its reality and its advantages," their rejection of the notion of the abstract individual in general and their sense that the "real, concrete man changes with the physical and social milieu which surrounds him, and, quite naturally, morality changes with men . . . ." (Durkheim 1888: 337–8). The "science of social phenomena" was "still too underdeveloped to be taught in the lower grades" of France's schools (there history was more appropriate) but "to become attached to society, the child must feel in it something that is real, alive and powerful, which dominates the person and to which he owes the best of himself" (Durkheim 1961: 275). It is true, in short, to say that the central message of *The Rules* reflected Durkheim's "frustration with the normative vocabulary of Cartesian rationalism" and that it had "moral as well as methodological force" (Jones and Kibbee 1993: 167).

In the context of Durkheim's life's work, *The Rules* looks both backward and forward. The first chapter ends with two defining criteria of a social fact: first, that it is "*capable of exerting over the individual an external constraint*" and, second, that it be "*general over the whole of a given society whilst having an existence of its own, independent of its individual manifestations*" (27). Durkheim saw the second criterion as "simply another formulation of the first," since "if a mode of action existing outside the consciousness of individuals becomes general, it can only do so by exerting pressure upon them" (25). The first criterion harks back to what is sometimes called the "index thesis" in *The Division of Labor* (see Cotterrell 1999), namely, the idea that the law is an index of social solidarity and, in particular, that the kind of sanctions imposed on individuals when the law is violated reveal the nature of that solidarity (repressive sanctions indicating "mechanical" solidarity and restitutive sanctions "organic" solidarity). The second criterion looks forward to the use of statistics in *Suicide* to indicate the relative extent of society-wide normative integration and regulation and thus the extent to which "suicidogenic currents" (anomie, egoism, altruism, fatalism) are present that will lead to the "individual manifestations" of vulnerable, suicide-prone individuals killing themselves. These "currents" are "tendencies of the whole social body" which "by affecting individuals cause them to commit suicide" (Durkheim 1951: 300).

The first chapter of *The Rules* proposes that social facts exhibit a range extending from the most to the least "crystallized." At one end are the most "structural": "collective *ways of being*, namely, social facts of an 'anatomical' or morphological nature," constituting "the substratum of social life," such as

> the number and nature of the elementary parts which constitute society, the way in which they are articulated, the degree of coalescence they have attained, the distribution of the population over the earth's surface, the extent and nature of the network of communications, the design of dwellings, etc. (26)

Then there were institutionalized norms, which could be more or less formal—"legal and moral rules, religious dogmas, financial systems, etc."—"beliefs and practices already well established" whose existence depends on "a well defined social organization." And beyond these are other less or non-crystallized facts which "possess the same objectivity and ascendancy over the individual, which Durkheim called "social currents": "more lasting movements of opinion . . . constantly being produced around us" and beyond these, at the other extreme, "free currents of social life"—"transitory outbreaks," such as are generated "in a public gathering" in the form of "great waves of enthusiasm, indignation and pity" (22–3).

Durkheim saw all these as "constraining," as "exerting pressure on individuals," and critics have disputed this claim ever since, some observing that the meaning of "constraint" shifts across the various examples he gives (see Parsons 1937: 378–90; Lukes 1972: 8–15). Thus he cites the constraint exercised through the authority of legal and moral rules and conventions manifested via sanctions when violated, the need to follow rules to achieve goals, such as rules of "economic technique" or having to speak a given language to be understood, the causal influence of social structures, the psychological pressure of crowds and the impact of socialization and acculturation. One answer to these criticisms is to interpret him as using "external constraint" to indicate the causal power of what he came to call "collective representations" (about which more below) and took to be at work in all these cases; in other words, that "all social facts constrain individuals in the same way, through the social forces to which collective representations give rise" (Schmaus 1994: 48). Or, as Sawyer puts it, that for Durkheim "constraint" is a kind of "downward causation" where "social facts constrain individuals, but at the same time they emerge from the "actions and interactions of those very same individuals" (Sawyer 2002: 238).

What is clearly true is that his focus of interest shifted away from the domain of structural, "morphological" social facts. *The Division of*

Labor contains more than a hint of "morphological determinism": the purely "material" factors of population volume and density are accorded considerable weight in his account of the developing division of labor with the growth of cities, markets and social differentiation. This is even said to occur as if "mechanically" (Durkheim 2013: 211). Indeed, "states of consciousness" derive from "the way in which men, once they associate together, exert a reciprocal effect upon one another according to their number and proximity" (Durkheim 2013: 273; see esp. bk II ch. 3).

His central thesis there was that "the division of labor progresses the more individuals there are who are sufficiently in contact with one another to be able mutually to act and react upon one another. If we agree to call dynamic or moral density this drawing together and the active exchanges that result from it, we can say that the progress of the division of labor is in direct proportion to the moral or dynamic density of society" (Durkheim 2013: 202). In *The Rules* he renounces the claim made in the earlier book that material density is an index of moral density. Yet he still maintained that the "primary origin of social processes of any importance must be sought in the constitution of the inner social environment," namely the manner in which its "anatomical elements" are "arranged in space." This was what for several years he continued to call the "material substratum of society," the domain of geography and demography (153). And yet, already in *The Rules* he was writing that the "active factor," the "vital forces of society" were "moral," not material. Thus what counted was "moral concentration," not physical proximity, "ways of being" were merely "ways of acting that have been consolidated," and so, for instance, "[t]he type of dwelling imposed upon us is merely the way in which everyone around us and, in part, previous generations have customarily built their houses"(26). Geographical factors, he wrote in 1899, "play a part as elements in the constitution of the social substratum" but they are not "the most vital ones" (184).

Here we can see what was the constant object of Durkheim's sociology from beginning to end: the domain of the moral. It was rightly said of him that morality was "the center and end of his work" (Davy 1920: 71). To appreciate this we need to realize that "moral" in French has an extra meaning largely absent from its English usage, signifying what pertains to the mind (*esprit*) and thought (*pensée*) and contrasting with material (*matériel*) and physical (*physique*) and that for Durkheim this embraced not only thought but also emotion, not only beliefs but also "sentiments."[4] He characterized this domain of the moral differently at different stages. In *The Division of Labor* the focus was on "social solidarity," which, he wrote, "is a wholly moral phenomenon which by itself is not amenable to exact observation and especially not to measurement . . . we must therefore substitute for this internal datum, which escapes us, an external one which symbolizes it, and then study the former through the latter" (Durkheim

2013: 52). *Suicide* is, in essence, a study in social pathology: a diagnosis of the consequences of inadequate solidarity (anomie and egoism) and excessive solidarity (mainly "altruism") in contemporary and earlier societies. As we have seen, he used law to study solidarity in the former book and suicide statistics to study its pathologies in the latter.

From 1897 he began to call the components of the moral domain "collective representations" (*représentations collectives*) and set out his understanding of these in his paper on "Individual and Collective Representations" in 1898 (Durkheim 1953a; see Descombes 2000). Here too we should be aware of a distinctively French usage. *"Représentation,"* common among French philosophers of the time, has a meaning absent from the English word, being used as a generic term for mental states of all kinds (meaning both the mental act and what is present to the mind). Thus, in the 1901 Preface he writes of studying, by "comparing mythical themes, legends and popular traditions, and languages, how social representations are attracted to or exclude each other" (12). It was in 1895, as he later explained in a letter to the *Revue néo-scolastique*, that he attained "a clear view of the capital role played by religion in social life" and found a means of tackling it sociologically. This led to a further means of access to collective representations through ritual practices and symbols and to his definition of religion in *Elementary Forms of Religious Life* as *"a unified system of beliefs and practices relative to sacred things, that is to say, things set apart and forbidden—beliefs and practices which unite into one single moral community called a Church all those who adhere to them"* (Durkheim 1995: 44). By this stage the initial focus on the "material substratum" had been long forgotten: as he wrote there, those theories were erroneous "which aim to derive all of social life from its material substrate (either economic or territorial)" (Durkheim 1995: 230 fn).

The Division of Labor had focused on social solidarity but its conclusion confronted Durkheim with a knotty problem. Its central thesis identified "collective consciousness" (*conscience collective*) with the "mechanical solidarity" of earlier societies, in which "the similarity of consciousnesses gives rise to legal rules which, under the threat of repressive measures, imposes upon everybody uniform beliefs and practices" (Durkheim 2013: 177). This had been replaced by "organic solidarity," which consisted in functional mutual interdependence of roles and occupations in ever more heterogeneous societies where "the collective consciousness is increasingly reduced to the cult of the individual" (317) and is ever more marginalized, abstract, indeterminate and general, allowing ever greater scope for individual initiative and reflection. But now the question arose: where, then, is the domain of the moral in accounting for the solidarity of advanced societies? After *The Division of Labor* Durkheim abandoned the typology of mechanical and organic solidarity and began, in *The Rules*, to reconceive collective beliefs and sentiments as functioning in all types of society including his own, to account for the fact that, "since it is indisputable today that most of our ideas and tendencies are not developed by ourselves, but come to us from outside, they can only penetrate us by imposing themselves upon us" (22). The outcome was his so-called "social realism" expounded in the first two chapters of *The Rules* and deployed throughout the rest of the text and defended against critics in the 1901 Preface.

The chapters

What is a social fact?

A new language of "the social" developed in the nineteenth century expressing "the notion of a relative thickness of human relations, a thematization of the endurance of habits, the sharedness of beliefs and, perhaps most importantly, the situatedness of both in time and space" (Terrier 2011: 175). It superseded an earlier vocabulary in which "society" carried "a range of essentially voluntaristic meanings, clustered around two poles: association of partnership for a common purpose, on the one hand; friendship, comradeship, companionship, on the other" (Baker 2001: 86). Thus Rousseau had maintained that societies could be transformed from mere aggregations ruled by strong men into free "associations" governed by reasonable citizens. It was Durkheim, in *The Rules* and elsewhere, who gave these new ways of conceiving "society" and "the social" "their theoretically most systematic and complex treatment" (Terrier 2011: 119; see Durkheim 1960).

That treatment was, however, beset by a dilemma. Durkheim's key insight was that "the social fact is distinct from its individual effects," so that "certain currents of opinion, whose intensity varies according to the time and country in which they occur, impel us, for example, toward marriage or suicide, toward higher or lower birth-rates, etc." (24). The dilemma was how to understand and portray this type of causal mechanism. On the one hand he viewed society as "not the mere sum of individuals" but "a specific reality which has its own characteristics" (86). On the other, he wrote that "social things are only realized by men; they are the product of human activity" (31). On the one hand, he takes "society" to exist as an entity "*sui generis*," a kind of super-individual organism, since, "not having the individual as their substratum, [social facts] can have none other than society, either political society in its entirety or one of the partial groups that it includes—religious denominations, political and literary schools, occupational corporations, etc." Thus by "aggregating together, by interpenetrating, by fusing together, individuals give birth to a being, psychical if you will, but one which constitutes a psychical individuality of a new kind" (86). On the other hand, he wrote in his 1901

Preface that "society comprises only individuals, together with "integrating elements" but individuals are its only "active elements." Thus he there strenuously denies the charges of suggesting that social consciousness was "substantial" and of advocating "realism" and engaging in "ontological thinking" (6). Sometimes, in short, Durkheim ties the reality of society to that of a substance, while at other times he takes a strong stand against this very view.

A solution to this dilemma is to view social facts—that is social properties and phenomena—as "emergent." The idea of emergence signifies that patterns and outcomes occurring at a higher level may not be explicable or predictable at a lower level.[5] Thus theories, concepts, laws and terminology at the social level may be irreducible to the level of interacting individuals, without any "ontological implication" of the existence of a "group mind" or the like. Philosophers of mind since the 1960s have appealed to the idea of emergence to suggest that concepts and laws at the psychological level are irreducible to the neurobiological level and, further, that mental events and properties can, in turn, have real effects at the social level, at the level of individuals and indeed upon the physical brain. (Thus one can hold this view while remaining a thoroughgoing materialist about ontology.) It is plausible to think that Durkheim was indeed reaching, *avant la lettre*, for this solution in the 1901 Preface when he denied engaging in "ontological thinking." This suggestion is strengthened by his repeated citing of natural science analogies where "elements combine" and "by virtue of this combination . . . give rise to new phenomena" (10). Thus he cites the living cell's relation to chemical particles; the hardness of bronze lying in neither copper, tin nor lead; the liquidity and other properties of water being absent from its component gases; and, most significantly, the independence of mental states from their neuronal substratum. Thus he was to write, in "Individual and Collective Representations," that

[e]ach mental condition is, as regards the neural cells, in the same condition of relative independence as social phenomena are in relation to individual people . . .Those, then, who accuse us of leaving social life in the air because we refuse to reduce it to the individual mind have not, perhaps, recognized all the consequences of their objection. If it were justified it would apply just as well to the relations between mind and brain. (Durkheim 1953a: 28)

This solution brings Durkheim's account of social facts remarkably close to that of another present-day philosopher, John Searle, who also writes (though quite uninfluenced by Durkheim) of "collective representations" (Searle 1995, 2006a, 2010). Searle is, unlike Durkheim, engaged in doing "social ontology" and as such has no time for the existence of multiple realities: his goal is to identify the distinguishing features of human social reality while insisting that it fits into the one world that "consists entirely of physical particles in fields of force" (Searle 1995: xi). For Searle "collective representations" are central to explaining "institutional" social facts, such as property, money, the state, markets, and so forth. These are real but only exist because people think they do: that is, because they "accept" (in some unspecified general sense) all kinds of "rights, duties, obligations, responsibilities, and so on." In this sense, Searle concludes that "social reality exists entirely in individual minds" (Searle 2006b: 59). Durkheim's goal, unlike Searle's, was the sociological one of studying and explaining how that "acceptance" is brought about and sustained, and accounting for the real effects of social facts both at the social level and, through "downward causation" on individuals, but, by viewing social realities as emergent, with real effects, Durkheim could agree with Searle's conclusion (see Lukes 2006, Searle 2006b and Lukes 2007).[6] He had, as he wrote in 1901, expressly "stated and reiterated in every way possible that social life was made up entirely of representations" (6). He could also agree with Searle that, therefore, "*we can have an epistemically objective science of a domain that is ontologically subjective*" (Searle 2006b: 63). This leads us to consider the second chapter of *The Rules*.

Rules for the Observation of Social Facts

This chapter is all about objectivity as Durkheim conceived it, as expressed by Durkheim's famous injunction to "consider social facts as things." The phrase does sound odd in English. "Thing" naturally suggests, as the *Oxford English Dictionary* indicates, "a material object, a body; a being or entity consisting of matter, or occupying space" and thus serves to compound the "misunderstandings and confusion" to which the 1901 Preface is addressed. "*Chose*" is less emphatic in this respect: according to *Le Petit Robert*, it means "a concrete or abstract reality perceived or conceivable as a unique object." Like the Latin word "*res*," what it signifies may be physical, mental, conceptual or linguistic. Moreover, the distinction drawn by Descartes between *res estensa* (referring to material substance extended in space) and *res cogitans* (referring to consciousness, without extension) was familiar to all those who had studied philosophy in the *lycée*, and thus to Durkheim and his contemporary readers. Hence the reality of social facts is added to them by collective representations. As Karen Fields has written, "we have something imagined, yet real, that is added to physical things or to people. What is added possesses the objectivity of things but not their materiality" (Fields 2005: 175).[7] And this makes sense of his idea of sacredness in his developing theory of religion. Sacredness for Durkheim cannot be present to only one mind; it must be present and shared across the minds of the faithful, thereby giving reality to their "moral community," just as a nation is, in Benedict Anderson's famous phrase, an "imagined community."

Durkheim himself asks "What indeed is a thing?" and answers:

The thing stands in opposition to the idea, just as what is known from the outside stands in opposition to what is known from the inside. A thing is any object of knowledge which is not naturally penetrable by the understanding. It is all that which we cannot conceptualize adequately as an idea by the simple process of intellectual analysis. It is all that which the mind cannot understand without going outside itself, proceeding progressively by way of observation and experimentation from those features which are the most external and most immediately accessible to those which are the least visible and most profound. To treat facts of a certain order as things is therefore not to place them in this or that category of reality; it is to observe toward them a certain attitude of mind. It is to embark upon the study of them by adopting the principle that one is entirely ignorant of what they are, that their characteristic properties, like the unknown causes on which they depend, cannot be discovered by even the most careful form of introspection. (7)

Social facts are to be treated as objects of potential knowledge: "to treat phenomena as things is to treat them as *data*" (36). They are both external to the observer—given, offered, indeed "imposing" themselves on observation (36). They are also external to individuals—resisting "modification through a mere act of will . . . like molds into which we are forced to cast our actions" (37)—in the sense that any given individual is surrounded, preceded and outlasted by them: by innumerable intermeshed expectations and requirements, to the study of which sociologists and anthropologists bring such terms as socialization, norms, roles, cultural imperatives, organizational and institutional logics, and the like. The remainder of *The Rules* consists in a meticulous and systematic statement of rules the following of which will lead from ignorance to knowledge and from what is most external and immediately accessible to what is least visible and most profound.

It is toward the end of the chapter that Durkheim makes clear exactly what his conception of objectivity for the sociologist is. The goal is to "capture that fleeting reality which the human mind will perhaps never grasp completely" (48). Starting from sense perception, and not from concepts formed independently from it, the first task is to "discard data which may be too personal to the observer," retaining those which "present a sufficient degree of objectivity." As opposed to "vague impressions," such as are produced by temperature or electricity, they should be *visually representable* as by a thermometer or voltmeter. They should be *stable*, since "we know that social reality possesses the property of crystallizing without changing its nature," by being isolatable from individual manifestations, from "particular events" and from fluctuations "from one moment to another." And they should be identifiable from a "fixed vantage point," capable of being fixed mentally by "the observer's scrutinizing gaze." The examples of such objective data he cites are legal rules, the "legal constitution of the family" such as "the right of succession," different organizational forms within which different types of crime will occur and proverbs and sayings which will express customs and popular beliefs (47). Elsewhere, as we have seen, he cites suicide statistics as indices of the state of social solidarity.

What this account of objectivity shows is that Durkheim was wedded to the regulative ideal of what has been called "mechanical" objectivity, prevalent in the natural sciences in the late nineteenth and early twentieth centuries, where, at the stage of observation, the goal was to register and represent the facts of nature "automatically," in ways that "minimize interpretation" and thus avoid the "distortion characteristic of the observer's personal tastes, commitments or ambitions." It was a conception of objectivity that "required a certain kind of scientist—long on diligence and self-restraint, scant on genial interpretation." The scientist as observer was to rely on indices and "objective measurement" (Daston and Galison 2008: 121, 122) and abstain from judgment and interpretation. Hence his quest for "indices" that would represent social facts by measuring them in ways analogous to the thermometer or voltmeter.

But there are serious objections to this austere doctrine of resolute avoidance of interpretation of data. Consider, for example, the proposal to treat legal rules as objective data. Durkheim makes the extraordinary assertion that a "legal rule is what it is and there are no two ways of perceiving it" (47). His claim in *The Division of Labor* that "we may be sure to find reflected in the law all the essential varieties of social solidarity" (Durkheim 2013: 52) made the assumption, rightly to be judged "fantastic," that one could achieve this knowledge by making a quantitative comparison of the number of rules imposing repressive sanctions and those imposing restitutive sanctions. As Cotterrell has observed:

> He seems unaware of problems of the individuation of laws—of what constitutes a distinct law . . . or indeed of the simple point that it may be quite arbitrary how many distinct provisions in relation to any particular topic a legal code contains. Legal provisions may be more or less detailed depending on the intentions or skill of the law creator, the extent to which common understandings governing circumstances in which the law is to apply can be assumed, and prevailing attitudes to interpretation of law. He fails to note that repressive and restitutive sanctions may often be mixed and that their relation to particular rules may be indirect and complex. (Cotterrell 1999: 33)

And consider his view that suicide statistics register the state of social solidarity. Here, of course, Durkheim does in practice interpret their meaning, since what they are taken to register depends on his very theory. But here too he seems unaware of the extent to which they are themselves constituted by contestable judgments, since they are the aggregate results of individual coroners" judgments, interpreting the meaning of modes of death (see Douglas 1967).

In general, Durkheim's image of the ideal social scientist served to prevent him from focusing on the significance of differences, sometimes irreconcilable, in the interpretation of meaning. Nor did he reflect, as did his contemporary Max Weber, on the perspectival character of knowledge and on the role of value choices in framing the questions on which social scientists bring their rules of sociological method to bear in order to arrive at objective answers. For Durkheim, as we have seen, explanation would yield "rules of action for the future," practical guidance for curing society's ills. But this too, he thought, could be done without departing from scientific objectivity.

Rules for Distinguishing the Normal from the Pathological

This is to be done, this chapter argues, by finding "an objective criterion, inherent in the facts themselves, to allow us to distinguish scientifically health from sickness in the various orders of social phenomena" (51). As he had written in *The Division of Labor*, "We would esteem our research not worth the labor of a single hour if its interest were merely speculative" (Durkheim 2013: 4). His central assumption was that, in principle, only one set of practical moral judgments is rationally possible in face of a fully scientific understanding of the present and foreseeable future. It is, he was later to argue, "never possible to desire a morality other than that required by the social conditions of a given time." We cannot, he thought, choose a criterion by an act of decision; we can only observe it and derive it from the facts. The state of society will provide "an objective standard to which our evaluations must always be brought back" (Durkheim 1953b: 38, 61). Otherwise, as he writes here, there would be "no limit . . . to the free inventions of the imagination in their search for the best." This goal then "recedes to infinity, discouraging not a few by its very remoteness, arousing and exciting others, on the other hand, who, so as to draw a little nearer to it, hasten their steps and throw themselves into revolutionary activity." His solution was to equate the desirable with the healthy, for "the state of health is something definite, inherent in things" and then "the extent of effort is given and defined . . . we need only to work steadily and persistently to maintain the normal state, to re-establish it if it is disturbed, and to rediscover the conditions of normality if they happen to change" (66).

As the last sentence of the chapter makes clear, Durkheim held to a diagnostic model of the relation between the sociologist and his object of study. Hence, for instance, his characterization of socialism as a "cry of grief, sometimes of anger uttered by men who feel most keenly our collective malaise" (Durkheim1958: 7)—a symptom of a pathological state of society for which sociology can provide the basis for prescribing suitable remedies. The practical role of social science lay in "helping contemporaries to become aware of themselves, their needs and their sentiments" (Durkheim 1953b: 64) by identifying the current conditions of social health and the causes of and remedies for social pathologies. Science alone could determine the existing state of moral health of society, which, however, is nowhere wholly attained but indicates an ideal toward which it is evolving: we can thus anticipate what would constitute progress toward it and what remedies such progress demands.

Clearly, this picture of the relation between science and practical judgment sets very severe limits to the scope of the latter and thus to the possibilities of social critique. But Durkheim evaded these, to some degree, in two ways. First, noting how far the nascent science of sociology was from being a guide to conduct, he came to allow for the need to engage in case-by-case judgment, guided only by the present state of knowledge. Second, he allowed that, when so judging, one could, in a complex and changing social world, distinguish those tendencies that are required by the conditions of collective existence from those that are *anachronistic* (as, for instance, the traditionalist morality of the anti-Dreyfusards at the time of the Dreyfus Affair) and also identify the *emerging* morals of the future (as exemplified by moral innovators such as Socrates and Jesus).

These, then, are the practical and political implications of Durkheim's diagnostic view of social science. It is, however, a view that rests on shaky foundations. Consider the very distinction between "the normal" and "the pathological." Is "normality" the same as "health"? Is "pathology" its contrary? Is "the pathological" properly to be contrasted with "the normal" as two objectively distinguishable "orders of facts" (55), the one the contrary of the other? Durkheim assumed an affirmative answer to these questions, arguing that health "establishes the norm which must serve as a basis for all our practical reasoning" (51). He assumed this because his usage of "normal" conflates two distinct meanings: designating, on the one hand, a desirable state or ideal condition enabling an individual to flourish—in the case of social life that of a well-ordered, solidary society; and, on the other hand, a statistically ascertainable fact in the form of "a kind of individual abstraction, the most frequently occurring characteristics of the species in their most frequent forms" at a given stage of its evolution (55). Adopting his usual practice, he treated the latter as an index of the former, on the basis of two further assumptions: that it would be "inexplicable that the most widespread forms of organization were not also—*at least in the aggregate*—the most advantageous" (57); and that their prevalence was to be explained by their "being bound up with the conditions of existence in the species under consideration, either as the mechanically essential effect of these conditions or as a means allowing the organism to adapt to these conditions" (57).

This picture of "the normal and the pathological" and the indicated supporting assumptions have had a considerable after-life and remain controversial to this day. Durkheim's conflation of the two senses of "normal"—the normative (indicating what ought to be) and the statistical—and his consequent belief in the possibility of establishing what is "normal" with scientific objectivity, as "inherent in the facts themselves" (51), were due to the influence of Claude Bernard. They have been powerfully contested in our time by the great historian-philosopher of science Georges Canguilhem, author of *Le Normal et le pathologique* (Canguilhem 1991). For Canguilhem what is normal for a living being is shown by its ability to adapt with activity and flexibility to changing circumstances. What counts as normal and what counts as pathological is, in this "vitalist" view, given in the experience of living beings who have shifting relationships to varying and variant environments; thus there can be no objective basis for identifying pathology on the basis of already established, "mechanistic" science. Subsequently the question of how to conceive of "normality" was further opened up in France by Foucault's various inquiries into "normalization" and in the Anglo-American sociology of deviance. Thus the opening pages of Howard Becker's classic study *Outsiders* propose four ways of conceiving of what is normal: the statistical (defining the normal as the average), the medical (defining it as health in opposition to disease), the functional (assigning a purpose or goal to a group)—very often, Becker observes, "a political question"—and the more "relativistic" view (defining it by reference to the group's rules) which we have come to call "constructivist." Interestingly, Becker's own, more interactionist view—that social groups create deviance (from normality) *"by making the rules whose infraction constitutes deviance,* and by applying those rules to particular people and labeling them as outsiders" (Becker 1963: 7, 9)—is close to Durkheim's own account of crime and punishment.

No less controversial today are the quasi-Darwinian assumptions that the statistically normal, or prevalent, forms of organization will be "the most advantageous" (advantageous to whom or what, and in what ways?) and the further ("functionalist") assumption that what is functional will be caused to occur, that is, that the "conditions of existence" of a given type of society, at a given stage of its development, are bound to generate those advantages. Both of these assumptions are often challenged but both also have considerable contemporary resonance. Thus neo-Darwinian theorists of gene-culture co-evolution argue that culture can influence natural selection processes, inducing genetic change that generates new selection processes such as group selection involving social conformity engendering cultural variation. And, also deriving from Darwinian ideas, recent work by Runciman (1998) proposes that, however they may be caused, a "selectionist paradigm" can best explain how some social practices and not others get selected over time.

All the foregoing claims are, of course, strongly influenced by analogy from biology, indeed the biology of Durkheim's time, but there is, of course, a major disanalogy, to which he himself drew attention, namely the existence of what he called "transition periods"—of evolution, so to speak, between species—where what is normal "relates to the past but no longer corresponds to the new conditions of existence" (58). Here what is statistically normal is anachronistic: that is, "no longer the sign that the phenomenon observed is closely linked to the general conditions of collective existence" (58). Then, to decide the question, one needs historical investigation to see whether past conditions of society "still pertain in the present, or, on the contrary, have changed" (58). It was this maneuver that enabled Durkheim to assert, for example, that the ideology of the anti-Dreyfusards was pathological and that the weakening of religious belief in advanced societies is normal.

The most interesting and striking section in this chapter, however, is the example he gives of identifying a normal social fact, namely the discussion of crime. Crime, he argues, is "a factor in public health, an integrative element in any healthy society" (61), strengthening collective sentiments through punishment. It is necessary, even useful. It can even be seen as a source of moral innovation, as with Socrates, "an anticipation of the morality to come" (64). These pages show Durkheim at his most provocative and they did indeed provoke Tarde to respond most vigorously and led to a fascinating debate between the two sociologists from which much can still be learnt (reproduced in Lukes and Scull 2013).

Rules for the Constitution of Social Types

In arguing that sociology needs typologies, Durkheim here distinguishes the sociological enterprise from history, which produces "purely descriptive monographs" (a criticism echoed in his debate with Seignobos), and from philosophy, concerned with "the unique, although ideal, concept of humanity" (69). Sociology's focus is rather to be on "intermediate entities: these are the social species" (69), thereby recognizing diversity within an overall unity. Here the biological analogy is plainly at work: comparative sociology, and indeed comparative history that is sociologically informed, is to view societies as bounded unities that are, moreover, classifiable within an evolutionary hierarchy that extends from the simplest to the ever more complex. The evolution was not, however, simply linear: as Schmaus observes, "Durkheim adopted the analogy of a branching tree for the evolution of human societies as well as for animal species" (Schmaus 1994: 105). In an earlier text Durkheim had made the comparison with "an immense family of which the different branches, increasingly divergent from one another, little by little detach themselves from a common stem in order to live their own lives" (Durkheim 1888 quoted in Schmaus 1994:

105–6). Nevertheless the overall picture is one of linear advance toward ever greater complexity: hence his continued use of the terminology, characteristic of the times, of "lower" and "higher," less and more "advanced" societies.

Read as a general plea for classification of types of society as a precondition for explanation, the topic addressed in the following chapter, the argument here is straightforward, making the case for "a small number" of criteria "carefully selected" which will identify "decisive or crucial facts" (71), "characteristics which are particularly essential" (72). But how are we to know which these are? His answer is that the appropriate classifications develop alongside the progress of explanatory theories.

Durkheim's own answer to this question is that the classification must be based on structural features. In an interesting footnote for the second edition he excludes economic and technological factors as insufficiently "permanent" and also civilizational criteria. It is social morphology that is "that part of sociology whose task it is to constitute and classify social types." Note, however, that here "morphological" does not denote "material" but rather "organizational" factors. Still reproducing the general idea of "mechanical" and "organic" solidarity (without the terminology), he suggests an overall progression from segmentary social structures, where the component segments retain their "own immediate life," to their eventual concentration and coalescence with the rise of city states and new forms of administrative and political organization.

Rules for the Explanation of Social Facts

This chapter begins with some ground clearing by establishing two distinctions. The first is that between cause and function. Explanation must be causal; teleology, in terms of ends, is non-explanatory. To "demonstrate the utility of a fact does not explain its origins, nor how it is what it is . . . Our need for things cannot cause them to be of a particular nature" (78). Indeed, a fact "can exist without serving any purpose, either because it has never been used to further any vital goal or because, having once been of use, it has lost all utility but continues to exist merely through force of custom" (79). Needs and desires can only explain social developments by virtue of efficient causes. There can, however, be reciprocal causation, as when the collective sentiments that crime offends cause the punishment that in turn reinforces them. The second distinction is between social and individual causation. The "constraining power" of social phenomena penetrates us or weighs on us more or less heavily (85): it thus dominates the individual "because it is a product of forces which transcend him and for which he consequently cannot account. It is not from within himself that can come the external pressure which he undergoes; it is not what is happening within himself that can explain it" (85). Hence the rule that the "*determining cause of a social fact must be sought among antecedent social facts and not among the states of the individual consciousness*" (90).

How, then, are we to understand explanation in terms of social causes? Durkheim does not tell us in this chapter how he understands causation. He does, however, address the question much later, in *Elementary Forms*. The idea of a causal relation, he there writes,

> implies efficacy, active power, or active force. We usually understand "cause" to mean "that which is able to produce a definite change." Cause is force before it has manifested the power that is in it. Effect is the same power, but actualized. Humanity has always imagined causality in dynamic terms. To be sure, some philosophers deny this conception any objective basis; they see it only as an arbitrary construction of imagination that relates to nothing in things. (Durkheim 1995: 367)

The philosophers he had in mind were the empiricists and, in particular John Stuart Mill, whom he criticizes in the following chapter of *The Rules* for believing that cause and effect are "absolutely heterogeneous and that there is between them no logical connection," that the relationship between them is "purely chronological." To hold this view, he argues, is to call "into question the intelligibility of the causal relationship." His view was that this relationship "results from the nature of things, the same effect can only sustain this relationship with one single cause, for it can express only one single nature" (102).

The upshot of all this is that for Durkheim *explanation* involves two elements: first, the identification of the efficient cause—that which brings about the effect; and second, the rendering "intelligible" of the relation, or "logical connection," between them, the "one single nature" that unites them. This view—that a single cause is a necessary and sufficient condition for a single effect—is for the present-day reader an unfamiliar way of thinking about causal explanation and one that is hard to accept. For one thing, it excludes multiple causation, where there are causal chains and networks: "this alleged axiom of the plurality of causes," he writes, "is a negation of the principle of causality"(102). For another, *a fortiori*, it excludes consideration of causation at multiple levels: hence his famous dictum that "every time a social phenomenon is directly explained by a psychological phenomenon, we may rest assured that the explanation is false" (86). Sociological explanation, we might think, should be able to encompass interactions between the macro and the micro and should encompass individual, structural and institutional processes. The doctrinal insistence on single-level explanation, from macro to macro, is as unreasonable as the insistence, common in Durkheim's time and still so today among proponents of "methodological individualism," that all proper explanation must be at the level of interacting individuals. And thirdly, Durkheim's view precludes consideration of the interest-relativity of the attribution of causation: the fact that what is causally *relevant* among causal factors depends on what puzzle we are trying to solve.

Nevertheless, this doctrine was Durkheim's way of addressing the problem, also confronted by Max Weber, of considering both the *cause* and the *meaning* of what he sought to explain. Schmaus even suggests that the French term "*explication*" in the title of this chapter encourages this conflation, since it has

> two different senses that today we would distinguish clearly but that Durkheim did not keep separate. In one of these senses to explain a *fact* means to subsume it under a more general expression, often one that provides the cause of the fact in question. To explain the meaning of a *concept*, on the other hand, means to analyze it or provide a definition. (Schmaus 1994: 59–60)

Durkheim does both in the examples he gives in this chapter of the ways in which the "inner social environment" influences the nature of social solidarity. Thus, echoing the analysis of *The Division of Labor,* he argues that "every increase in the volume and dynamic density of societies" has the effect of "making social life more intense and widening the horizons of thought and action of each individual" (93). Likewise the character of domestic life will vary "depending on whether the family is large or small, or more or less turned in upon itself" and "professional life" will vary according to whether social bonds are "strongly developed" or "loose" (93). Similarly, in *Suicide*, "anomie" and "egoism" are concepts which render intelligible—that is, interpret the meaning of—the impact of loosening social bonds in modern societies.

Rules for the Demonstration of Sociological Proof

Human social life was not for Durkheim, as it was for Weber, distinct from the rest of nature by virtue of its meaningfulness: "social phenomena," he writes, "are only distinguishable from the other phenomena by virtue of their greater complexity" (102). But there are reasons why the "demonstration of proof"—that is, the elimination of alternative hypotheses—should be different in social as opposed to natural science. First there is no scope for direct experimentation, artificially intervening by manipulating the world to eliminate "adventitious" elements (104). And second, therefore, the social scientist is confined to observing and interpreting the limited range of cases that history throws up, unlike the experimental physicist or chemist or biologist, who can replicate results "a very great number of times" (106). He was, as we have seen, strongly influenced by the physiologist Claude Bernard's views of scientific method and accepted Bernard's insistence that the key to the experimental method was the search for relevant comparisons.

But this led him to reject four of the five modes of "eliminative induction" discussed by Mill: the method of residues, the methods of agreement and of difference and the combined method of agreement and difference. The point of all these was to eliminate hypothesized causes: the first by eliminating all that is known already and the others by setting up experiments in order to isolate conditions under which an antecedent can be identified as the cause by comparing cases that either agree or differ in only one respect. Apart from the unavailability of experimentation, the sheer complexity of social life rendered these methods inapplicable to its scientific study. We could never be sure that "all the facts had been reviewed" (106). The only alternative was Mill's fifth method: the method of concomitant variation.

This does not rely on comparing instances of a phenomenon alike in all but one respect, through the rigorous exclusion, which experimentation makes possible, of alternative explanatory factors. Nor does it require a large number of confirming cases. This method alone, he thought, could establish a sociological law, by showing "us the facts connecting with each other in a continuous fashion, at least as regards their quantitative aspects. Now this connection alone suffices to demonstrate that they are not foreign to each other" (104). He thought that well-established serial and systematic variation is a basis for confidence, compensating for the replicability of data through experimentation in the natural sciences; and it renders unnecessary the use of "incomplete enumerations or superficial observations" (106) relied on by many historians and social scientists, who engaged in the unsystematic accumulation of unchecked and second-hand evidence garnered from here and there, comprising both "the confused and cursory observations of travelers" or "the more precise texts of history" (106).

The key here was to exploit, within the limited range of the evidence from past and present societies, "the wealth of variations which are spontaneously available . . . riches without example in any other domain of nature." This is Durkheim's immediate research program, as set out in *The Rules,* of comparing "uninterrupted series of transformations" within a given society that assume "various forms according to regions, occupations, religious faiths, etc." in order to explain "crime, suicide, birth and marriage, savings, etc." (107). In practice, he only pursued this method (and that to only a limited extent) in *Suicide.*

This final chapter concludes by expounding the idea of comparative sociology, which, Durkheim proclaims, "is not a special branch of sociology; it is sociology itself, in so far as it ceases to be purely descriptive and aspires to account for facts" (109). This requires a far wider, more ambitious research program by embracing broader comparisons. Thus one must go beyond comparisons within a single society to those across societies of the same type (at a given stage of development). As an example, he cites tracing the evolution of the patriarchal family through the history of Rome, Athens and Sparta. But beyond this one should compare across types of society to reach "the more fundamental phenomena," so as to explain, for instance, "the present state of the family, marriage and property, etc." (109). This proposed method, which he labels "genetic," is not elaborated upon here. All we learn, in the chapter's tantalizing penultimate paragraph, is that it involves studying a "fundamental phenomenon" such as "domestic organization" by comparing the different forms which it assumes across all species. This would show us such a phenomenon in its "most rudimentary" form, so that we could then "follow step by step the way in which it has progressively grown more complex," exposing "in dissociated state its component elements" (109). Here we can see dimly foreshadowed the method for demonstrating sociological proof that Durkheim was to employ in his last great work, *Elementary Forms of Religious Life*. Karen Fields has commented on the significance of the ambiguity of the French word "*élémentaire,*" meaning both elementary and elemental (Fields 1995: lix–lx). Durkheim was, plainly and significantly, intending the second sense as well as the first. Thus *Elementary Forms*, contrary to what is advocated in *The Rules*, relies exclusively on ethnographic data, argues that while "an extended test can add to the persuasiveness of a theory" it is "no less true that when a law has been proved by a single well-made experiment, this proof is universally valid" (Durkheim 1995: 418) and claims that "a science in its infancy must pose problems in their simplest form, and only later make them gradually more complicated. When we have understood very elementary religions, we will be able to move on to others" (Durkheim 1919: 142–3).

Thirty years ago I concluded an earlier introduction to this work with the following summary judgment:

> *The Rules* is not a deep work of theory, or meta-theory; nor is it Durkheim's finest work. Nor does it give an accurate guide to his own sociological practice. It is, however, a highly *instructive* text, especially when read in the light of that practice. For, along with his subsequent methodological statements, it represents both a typically bold and clear statement of the aspiration toward a social science that is objective, specific (to social reality) and autonomous (of non-scientific influences) and a demonstration of why that aspiration was, and must remain, frustrated. (Durkheim 1982: 23)

But that judgment is, indeed, far too summary. It has been justly criticized for its suggestion that "it is valuable to read the *Rules* for purely negative reasons" (Gane 1988: 12).[8] That is to assume that the issues its six chapters so boldly and clearly confront have been resolved. It further assumes that Durkheim's attempts to resolve them stand refuted or at least seriously weakened. Neither of these assumptions is warranted. The issues remain live issues for practitioners of social science and *The Rules* remains, for the reasons I have sought to suggest, a highly instructive aid to reflection upon them.

Notes

1. Patricia Cormack's subtle account of *The Rules* as a manifesto (Cormack 1996) presents Durkheim as here attacking "conventional pre-modern as well as contemporary competing explanations of the human world," as employing hyperbole and polemics to "make the 'social' a real imaginative possibility for his audience" and as providing a discussion of representations as collective phenomena which, however, "cannot be fully grasped by the collective that generates them" (89, 93–4, 98).
2. On the contested issue of Durkheim's reading of Spencer, see Offer 2010: 178–83, Corning 1982, Perrin 1995 and Zafirovski 2000. On Durkheim's differences with Tarde see Jones 1999: 259–268 and Candea 2010, in which an imagined debate between the two is reconstructed from their published writings, and Lukes 1972 ch. 16 for a summary and discussion of their debate over criminality and the law. This is reproduced in Lukes and Scull 2013.
3. Monnerot's critique viewed "the sciences of man from a phenomenological point of view" (p. 62) under the influence of the philosopher Husserl. And the debate continues: see Kaufmann 1999.
4. See the brilliant discussions of these and other issues of translating Durkheim by Karen Fields, the latest and most successful translator of *Les Formes élémentaires de la vie religieuse*, in Fields 2005 and Fields 1995: li–lxi. See also Lukes 2012.
5. For an excellent exposition and defence of emergence as applied to the analysis of the social world see Elder-Vass 2010. Emergence occurs "when a whole possesses *emergent properties*," that is properties "not possessed by any of the parts individually and that would not be possessed by the full set of parts in the absence of a structuring set of relations between them" (15). Emergence is "a synchronic relation among the parts of an entity that gives the entity as a whole the ability to have a particular (diachronic) causal impact" (23).
6. Searle does not, however, follow Durkheim in accepting the analogy between neurological/mental emergence to the individual/social case and thus the idea of downward social causation (though his account of what he calls "the background" suggests that he should do so).
7. See Fields and Fields 2012 for a vivid and extended application of this idea to the "invisible ontology" of race.
8. Others have been much harsher. Thus William Pickering writes that *The Rules* is "full of serious defects in many people's eyes and shows a very limited knowledge of scientific procedure" (Pickering 1984: 288) and Robert Alun Jones describes the book as "Durkheim at his worst" (Jones 1986: 77).

References

Baker, Keith Michael 2001. "Enlightenment and the institution of society: notes for a conceptual history" in Sudipta Kaviraj and Sunil Khilnani (eds.), *Civil Society: History and Possibilities*. Cambridge and New York: Cambridge University Press.

Becker, Howard S. 1963. *Outsiders: Studies in the Sociology of Deviance*. New York: Free Press.

Borlandi, Massimo and Mucchielli, Laurent 1995. *La Sociologie et sa méthode: Les règles de Durkheim un siècle après*. Paris: Editions L'Harmattan.

Candea, M. (ed.) 2010. *The Social after Gabriel Tarde: Debates and Assessments*. London: Routledge.

Canguilhem, Georges 1991 (1943, 1966). *The Normal and the Pathological*, translated by Carolyn R. Fawcett with an introduction by Michel Foucault. New York: Zone Books.

Cormack, Patricia 1996. "The paradox of Durkheim's manifesto: Reconsidering *The Rules of Sociological Method*" *Theory and Society* 25.1: 85–104.

Corning, P. A. 1982. "Durkheim and Spencer," *British Journal of Sociology* 33.3: 359–82.

Cotterrell, Roger 1999. *Emile Durkheim: Law in a Moral Domain*. Edinburgh: University of Edinburgh Press.

Daston, Lorraine and Galison, Peter 2008. *Objectivity*. New York: Zone Books.

Davy, Georges 1920. "Emile Durkheim: l'oeuvre," *Revue de métaphysique et de morale* 27: 71–112.

Descombes, Vincent 2000. "The Philosophy of Collective Representations," *History of the Human Sciences* 13.1: 37–49.

Douglas, J. D. 1967. *The Social Meanings of Suicide*. Princeton: Princeton University Press.

Durkheim, Emile 1887. "La philosophie dans les universités allemandes," *Revue internationale de l'ensignement* 13: 313–38, 423–40.

Durkheim, Emile 1888. "Cours de science sociale: leçon d'ouverture," *Revue Internationale de l'enseignement* 15: 23–48.

Durkheim, Emile 1919 (1914). Contribution to discussion in F. Abauzit, *Le Sentiment religieux à l'heure actuelle*. Paris: Vrin.

Durkheim, Emile 1951 (1897). *Suicide: A Study in Sociology*. Translated by J. A. Spaulding and G. Simpson and edited with an introduction by G. Simpson. Glencoe, IL: Free Press of Glencoe and (1952) London: Routledge & Kegan Paul.

Durkheim, Emile 1953 (1925). *Sociology and Philosophy*. Translated by D. F. Pocock with an introduction by J. G. Peristiany. London: Cohen & West and Glencoe, IL: Free Press of Glencoe.

Durkheim, Emile 1953a (1898). "Individual and Collective Representations" in Durkheim 1953.

Durkheim, Emile 1953b (1906). "The Determination of the Moral Fact" in Durkheim 1953.

Durkheim, Emile 1958 (1928). *Socialism and Saint-Simon*, translated by C. Sattler with an introduction by Alvin W. Gouldner. Yellow Springs, OH: Antioch Press and (1959) London: Routledge & Kegan Paul.

Durkheim, Emile 1960 (1918). "Rousseau's *Social Contract*" in Emile Durkheim, *Montesquieu and Rousseau: Forerunners of Sociology*, translated by R. Mannheim with Foreword by Henri Peyre. Ann Arbor, MI: University of Michigan Press.

Durkheim, Emile 1961 (1925). *Moral Education: A Study in the Theory and Application of the Sociology of Education*. New York: The Free Press of Glencoe.

Durkheim, Emile 1977 (1938). *The Evolution of Educational Thought in France*. London: Routledge & Kegan Paul.

Durkheim, Emile 1982. *The Rules of Sociological Method and Selected Texts on Sociology and Its Method*, edited with an introduction by Steven Lukes. Translation by W. D. Halls. London: Macmillan and New York: Free Press.

Durkheim, Emile 1995 (1912). *Elementary Forms of Religious Life*, translated by Karen E. Fields. New York: Free Press.

Durkheim, Emile 2013. *The Division of Labor in Society*, Steven Lukes (ed.). Basingstoke: Palgrave Macmillan.

Elder-Vass, Dave 2010. *The Causal Power of Social Structures: Emergence, Structure and Agency*. Cambridge: Cambridge University Press.

Emirbayer, Mustafa 1996. "Useful Durkheim," *Sociological Theory*, 14.2: 109–130.

Fields, Karen E. (1995) Translator's Introduction, "Religion as an eminently social thing," *Elementary Forms of Religious Life*, xvii–lxxiii.

Fields, Karen E. 2005. "What difference does translation make? *Les Formes élémentaires de la vie religieuse* in French and English" in Jeffrey C. Alexander and Philip Smith (eds.), *The Cambridge Companion to Durkheim*. Cambridge and New York: Cambridge Univesity Press.

Fields, Karen E. and Fields, Barbara J. 2012. *Racecraft: The Soul of Inequality in American Life*. London and New York: Verso.

Gane, Mike 1988. *On Durkheim's Rules of Sociological Method*. London and New York: Routledge.

Gross, Neil 2006. "Comment on Searle," *Anthropological Theory* 6.1: 45–56.

Jones, Robert Alun 1986. *Emile Durkheim: An Introduction to Four Major Works*. London: Sage.

Jones, Robert Alun 1999. *The Development of Durkheim's Social Realism*. Cambridge: Cambridge University Press.

Jones, Robert Alun and Kibbee, Douglas A. 1993. "Durkheim, Language and History," *Sociological Theory* 11: 152–70.

Kaufmann, Laurence 1999. "Les faits sociaux sont-ils des choses?" *Critique* 630: 890–911.

Lukes, Steven 1972. *Emile Durkheim: His Life and Work*. New York: Harper & Row and (1973) London: Allen Lane, The Penguin Press.

Lukes, Steven 2006. "Searle and His Critics," *Anthropological Theory* 6.1: 5–11.

Lukes, Steven 2007. "Searle versus Durkheim" in Savas L. Tsohatzidis (ed.), *Intentional Acts and Institutional Facts: Essays on John Searle's Social Ontology*. Dordrecht: Springer.

Lukes, Steven 2012. "On Translating Durkheim" in Martin J. Burke and Melvin Richter (eds.), *Why Concepts Matter: Translating Social and Political Thought*. Leiden and Boston: Brill.

Lukes, Steven and Scull, Andrew (eds.) 2013. *Durkheim and the Law*. Basingstoke: Palgrave Macmillan.

Monnerot, Jules 1946. *Les faits sociaux ne sont pas des choses.* Paris: Galimard.

Offer, John 2010. *Herbert Spencer and Social Theory.* Basingstoke: Palgrave Macmillan.

Parsons, Talcott 1937. *The Structure of Social Action.* New York: Free Press. Second Edition 1949.

Perrin, R. G. 1995. "Emile Durkheim's *Division of Labor* and the shadow of Herbert Spencer," *Sociological Quarterly* 36.4: 791–808.

Pickering, William S. F. 1984. *Durkheim's Sociology of Religion.* London: Routledge & Kegan Paul.

Runciman, W. G. 1998. "The selectionist paradigm and its implications for sociology," *Sociology* 32.1: 163–188.

Sawyer, R. Keith 2002. "Durkheim's dilemma: toward a sociology of emergence," *Sociological Theory* 20.2: 227–47.

Schmaus, Warren 1994. *Durkheim's Philosophy of Science and the Sociology of Knowledge: Creating an Intellectual Niche.* Chicago and London: The University of Chicago Press.

Searle, John R. 1995. *The Construction of Social Reality.* New York: Free Press.

Searle, John R. 2006. "Searle versus Durkheim and the waves of thought," *Anthropological Theory* 6.1: 57–69.

Searle, John R. 2006a. "Social Ontology: some basic principles," *Anthropological Theory* 6.1: 12–29.

Searle, John R. 2006b. "Lukes and 'substantial scientific work,'" *Anthropological Theory* 6.1: 122–5.

Searle, John R. 2010. *Making the Social World: The Structure of Human Civilization.* Oxford and New York: Oxford University Press.

Terrier, Jean 2011. *Visions of the Social: Society as a Political Project in France, 1750–1950.* Leiden and Boston: Brill.

Zafirovski, M. Z. 2000. "Spencer is dead, long live Spencer: individualism, holism and the problem of norms," *British Journal of Sociology* 51.3: 553–579.

Emile Durkheim's Life and Works: Timeline 1858–1917

1858   Born David Emile Durkheim in Epinal, capital of the depart-
        ment of Vosges, in Lorraine. His father is Chief Rabbi of the
        Vosges and Haute-Marne, descending from a line of rabbis, and
        the family close-knit, orthodox and traditional, part of a long-
        established Jewish community.
        Attends the Collège d'Epinal.

1870–   The Franco-Prussian War: the Prussian army occupies the town
1871   of Epinal, which becomes a French frontier town after the
        armistice.

1876   Arrives in Paris to study for admission to the *Ecole normale
        supérieure* at the Lycée Louis-le-Grand.

1879   Admitted to the *Ecole normale supérieure* after failing in 1877 and
        1878. His fellow-students include the philosopher Henri Bergson
        and the future socialist leader Jean Jaurès. His love of philosoph-
        ical debate leads to his being nicknamed "the Metaphysician."

1882   Takes the final examination, the *agrégation* (but placed second-
        last in his cohort), entitling him to teach philosophy in secondary
        schools.
        Nominated to teach at the Lycée de Sens.

1884   Moves to teach at the Lycée de Saint-Quentin.

1885   Granted a year's leave by Louis Liard, reforming Director of
        Higher Education, and undertakes a mission to study the state
        of the social sciences, in particular experimental psychology, in
        Germany. The work of Wilhelm Wundt, practicing the "positive
        science of morality," greatly influences him.

1886   Suicide of his close student friend, Victor Hommay, of whom he
        publishes an obituary, noting that Hommay suffered from "social
        isolation" and that his life "lacked an object transcending it."
        On returning to France is nominated to teach at the Lycée de
        Troyes.

1887   Publishes two articles reporting on his mission to Germany on "*La science positive de la morale*" and philosophy in German universities.

  Nominated to the first teaching post (*chargé de cours*) in the social sciences in France to teach sociology and pedagogy at the University of Bordeaux.

  Marries Louise Dreyfus (from Alsace) who, according to his nephew, Marcel Mauss, "kept every material care far from him." They will have a daughter, Marie, and a son, André.

1888   Inaugural lecture at Bordeaux opening his first course on "*La solidarité sociale.*"

1889   First studies of suicide and the family.

1890   Initiates first course on "*Physique des moeurs et du droit*" (to be published posthumously as *Leçons de sociologie: physique des moeurs et du droit*), concerning professional ethics, civic morals, property and contract.

  Mauss joins him in Bordeaux as a student. He will later work closely with his uncle on suicide, preparing the literature review and helping compile the statistics.

1892   Publishes his Latin dissertation on Montesquieu's contributions to social science, *Quid Secondatus Politicae Scientiae Instituendae Contulerit.*

1893   Defends and publishes his principal dissertation at the Sorbonne: *De la division du travail social: Etude sur l'organisation des sociétés supérieures.*

1894   Publishes "*Les règles de la méthode sociologique*" as articles in the *Revue philosophique.*

1895   Publication of *Les règles* in book form. It receives largely hostile reviews. Inaugurates his course on the history of socialism (published posthumously as *Le socialisme*).

1896   Durkheim's father dies.

  Nominated *Professeur titulaire* at Bordeaux, the first social science chair in France.

1897   Publishes *Le suicide.*

1898   Founds *L'Année sociologique,* of which the first of twelve volumes (1898–1913) appears containing his article "*La prohibition de l'inceste et ses origines.*"

  Also publishes "*Représentations individuelles et représentations collectives*" (published posthumously in *Sociologie et philosophie*).

The Dreyfus Affair explodes with the publication of Emile Zola's letter "J'accuse." Durkheim becomes secretary of the Bordeaux section of the *Ligue des droits de l'homme* and intervenes in the polemics of the Affair with his article "*L'individualisme et les intellectuels,*" defending the "religion of individualism" as a precondition of social cohesion under modern conditions.

1899   Second volume of the *Année* includes his article "*De la définition des phénomènes religieux.*"

1901   Second edition of *Les règles de la méthode sociologique,* with a new preface.

1902   Second edition of *De la division du travail social,* with a new preface entitled "*Quelques remarques sur les groupements professionels.*"
    Nominated *chargé de cours* at the Sorbonne in the Science of Education. Viewed as an appointee of the secular left, he comes under attack by Catholics and conservatives.
    Inaugural lecture on "*Pédagogie et sociologie.*"

1903   Publication of "*De quelques formes primitives de la classification*" by Durkheim and Marcel Mauss in the sixth volume of the *Année.*

1905   Nominated *chargé de cours* to teach schoolteachers and inaugurates course on "*L'évolution pédagogique en France*" (published posthumously with the same title). This course is compulsory for all students seeking to be teachers in the humanities.

1906   Nominated *Professeur titulaire* at the Sorbonne and lectures on "*La détermination du fait moral*" (published posthumously in *Sociologie et philosophie*).

1907–
1910   Numerous articles, book reviews and published contributions to discussions.

1911   Lecture on "*Jugements de valeur et jugements de réalité*" (published posthumously in *Sociologie et philosophie*) at the International Congress of Philosophy in Bologna.

1912   Publication of *Les formes élémentaires de la vie religieuse.*

1914   Outbreak of First World War and assassination of Jean Jaurès. Many members of the Durkheimian group centerd on the *Année sociologique* go to fight in the war.

1915   Publishes two war pamphlets: "*Qui a voulu la guerre? Les origines de la guerre d'après les documents diplomatiques*" and

"L'Allemagne au-dessus de tout: La mentalité allemande et la guerre."

Death on the battlefield in the retreat from Serbia of André, Durkheim's son and student at the *Ecole normale.*

1916   Publishes and partially contributes to *Lettres à tous les Français* but subjected to anti-Semitic attack in the Senate, accused of being a German spy.

1917   Dies at the age of 59. On his deathbed he is at work on a planned major work in which he intends to take up again the topic of morality, completing only drafts of the introduction.

Suggestions for Further Reading

The scholarly literature on Durkheim (and the Durkheimians) is increasingly vast and various, in several languages. The Anglophone reader in search of bearings may find it helpful to begin with the chapter on Durkheim in Lewis Coser's *Masters of Sociological Thought* (New York: Harcourt, 1971, second edition 1977); the chapters on Durkheim in Talcott Parsons's classic *The Structure of Social Action* (New York: Free Press, 1937, second edition 1949) and in Raymond Aron's *Main Currents in Sociological Thought* (London: Weidenfeld & Nicolson, 1965 and 1968, reprinted by Transaction, 1998); the present author's *Emile Durkheim: His Life and Work* (New York: Harper & Row, 1972 and Allen Lane, The Penguin Press, 1973); the exhaustive biography by Marcel Fournier first published in French as *Emile Durkheim* (Paris: Fayard 2007) and in English as *Emile Durkheim: A Biography* (Cambridge, England, and Malden, MA: Polity, 2013); and shorter studies of Durkheim by Frank Parkin (Oxford and New York: Oxford University Press, 1992), Gianfranco Poggi (Oxford and New York: Oxford University Press, 2000), Robert Nisbet (Englewood Cliffs, NJ: Prentice-Hall, 1965), Robert Alun Jones (Beverly Hills and London: Sage, 1986), Dominick LaCapra (Aurora, CO: Davies) and Kenneth Thompson (Chichester and New York: Tavistock, 1982). Among recent general collections of writings about his work are Jeffrey C. Alexander (ed.), *Durkheimian Sociology* (Cambridge: Cambridge University Press, 1988), Jeffrey C. Alexander and Philip Smith (eds.), *The Cambridge Companion to Durkheim* (Cambridge and New York: Cambridge University Press, 2005) and Stephen Turner (ed.), *Emile Durkheim: Sociologist and Moralist* (London and New York: Routledge, 1993).

Among recent writings relevant to *The Rules of Sociological Method* the following are to be noted:

Berthelot, Jean-Michel 1988. Introduction to *Les Règles de la méthode sociologique* (ed. J.-M. Berthelot). Paris: Flammarion.

Borlandi, Massimo and Mucchielli, Laurent (eds.) 1995. *La Sociologie et la méthode: Les Règles de Durkheim un siècle après*. Paris: Editions L'Harmattan.

Cherkaoui, Mohamed 1998. *Naissance d'une science sociale: la sociologie selon Durkheim*. Geneva and Paris: Droz.

Cherkaoui, Mohamed, Hamilton, Peter and Matthews, Toby 2008. *Durkheim and the Puzzle of Social Complexity*. Oxford: Bardwell Press.

Cuin, Charles-Henri (ed.) 1997. *Durkheim d'un siècle à l'autre: lectures actuelles des Règles de la méthode sociologique*. Paris: Presses Universitaires de France.

Gane, Mike 1988. *On Durkheim's Rules of Sociological Method*. London and New York: Routledge.

Jones, Robert Alun 1995. *The Development of Durkheim's Social Realism*. Cambridge and New York: Cambridge University Press.

Mucchielli, Laurent 2010. Introduction to *Les Règles de la méthode sociologique* (ed. J.-M. Berthelot). Paris: Flammarion.

Schmaus, Warren 1994. *Durkheim's Philosophy of Science and the Sociology of Knowledge: Creating an Intellectual Niche*. Chicago and London: Chicago University Press.

Stedman Jones, Susan 2001. *Durkheim Reconsidered*. Oxford: Polity.

Terrier, Jean 2011. *Visions of the Social Society as a Political Project in France 1750–1950*. Leiden and Boston: Brill.

Original Translator's Note

References to works cited in the Notes have been checked in editions available and in some cases additions and amendments have been made.

W. D. H.

The Rules of
Sociological Method

Preface to the First Edition
(1895)

We are so little accustomed to treating social facts scientifically that certain propositions contained in this book may well surprise the reader. However, if a science of societies exists, one must certainly not expect it to consist of a mere paraphrase of traditional prejudices. It should rather cause us to see things in a different way from the ordinary man, for the purpose of any science is to make discoveries, and all such discoveries more or less upset accepted opinions. Thus unless in sociology one ascribes to common sense an authority that it has lost for a long time in the other sciences—and it is not clear whence that might be derived—the scholar must determinedly resolve not to be intimidated by the results to which his investigations may lead, provided that they have been methodically carried out. If the search for paradox is the mark of the sophist, to flee from it when the facts demand it is that of a mind that possesses neither courage nor faith in science.

Unfortunately it is easier to accept this rule in principle or theory than to apply it consistently. We are still too used to deciding all such questions according to the promptings of common sense to exclude the latter easily from sociological discussion. Whilst we believe ourselves to be emancipated from it, it imposes its judgments upon us unawares. Only sustained and special practice can prevent such shortcomings. We would ask our reader not to lose sight of this. His mind should always be conscious that the modes of thought with which he is most familiar are adverse, rather than favorable, to the scientific study of social phenomena, so that he must consequently be on his guard against first impressions. If he yields to these without resistance he may well have judged our work without having understood us. He might, for example, charge us with seeking to justify crime, on the specious grounds that we treat it as a phenomenon of normal sociology. Yet such an objection would be childish. For if it is normal for crimes to occur in every society, it is no less normal for them to be punished. The institution of a system of repression is as universal a fact as the existence of criminality, and one no less indispensable to the collective health. An absence of crime would require eliminating the differences between individual consciences to a degree which, for reasons set out later, is neither possible nor desirable. Yet for a repressive system not to exist there would have to be an absence of moral homogeneity incompatible with the existence of society. Yet, proceeding from the fact that crime is both abhorred and abhorrent, common sense mistakenly concludes that it could not die out swiftly enough. With customary naïveté it cannot conceive that something repugnant may nevertheless have a useful reason for existing. Nevertheless, here there is no contradiction. Has not the physical organism repugnant functions whose regular action is necessary to the health of the individual? Do we not shrink from suffering? Yet a being to whom it was unknown would be a monster. The normality of something and the sentiments of revulsion that it inspires may even be closely joined. If pain is a normal fact, it is none the less disliked; if crime is normal, it is none the less detested.[1] Thus our method is by no means revolutionary. In one sense it is even essentially conservative, since it treats social facts as things whose nature, however flexible and malleable it may be, is still not modifiable at will. How much more dangerous is the doctrine which sees in them the mere resultant of mental combinations which a simple dialectic artifice can, in a trice, upset from top to bottom!

Likewise, because we are accustomed to representing social life as the logical development of ideal concepts, a method which makes collective evolution dependent on objective conditions, spatially delineated, may perhaps be condemned as rough and ready, and we may even be called materialist. However, we might more accurately claim to be the opposite. Does not the essence of spiritualism in fact depend upon the idea that psychical phenomena cannot be derived directly from organic ones? Our method is in part only an application of this principle to social facts. Just as spiritualists separate the psychological from the biological domain, so we also separate the psychological domain from the social one; like them, we refuse to explain the more complex in terms of the more simple. Yet, to tell the truth, neither designation fits us precisely: the only one we accept is that of *rationalist*. Indeed, our main objective is to extend the scope of scientific rationalism to cover human behavior by demonstrating that, in the light of the past, it is capable of being reduced to relationships of cause and effect, which, by an operation no less rational, can then be transformed into rules of action for the future. What has been termed our positivism is merely a consequence of this rationalism.[2] One will not be tempted to go beyond the facts, either in order to account for them or to guide the direction in which they might go, save to the extent that one believes them to be irrational. If they are wholly intelligible, they suffice for both science and practice; for science, because there is then no motive for seeking outside them the reasons why they exist; for practice, because their usefulness is one of these reasons. It therefore seems to us, particularly in this time of resurgent mysticism, that such an undertaking can and should be greeted without apprehension and indeed with sympathy by all those who, although they part company with us on certain points, share our faith in the future of reason.

Notes

1. The objection may be made that, if health contains some repugnant elements, how can it be presented, as we do later, as the immediate object of behavior? But there is no contradiction here. Although it may be harmful in some of its consequences, it is common for a thing to be, through others, useful or even vital to life. If the evil effects which arise from it are regularly counteracted by an opposing influence, it is in fact useful without being harmful. It nevertheless remains repugnant, for in itself it does not cease to constitute a possible danger, one which is only exorcised by the action of a hostile force. Such is the case with crime. The wrong that it inflicts upon society is nullified by the punishment, if this functions regularly. It therefore follows that, without engendering the evil that it implies, it sustains, as we shall see, positive relationships, together with the basic conditions of social life. But since, so to speak, it is rendered harmless despite itself, the sentiments of revulsion that it gives rise to are none the less well founded.
2. Namely, it must not be confused with the positive metaphysics of Comte and Spencer.

Preface to the Second Edition (1901)

When this book first appeared, it aroused some fairly lively controversy. Current ideas, as if put out of joint, at first offered such vigorous resistance that it was for a while almost impossible for us to gain a hearing. On the very points about which we had expressed ourselves most explicitly, views were gratuitously ascribed to us which lacked anything in common with our own and, by refuting them, it was believed that we were also refuted. Whereas we had repeatedly declared that consciousness, both individual and social, did not signify for us anything substantial, but merely a collection of phenomena *sui generis*, more or less systematized, we were accused of realism and ontological thinking. While we had expressly stated and reiterated in every way possible that social life was made up entirely of representations, we were accused of eliminating from sociology the element of mind. Critics even went so far as to revive against us ways of argument that one might well think had definitively disappeared. Indeed, certain opinions were imputed to us that we had not put forward, on the pretense that they were "in conformity with our principles." Yet experience has demonstrated all the dangers of this method which, by allowing one to construct in arbitrary fashion the systems under discussion, also allows one to triumph without difficulty over them.

We do not think that we are deluding ourselves when we assert that, since then, resistance has progressively weakened. More than one proposition we advanced is doubtless still under attack. But we cannot be surprised or complain about this opposition, which is salutary because it is indeed very apparent that our formulas are destined to be revised in the future. Summarizing, as they do, an individual practice that is inevitably restricted, they must necessarily evolve as wider and deeper experience of social reality is gained. Furthermore, as regards methods, not one can ever be used that is not provisional, for they change as science progresses. Nevertheless, during recent years, in spite of opposition, the cause of a sociology that is objective, specific and methodical has continually gained ground. The founding of the *Année sociologique* has certainly contributed much to this result. Since it embraces at one and the same time the whole field of the science, the *Année*, better than any more specialized publication, has been able to impart a feeling of what sociology must and can become. Thus it has made plain that sociology is not condemned to remain a branch of general philosophy and that, moreover, it can come to grips in detail with facts without degenerating into pure erudition. And so we cannot pay tribute enough to the enthusiasm and devotion of our colleagues; it is thanks to them that this demonstration by facts could be attempted and can continue.

However, no matter how real the progress made, one cannot deny that past misunderstandings and confusion have not been entirely dispelled. This is why we should like to seize the opportunity of this second edition to put forward additional explanations to those already stated, to reply to certain criticisms and to give fresh clarification of certain points.

I

The proposition which states that social facts must be treated as things—the proposition which is at the very basis of our method—is among those which have stirred up the most opposition. It was deemed paradoxical and scandalous for us to assimilate to the realities of the external world those of the social world. This was singularly to misunderstand the meaning and effect of this assimilation, the object of which was not to reduce the higher forms of being to the level of lower ones but, on the contrary, to claim for the former a degree of reality at least equal to that which everyone accords to the latter. Indeed, we do not say that social facts are material things, but that they are things just as are material things, although in a different way.

What indeed is a thing? The thing stands in opposition to the idea, just as what is known from the outside stands in opposition to what is known from the inside. A thing is any object of knowledge which is not naturally penetrable by the understanding. It is all that which we cannot conceptualize adequately as an idea by the simple process of intellectual analysis. It is all that which the mind cannot understand without going outside itself, proceeding progressively by way of observation and experimentation from those features which are the most external and the most immediately accessible to those which are the least visible and the most profound. To treat facts of a certain order as things is therefore not to place them in this or that category of reality; it is to observe toward them a certain attitude of mind. It is to embark upon the study of them by adopting the principle that one is entirely ignorant of what they are, that their characteristic properties, like the unknown causes upon which they depend, cannot be discovered by even the most careful form of introspection.

The terms being so defined, our proposition, far from being a paradox, might almost pass for a truism if it were not too often still unrecognized in those sciences which deal with man, and above all in sociology. Indeed, in this sense it may be said that any object of knowledge is a thing, except perhaps for mathematical objects. Regarding the latter, since we construct them ourselves, from the most simple to the most complex, it is enough to look within ourselves and to analyze internally the mental process from which they arise, in order to know what they are. But as soon as we consider facts *per se*, when we undertake to make a science of them, they are of necessity unknowns for us, *things* of which we are ignorant, for the representations that we have been able to make of them in the course of our lives, since they have been made without method and uncritically, lack any scientific value and must be discarded. The facts of individual psychology themselves are of this nature and must be considered in this light. Indeed, although by definition they are internal to ourselves, the consciousness that we have of them reveals to us neither their inmost character nor their origin. Consciousness allows us to know them well up to a certain point, but only in the same way as our senses make us aware of heat or light, sound or electricity. It gives us muddled impressions of them, fleeting and subjective, but provides no clear, distinct notions or explanatory concepts. This is precisely why during this century an objective psychology has been founded whose fundamental rule is to study mental facts from the outside, namely as things. This should be even more the case for social facts, for consciousness cannot be more capable of knowing them than of knowing its own existence.[1] It will be objected that, since they have been wrought by us, we have only to become conscious of ourselves to know what we have put into them and how we shaped them. Firstly, however, most social institutions have been handed down to us already fashioned by previous generations; we have had no part in their shaping; consequently it is not by searching within ourselves that we can uncover the causes which have given rise to them. Furthermore, even if we have played a part in producing them, we can hardly glimpse, save in the most confused and often even the most imprecise way, the real reasons which have impelled us to act, or the nature of our action. Already, even regarding merely the steps we have taken personally, we know very inaccurately the relatively simple motives that govern us. We believe ourselves disinterested, whereas our actions are egoistic; we think that we are commanded by hatred whereas we are giving way to love, that we are obedient to reason whereas we are the slaves of irrational prejudices, etc. How therefore could we possess the ability to discern more clearly the causes, of a different order of complexity, which inspire the measures taken by the collectivity? For at the very least each individual shares in only an infinitesimally small part of them; we have a host of fellow-fashioners, and what is occurring in the consciousness of others eludes us.

Thus our rule implies no metaphysical conception, no speculation about the innermost depth of being. What it demands is that the sociologist should assume the state of mind of physicists, chemists and physiologists when they venture into an as yet unexplored area of their scientific field. As the sociologist penetrates into the social world he should be conscious that he is penetrating into the unknown. He must feel himself in the presence of facts governed by laws as unsuspected as those of life before the science of biology was born. He must hold himself ready to make discoveries which will surprise and disconcert him. Yet sociology is far from having arrived at this degree of intellectual maturity. While the scientist who studies physical nature feels very keenly the resistances that it proffers, ones which he has great difficulty in overcoming, it really seems as if the sociologist operates among things immediately clear to the mind, so great is the ease with which he seems to resolve the most obscure questions. In the present state of the discipline, we do not really know the nature of the principal social institutions, such as the state or the family, property rights or contract, punishment and responsibility. We are virtually ignorant of the causes upon which they depend, the functions they fulfill and their laws of evolution. It is as if, on certain points, we are only just beginning to perceive a few glimmers of light. Yet it suffices to glance through works of sociology to see how rare is any awareness of this ignorance and these difficulties. Not only is it deemed mandatory to dogmatize about every kind of problem at once, but it is believed that one is capable, in a few pages or sentences, of penetrating to the inmost essence of the most complex phenomena. This means that such theories express, not the facts, which could not be so swiftly fathomed, but the preconceptions of the author before he began his research. Doubtless the idea that we form of collective practices, of what they are, or what they should be, is a factor in their development. But this idea itself is a fact which, in order to be properly established, needs to be studied from the outside. For it is important to know not the way in which a particular thinker individually represents a particular institution, but the conception that the group has of it. This conception is indeed the only socially effective one. But it cannot be known through mere inner observation, since it is not wholly and entirely within any one of us; one must therefore find some external signs which make it perceptible. Furthermore, it did not arise from nothing: it is itself the result of external causes which must be known in order to be able to appreciate its future role. Thus, no matter what one does, it is always to the same method that one must return.

II

Another proposition has been no less hotly disputed than the previous one. It is the one which presents social phenomena as external to individuals. Today it is fairly willingly accepted that the facts of individual life and those of collective life are to some extent heterogeneous. It can be stated that agreement, although not unanimous but at least very widespread, is beginning to be reached on this point. There are now hardly any sociologists who deny to sociology any kind of specificity. Yet since society comprises only individuals[2] it seems in accordance with common sense that social life can have no other substratum than the individual consciousness. Otherwise it would seem suspended in the air, floating in the void.

Yet what is so readily deemed unacceptable for social facts is freely admitted for other domains of nature. Whenever elements of any kind combine, by virtue of this combination they give rise to new phenomena. One is therefore forced to conceive of these phenomena as residing, not in the elements, but in the entity formed by the union of these elements. The living cell contains nothing save chemical particles, just as society is made up of nothing except individuals. Yet it is very clearly impossible for the characteristic phenomena of life to reside in atoms of hydrogen, oxygen, carbon and nitrogen. For how could living movements arise from amidst non-living elements? Furthermore, how would biological properties be allocated amongst these elements? They could not be found equally in them all, since they are not of the same nature: carbon is not nitrogen and thus cannot possess the same properties or play the same part. It is no less unacceptable for every facet of life, for each of its main characteristics, to be incorporated in a distinct group of atoms. Life cannot be split up in this fashion. It is one, and consequently cannot be located save in the living substance in its entirety. It is in the whole and not in the parts. It is not the non-living particles of the cell which feed themselves and reproduce—in a word, which live; it is the cell itself and it alone. And what we maintain regarding life could be reaffirmed for every possible kind of synthesis. The hardness of bronze lies neither in the copper, nor in the tin, nor in the lead which have been used to form it, which are all soft or malleable bodies. The hardness arises from the mixing of them. The liquidity of water, its sustaining and other properties, are not in the two gases of which it is composed, but in the complex substance which they form by coming together.

Let us apply this principle to sociology. If, as is granted to us, this synthesis *sui generis*, which constitutes every society, gives rise to new phenomena, different from those which occur in consciousnesses in isolation, one is forced to admit that these specific facts reside in the society itself that produces them and not in its parts—namely its members. In this sense therefore they lie outside the consciousness of individuals as such, in the same way as the distinctive features of life lie outside the chemical substances that make up a living organism. They cannot be reabsorbed into the elements without contradiction, since by definition they presume something other than what those elements contain. Thus yet another reason justifies the distinction we have established later between psychology proper—the science of the individual mind—and sociology. Social facts differ not only in quality from psychical facts; *they have a different substratum*, they do not evolve in the same environment or depend on the same conditions. This does not mean that they are not in some sense psychical, since they all consist of ways of thinking and acting. But the states of the collective consciousness are of a different nature from the states of the individual consciousness; they are representations of another kind. The mentality of groups is not that of individuals: it has its own laws. The two sciences are therefore as sharply distinct as two sciences can be, whatever relationships may otherwise exist between them.

Nevertheless, on this point it is proper to make a distinction which will perhaps shed some light on the argument.

That the *content* of social life cannot be explained by purely psychological factors, namely by states of the individual consciousness, seems to us to be as plain as can be. Indeed what collective representations express is the way in which the group thinks of itself in its relationships with the objects which affect it. Now the group is constituted differently from the individual and the things which affect it are of another kind. Representations which express neither the same subjects nor the same objects cannot depend upon the same causes. In order to understand the way in which society conceives of itself and the world that surrounds it, it is the nature of society and not that of individuals which must be considered. The symbols in which it thinks of itself alter according to what it is. If, for example, it conceives of itself as deriving from an eponymous animal, it is because it forms one of those special groups known as clans. Where the animal is replaced by a human ancestor, but one that is also mythical, it is because the clan has changed its nature. If, above local or family divinities, it imagines others on whom it fancies it is dependent, it is because the local and family groups of which it is made up tend to concentrate and unite together, and the degree of unity presented by a pantheon of gods corresponds to the degree of unity reached at the same time in society. If it condemns certain modes of behavior it is because they offend certain of its basic sentiments; and these sentiments relate to its constitution, just as those of the individual relate to his physical temperament and his mental makeup. Thus, even if individual psychology held no more secrets for us, it could not provide the solution to any one of these problems, since they relate to orders of facts of which it is ignorant.

But once this difference in nature is acknowledged one may ask whether individual representations and collective representations do not nevertheless resemble each other, since both are equally representations; and whether, as a consequence of these similarities, certain abstract laws might not be common to the two domains. Myths, popular legends, religious conceptions of every kind, moral beliefs, etc., express a different reality from individual reality. Yet it may be that the manner in which the two attract or repel, join together or separate, is independent of their content and relates solely to their general quality of being representations. While having a different content they could well behave in their interrelation-ships as do feelings, images or ideas in the individual. Could not one, for example, believe that proximity and similarity, contrasts and logical oppositions act in the same way, no matter what things are being repre-sented? Thus one arrives at the possibility of an entirely formal psychology which might form a common ground between individual psychology and sociology. This is maybe why certain minds feel scruples at distinguishing too sharply between the two sciences.

Strictly speaking, in our present state of knowledge, the question posed in this way can receive no categorical answer. Indeed, all that we know, moreover, about the manner in which individual ideas combine together is reduced to those few propositions, very general and very vague, which are commonly termed the laws of the association of ideas. As for the laws of the collective ideation, these are even more completely unknown. Social psychology, whose task it should be to determine them, is hardly more than a term which covers all kinds of general questions, various and imprecise, without any defined object. What should be done is to investigate, by comparing mythical themes, legends and popular traditions, and languages, how social representations are attracted to or exclude each other, amalgamate with or are distinguishable from each other, etc. Now, although the problem is one that is worthy of tempting the curiosity of researchers, one can hardly say that is has been tackled. So long as some of these laws remain undiscovered, it will clearly be impossible to know with certainty whether they do or do not repeat those of individual psychology.

Yet in the absence of certainty, it is at the very least probable that, if there exist resemblances between these two kinds of laws, the differences between them must be no less marked. Indeed it does not seem legitimate to claim that the matter from which the representations are formed has no effect upon the various ways in which they combine together. It is true that psychologists sometimes speak of the laws of association of ideas, as if they were the same for all the various kinds of individual representations. But nothing is less likely: images do not combine with each other as do the senses, nor concepts in the same way as images. If psychology were more advanced it would doubtless establish that each category of mental states has its own formal laws which are peculiar to it. If this is so, *a fortiori* one must expect that the corresponding laws of social thinking are specific, as is the thinking itself. Indeed, little as this order of facts has been explored, it is difficult not to be aware of this specificity. Is it not really this which makes appear so strange to us the very special manner in which religious conceptions (which are essentially collective) intermingle or, alternatively, distinguish themselves from each other, are transformed one into another, giving birth to composites which are contradictory, in contrast to the usual outcomes of our own individual thinking? If therefore, as one may presume, certain laws regarding social states of mind are in fact reminiscent of certain of those established by the psychologists, it is not because the former are simply a special case of the latter. It is rather because between the one and the other, setting on one side differences which are certainly important, there are similarities which may be adduced by abstraction, but which are as yet unknown. This means that in no way can sociology borrow purely and simply from psychology this or that proposition in order to apply it as such to social facts. But collective thinking in its entirety, in form as in substance, must be studied in itself and for itself, with a feeling for what is special to it, and one must leave to the future the task of discovering to what extent it resembles the thought of individuals. This is even a problem which pertains rather to general philosophy and abstract logic than to the scientific study of social facts.[3]

III

It remains for us to say a few words about the definition of social facts that we have given in our first chapter. We represent them as consisting of manners of acting or thinking, distinguishable through their special characteristic of being capable of exercising a coercive influence on the consciousness of individuals. A confusion has arisen about this which is worthy of note.

So strong has been the habit of applying to sociological matters the forms of philosophical thought that this preliminary definition has often been seen as a sort of philosophy of the social fact. It has been maintained that we were explaining social phenomena in terms of constraint, just as Tarde explains them by imitation. We harbor no such ambition, and it did not even occur to us that this could be imputed to us, so directly is it contrary to all method. What we set out to do was not to anticipate the conclusions of the discipline by stating a philosophical view, but merely to indicate how, by outward signs, it is possible to identify the facts that the science must deal with, so that the social scientist may learn how to pick out their location and not to confuse them with other facts. It was intended to mark out the field of research as clearly as possible, and not for philosophy and sociology to embrace each other in some kind of comprehensive intuition. Thus we readily admit the charge that this definition does not express all aspects of the social fact and consequently that it is not the sole possible one. Indeed it is not at all inconceivable for it to be characterized in several different ways, for there is no reason why it should possess only the one distinctive property.[4] All that matters is to select the characteristic which seems to suit best the purpose one has in mind. It is even highly possible to employ several criteria at the same time, according to circumstances. We have ourselves recognized this sometimes to be necessary in sociology (see p. 58). Since we are dealing with a preliminary definition, all that is necessary is that the characteristics which are being used are immediately recognizable and can be identified before the investigation begins. Such a condition is not fulfilled in the definitions that have sometimes been advanced in opposition to our own. It has been said, for example, that the social fact is "all that is produced in and by society," or "that which in some way concerns and affects the group." But one cannot know whether society is or is not the cause of a fact or if this fact has social consequences until further knowledge has already been obtained. Such definitions could not therefore serve to determine initially the object of the investigation. In order to be able to use them, the study of social facts must therefore already have been carried somewhat further, and consequently some other means previously discovered for recognizing the facts in context.

At the same time as our definition has been found to be too narrow, it has also been accused of being too broad and of encompassing almost all reality. It has indeed been said that any physical environment exercises constraint upon those who are subjected to it, for, to a certain degree, they are forced to adapt themselves to it. But as between these two types of coercion, there is a world of difference separating a physical from a moral environment. The pressure exerted by one or several bodies on other bodies or even on other wills should not be confused with that which the group consciousness exercises on the consciousness of its members. What is exclusively peculiar to social constraint is that it stems not from the unyieldingness of certain patterns of molecules, but from the prestige with which certain representations are endowed. It is true that habits, whether unique to individuals or hereditary, in certain respects possess this same property. They dominate us and impose beliefs and practices upon us. But they dominate us from within, for they are wholly within each one of us. By contrast, social beliefs and practices act upon us from the outside; thus the ascendancy exerted by the former as compared with the latter is basically very different.

Furthermore, one should not be surprised that other natural phenomena present in different forms the very characteristic by which we have defined social phenomena. This similarity springs merely from the fact that both are real. For everything which is real has a definite nature which makes itself felt, with which one must reckon and which, even if one succeeds in neutralizing it, is never completely overcome. And, after all, this is what is most essential in the notion of social constraint. For all that it implies is that collective ways of acting and thinking possess a reality existing outside individuals, who, at every moment, conform to them. They are things which have their own existence. The individual encounters them when they are already completely fashioned and he cannot cause them to cease to exist or be different from what they are. Willy-nilly he is therefore obliged to take them into account; it is all the more difficult (although we do not say that it is impossible) for him to modify them because in varying degrees they partake of the material and moral supremacy that society exerts over its members. No doubt the individual plays a part in their creation. But in order for a social fact to exist, several individuals at the very least must have interacted together and the resulting combination must have given rise to some new production. As this synthesis occurs outside each one of us (since a plurality of consciousnesses are involved) it has necessarily the effect of crystallizing, of instituting outside ourselves, certain modes of action and certain ways of judging which are independent of the particular individual will considered separately. As has been remarked,[5] there is one word which, provided one extends a little its normal meaning, expresses moderately well this very special kind of existence; it is that of *institution*. In fact, without doing violence to the meaning of the word, one may term an *institution* all the beliefs and modes of behavior instituted by the collectivity; sociology can then be defined as the science of institutions, their genesis and their functioning.[6]

It seems pointless for us to revert to the other controversies that this book has given rise to, for they do not touch upon anything essential. The general orientation of the method does not depend upon the procedures preferred to classify social types or distinguish the normal from the pathological. Moreover, such objections very often arise from the fact that one has refused to admit, or not admitted without reservations, our basic principle, that of the objective reality of social facts. It is therefore upon this principle that in the end everything rests, and everything comes back to it. This is why it has seemed fruitful for us to highlight it yet again, while distinguishing it from any secondary question. And we are certain that in attributing this paramountcy to it we remain faithful to sociological tradition: for, after all, it is from this conception that the whole of sociology has sprung. Indeed the science could not see the light of day until it had been grasped that social phenomena, although not material things, are nevertheless real ones requiring to be studied. To arrive at thinking that it is appropriate to investigate what they are, it was necessary to understand that they exist in a definite way, that their mode of existence is constant and that they possess a character independent of individual arbitrariness, yet one from which flow necessary relationships. Thus the history of sociology has been simply the long effort to define this sentiment, to give it depth, and to elaborate all the consequences that it entails. But in spite of the great progress that has been made in this direction, we shall see later in this work that there still subsist numerous vestiges of that anthropocentric postulate which, here as elsewhere, blocks the path to science. It is disagreeable for man to have to renounce the unlimited power over the social order that for so long he ascribed to himself. Moreover it appears to him that, if collective forms really exist, he is necessarily condemned to be subjected to them without being able to modify them. This is what inclines him to deny their existence. Repeated experiences have in vain attempted to teach him that this all-powerfulness, the illusion of which he so willingly entertains, has always been for him a cause of weakness; that his dominion over things only really began when he recognized that they have a nature of their own, and when he resigned himself to learning from them what they are. Banished from all other sciences, this deplorable prejudice stubbornly survives in sociology. Hence there is nothing more urgent than to seek to free our science from it: this is the main purpose of our efforts.

Notes

1. It can be seen that to concede this proposition it is unnecessary to maintain that social life is made up of anything save representations. It is sufficient to posit that representations, whether individual or collective, cannot be studied scientifically unless they are studied objectively.
2. Moreover, this proposition is only partially accurate. As well as individuals, there are things which are integrating elements in society. It is merely true that individuals are the only active elements in it.
3. It is superfluous to demonstrate how, from this viewpoint, the necessity for studying facts from the outside appears even more apparent, since they result from syntheses which take place outside us and about which we have not even the hazy perception which consciousness can give us of internal phenomena.
4. The coercive power that we attribute to the social fact represents so small a part of its totality that it can equally well display the opposite characteristic. For, while institutions bear down upon us, we nevertheless cling to them; they impose obligations upon us, and yet we love them; they place constraints upon us, and yet we find satisfaction in the way they function, and in that very constraint. This antithesis is one that moralists have often pointed out as existing between the two notions of the good and of duty, which express two different aspects, but both equally real, of moral life. Now there are perhaps no collective practices which do not exert this dual influence upon us, which, moreover, is only apparent in contradiction. If we have not defined them in terms of this special attachment, which is both interested and disinterested, it is purely and simply because it does not reveal itself in easily perceptible external signs. The good possesses something more internal and intimate than duty, and is in consequence less tangible.
5. Cf. the article "Sociologie" by Fauconnet and Mauss, published in the *Grande Encyclopédie*.
6. Despite the fact that beliefs and social practices permeate us in this way from the outside, it does not follow that we receive them passively and without causing them to undergo modification. In thinking about collective institutions, in assimilating ourselves to them, we individualize them, we more or less impart to them our own personal stamp. Thus in thinking about the world of the senses each one of us colors it in his own way, and different

people adapt themselves differently to an identical physical environment. This is why each one of us creates to a certain extent *his own* morality, *his own* religion, *his own* techniques. Every type of social conformity carries with it a whole gamut of individual variations. It is nonetheless true that the sphere of permitted variations is limited. It is nonexistent or very small as regards religious and moral phenomena, where deviations may easily become crimes. It is more extensive for all matters relating to economic life. But sooner or later, even in this last case, one encounters a limit that must not be overstepped.

Introduction

Up to now sociologists have scarcely occupied themselves with the task of characterizing and defining the method that they apply to the study of social facts. Thus in the whole of Spencer's work the methodological problem has no place. *The Study of Sociology*, the title of which could be misleading, is devoted to demonstrating the difficulties and possibilities of sociology, not to setting out the procedures it should employ. It is true that Mill dealt with the question at some length.[1] But he merely submitted to the sieve of his own dialectic what Comte had said upon it, without adding any real contribution of his own. Therefore to all intents and purposes a chapter of the *Cours de philosophie positive*[2] is the only original and important study which we possess on the subject.

Yet there is nothing surprising in this apparent neglect. This is because the great sociologists just cited hardly went beyond generalities concerning the nature of societies, the relationships between the social and biological realms, and the general march of progress. Even Spencer's voluminous sociological work has hardly any other purpose than to show how the law of universal evolution is applied to societies. In order to deal with these philosophical questions, no special, complex procedures are necessary. Sociologists have therefore been content to weigh up the comparative merits of deduction and induction and to make a cursory inquiry into the most general resources that sociological research has at its command. But the precautions to be taken in the observation of facts, the manner in which the main problems should be set out, the direction that research should take, the particular procedures which may make it successful, the rules that should govern the demonstration of proof—all these remained undetermined.

A happy conjunction of circumstances, among which pride of place must rightly be assigned to the initiative which set up on our behalf a regular course in sociology at the Faculty of Letters at Bordeaux, allowed us to devote ourselves early on to the study of social science and even to make it our professional concern. Thus we have been able to move on from these over-general questions and tackle a certain number of specific problems. The very nature of things has therefore led us to work out a better-defined method, one which we believe to be more exactly adapted to the specific nature of social phenomena. It is the results of our work which we wish to set down here and submit to debate. They are undoubtedly implicit in our recently published book *La Division du Travail Social*. But it seems to us to have some advantage to single them out here, formulate them separately and accompany them with proofs, illustrating them with examples culled from that book or taken from work as yet unpublished. One will then be able to judge better the direction we are seeking to give to sociological studies.

Notes

1. J.S. Mill, *System of Logic*, vol. I, book VI, chs VII–XII (London: Longmans, Green, Reader & Dyer, 1872).
2. Cf. 2nd ed., Paris, pp. 294–336.

CHAPTER I

What Is a Social Fact?

Before beginning the search for the method appropriate to the study of social facts it is important to know what are the facts termed "social."

The question is all the more necessary because the term is used without much precision. It is commonly used to designate almost all the phenomena that occur within society, however little social interest of some generality they present. Yet under this heading there is, so to speak, no human occurrence that cannot be called social. Every individual drinks, sleeps, eats, or employs his reason, and society has every interest in seeing that these functions are regularly exercised. If therefore these facts were social ones, sociology would possess no subject matter peculiarly its own, and its domain would be confused with that of biology and psychology.

However, in reality there is in every society a clearly determined group of phenomena separable, because of their distinct characteristics, from those that form the subject matter of other sciences of nature.

When I perform my duties as a brother, a husband or a citizen and carry out the commitments I have entered into, I fulfill obligations which are defined in law and custom and which are external to myself and my actions. Even when they conform to my own sentiments and when I feel their reality within me, that reality does not cease to be objective, for it is not I who have prescribed these duties; I have received them through education. Moreover, how often does it happen that we are ignorant of the details of the obligations that we must assume, and that, to know them, we must consult the legal code and its authorized interpreters! Similarly the believer has discovered from birth, ready fashioned, the beliefs and practices of his religious life; if they existed before he did, it follows that they exist outside him. The system of signs that I employ to express my thoughts, the monetary system I use to pay my debts, the credit instruments I utilize in my commercial relationships, the practices I follow in my profession, etc., all function independently of the use I make of them. Considering in turn each member of society, the foregoing remarks can be repeated for each single one of them. Thus there are ways of acting, thinking and feeling which possess the remarkable property of existing outside the consciousness of the individual.

Not only are these types of behavior and thinking external to the individual, but they are endued with a compelling and coercive power by virtue of which, whether he wishes it or not, they impose themselves upon him. Undoubtedly when I conform to them of my own free will, this coercion is not felt or felt hardly at all, since it is unnecessary. None the less it is intrinsically a characteristic of these facts; the proof of this is that it asserts itself as soon as I try to resist. If I attempt to violate the rules of law they react against me so as to forestall my action, if there is still time. Alternatively, they annul it or make my action conform to the norm if it is already accomplished but capable of being reversed; or they cause me to pay the penalty for it if it is irreparable. If purely moral rules are at stake, the public conscience restricts any act which infringes them by the surveillance it exercises over the conduct of citizens and by the special punishments it has at its disposal. In other cases the constraint is less violent; nevertheless, it does not cease to exist. If I do not conform to ordinary conventions, if in my mode of dress I pay no heed to what is customary in my country and in my social class, the laughter I provoke, the social distance at which I am kept, produce, although in a more mitigated form, the same results as any real penalty. In other cases, although it may be indirect, constraint is no less effective. I am not forced to speak French with my compatriots, nor to use the legal currency, but it is impossible for me to do otherwise. If I tried to escape the necessity, my attempt would fail miserably. As an industrialist nothing prevents me from working with the processes and methods of the previous century, but if I do I will most certainly ruin myself. Even when in fact I can struggle free from these rules and successfully break them, it is never without being forced to fight against them. Even if in the end they are overcome, they make their constraining power sufficiently felt in the resistance that they afford. There is no innovator, even a fortunate one, whose ventures do not encounter opposition of this kind.

Here, then, is a category of facts which present very special characteristics: they consist of manners of acting, thinking and feeling external to the individual, which are invested with a coercive power by virtue of which they exercise control over him. Consequently, since they consist of representations and actions, they cannot be confused with organic phenomena, nor with psychical phenomena, which have no existence save in and through the individual consciousness. Thus they constitute a new species and to them must be exclusively assigned the term *social*. It is appropriate, since it is clear that, not having the individual as their substratum, they can have none other than society, either political society in its entirety or one of the partial groups that it includes—religious denominations, political and literary schools, occupational corporations, etc. Moreover, it is for such as these alone that the term is fitting, for the word "social" has the sole meaning of designating those phenomena which fall into none of the categories of facts already constituted and labeled. They are consequently the proper field of sociology. It is true that this word "constraint," in terms of which we define them, is in danger of infuriating those who zealously uphold out-and-out individualism. Since they maintain that the individual is completely autonomous, it seems to them that he is diminished every time he is made aware that he is not dependent on himself alone. Yet since it is indisputable today that most of our ideas and tendencies are not developed by ourselves, but come to us from outside, they can only penetrate us by imposing themselves upon us. This is all that our definition implies. Moreover, we know that all social constraints do not necessarily exclude the individual personality.[1]

Yet since the examples just cited (legal and moral rules, religious dogmas, financial systems, etc.) all consist of beliefs and practices already well established, in view of what has been said it might be maintained that no social fact can exist except where there is a well-defined social organization. But there are other facts which do not present themselves in this already crystallized form but which also possess the same objectivity and ascendancy over the individual. These are what are called social "currents." Thus in a public gathering the great waves of enthusiasm, indignation and pity that are produced have their seat in no one individual consciousness. They come to each one of us from outside and can sweep us along in spite of ourselves. If perhaps I abandon myself to them I may not be conscious of the pressure that they are exerting upon me, but that pressure makes its presence felt immediately I attempt to struggle against them. If an individual tries to pit himself against one of these collective manifestations, the sentiments that he is rejecting will be turned against him. Now if this external coercive power asserts itself so acutely in cases of resistance, it must be because it exists in the other instances cited above without our being conscious of it. Hence we are the victims of an illusion which leads us to believe we have ourselves produced what has been imposed upon us externally. But if the willingness with which we let ourselves be carried along disguises the pressure we have undergone, it does not eradicate it. Thus air does not cease to have weight, although we no longer feel that weight. Even when we have individually and spontaneously shared in the common emotion, the impression we have experienced is utterly different from what we would have felt if we had been alone. Once the assembly has broken up and these social influences have ceased to act upon us, and we are once more on our own, the emotions we have felt seem an alien phenomenon, one in which we no longer recognize ourselves. It is then we perceive that we have undergone the emotions much more than generated them. These emotions may even perhaps fill us with horror, so much do they go against the grain. Thus individuals who are normally perfectly harmless may, when gathered together in a crowd, let themselves be drawn into acts of atrocity. And what we assert about these transitory outbreaks likewise applies to those more lasting movements of opinion which relate to religious, political, literary and artistic matters, etc., and which are constantly being produced around us, whether throughout society or in a more limited sphere.

Moreover, this definition of a social fact can be verified by examining an experience that is characteristic. It is sufficient to observe how children are brought up. If one views the facts as they are and indeed as they have always been, it is patently obvious that all education consists of a continual effort to impose upon the child ways of seeing, thinking and acting which he himself would not have arrived at spontaneously. From his earliest years we oblige him to eat, drink and sleep at regular hours, and to observe cleanliness, calm and obedience; later we force him to learn how to be mindful of others, to respect customs and conventions, and to work, etc. If this constraint in time ceases to be felt it is because it gradually gives rise to habits, to inner tendencies which render it superfluous; but they supplant the constraint only because they are derived from it. It is true that, in Spencer's view, a rational education should shun such means and allow the child complete freedom to do what he will. Yet as this educational theory has never been put into practice among any known people, it can only be the personal expression of a *desideratum* and not a fact which can be established in contradiction to the other facts given above. What renders these latter facts particularly illuminating is that education sets out precisely with the object of creating a social being. Thus there can be seen, as in an abbreviated form, how the social being has been fashioned historically. The pressure to which the child is subjected unremittingly is the pressure itself of the social environment which seeks to shape him in its own image, and in which parents and teachers are only the representatives and intermediaries.

Thus it is not the fact that they are general which can serve to characterize sociological phenomena. Thoughts to be found in the consciousness of each individual and movements which are repeated by all individuals are not for this reason social facts. If some have been content with using this characteristic in order to define them it is because they have been confused, wrongly, with what might be termed their individual incarnations. What constitutes social facts are the beliefs, tendencies and practices of the group taken collectively. But the forms that these collective states may assume when they are "refracted" through individuals are things of a different kind. What irrefutably demonstrates this duality of nature is that these two categories of facts frequently are manifested dissociated from each other. Indeed some of these ways of acting or thinking acquire, by dint of repetition, a sort of consistency which, so to speak, precipitate them, isolating them from the particular events which reflect them. Thus they assume a shape, a tangible form peculiar to them and constitute a reality *sui generis* vastly distinct from the individual facts which manifest that reality. Collective custom does not exist only in a state of immanence in the successive actions which it determines, but, by a privilege without example in the biological kingdom, expresses itself once and for all in a formula repeated by word of mouth, transmitted by education and even enshrined in the written word. Such are the origins and nature of legal and moral rules, aphorisms and popular sayings, articles of faith in which religious or political sects epitomize their beliefs, and standards of taste drawn up by literary schools, etc. None of these modes of acting and thinking are to be found wholly in the application made of them by individuals, since they can even exist without being applied at the time.

Undoubtedly this state of dissociation does not always present itself with equal distinctiveness. It is sufficient for dissociation to exist unquestionably in the numerous important instances cited, for us to prove that the social fact is distinct from its individual effects. Moreover, even when the dissociation is not immediately observable, it can often be made so with the help of certain methodological devices. Indeed it is essential to embark on such procedures if one wishes to refine out the social fact from any amalgam and so observe it in its pure state. Thus certain currents of opinion, whose intensity varies according to the time and country in which they occur, impel us, for example, toward marriage or suicide, toward higher or lower birth-rates, etc. Such currents are plainly social facts. At first sight they seem inseparable from the forms they assume in individual cases. But statistics afford us a means of isolating them. They are indeed not inaccurately represented by rates of births, marriages and suicides, that is, by the result obtained after dividing the average annual total of marriages, births, and voluntary homicides by the number of persons of an age to marry, produce children, or commit suicide.[2] Since each one of these statistics includes without distinction all individual cases, the individual circumstances which may have played some part in producing the phenomenon cancel each other out and consequently do not contribute to determining the nature of the phenomenon. What it expresses is a certain state of the collective soul.

That is what social phenomena are when stripped of all extraneous elements. As regards their private manifestations, these do indeed have something social about them, since in part they reproduce the collective model. But to a large extent each one depends also upon the psychical and organic constitution of the individual, and on the particular circumstances in which he is placed. Therefore they are not phenomena which are in the strict sense sociological. They depend on both domains at the same time, and could be termed socio-psychical. They are of interest to the sociologist without constituting the immediate content of sociology. The same characteristic is to be found in the organisms of those mixed phenomena of nature studied in the combined sciences such as biochemistry.

It may be objected that a phenomenon can only be collective if it is common to all the members of society, or at the very least to a majority, and consequently, if it is general. This is doubtless the case, but if it is general it is because it is collective (that is, more or less obligatory); but it is very far from being collective because it is general. It is a condition of the group repeated in individuals because it imposes itself upon them. It is in each part because it is in the whole, but far from being in the whole because it is in the parts. This is supremely evident in those beliefs and practices which are handed down to us ready fashioned by previous generations. We accept and adopt them because, since they are the work of the collectivity and one that is centuries old, they are invested with a special authority that our education has taught us to recognize and respect. It is worthy of note that the vast majority of social phenomena come to us in this way. But even when the social fact is partly due to our direct cooperation, it is no different in nature. An outburst of collective emotion in a gathering does not merely express the sum total of what individual feelings share in common, but is something of a very different order, as we have demonstrated. It is a product of shared existence, of actions and reactions called into play between the consciousnesses of individuals. If it is echoed in each one of them it is precisely by virtue of the special energy derived from its collective origins. If all hearts beat in unison, this is not as a consequence of a spontaneous, pre-established harmony; it is because one and the same force is propelling them in the same direction. Each one is borne along by the rest.

We have therefore succeeded in delineating for ourselves the exact field of sociology. It embraces one single, well-defined group of phenomena. A social fact is identifiable through the power of external coercion which it exerts or is capable of exerting upon individuals. The presence of this power is in turn recognizable because of the existence of some pre-determined sanction, or through the resistance that the fact opposes to any individual action that may threaten it. However, it can also be defined by ascertaining how widespread it is within the group, provided that, as noted above, one is careful to add a second essential characteristic; this is, that it exists independently of the particular forms that it may assume in the process of spreading itself within the group. In certain cases this latter criterion can even be more easily applied than the former one. The presence of constraint is easily ascertainable when it is manifested externally through some direct reaction of society, as in the case of law, morality, beliefs, customs and even fashions. But when constraint is merely indirect, as with that exerted by an economic organization, it is not always so clearly discernible. Generality combined with objectivity may then be easier to establish. Moreover, this second definition is simply another formulation of the first one: if a mode of behavior existing outside the consciousnesses of individuals becomes general, it can only do so by exerting pressure upon them.[3]

However, one may well ask whether this definition is complete. Indeed the facts which have provided us with its basis are all *ways of functioning*:

they are "physiological" in nature. But there are also collective *ways of being*, namely, social facts of an "anatomical" or morphological nature. Sociology cannot dissociate itself from what concerns the substratum of collective life. Yet the number and nature of the elementary parts which constitute society, the way in which they are articulated, the degree of coalescence they have attained, the distribution of population over the earth's surface, the extent and nature of the network of communications, the design of dwellings, etc., do not at first sight seem relatable to ways of acting, feeling or thinking.

Yet, first and foremost, these various phenomena present the same characteristic which has served us in defining the others. These ways of being impose themselves upon the individual just as do the ways of acting we have dealt with. In fact, when we wish to learn how a society is divided up politically, in what its divisions consist and the degree of solidarity that exists between them, it is not through physical inspection and geographical observation that we may come to find this out: such divisions are social, although they may have some physical basis. It is only through public law that we can study such political organization, because this law is what determines its nature, just as it determines our domestic and civic relationships. The organization is no less a form of compulsion. If the population clusters together in our cities instead of being scattered over the rural areas, it is because there exists a trend of opinion, a collective drive which imposes this concentration upon individuals. We can no more choose the design of our houses than the cut of our clothes—at least, the one is as much obligatory as the other. The communication network forcibly prescribes the direction of internal migrations or commercial exchanges, etc., and even their intensity. Consequently, at the most there are grounds for adding one further category to the list of phenomena already enumerated as bearing the distinctive stamp of a social fact. But as that enumeration was in no wise strictly exhaustive, this addition would not be indispensable.

Moreover, it does not even serve a purpose, for these ways of being are only ways of acting that have been consolidated. A society's political structure is only the way in which its various component segments have become accustomed to living with each other. If relationships between them are traditionally close, the segments tend to merge together; if the contrary, they tend to remain distinct. The type of dwelling imposed upon us is merely the way in which everyone around us and, in part, previous generations, have customarily built their houses. The communication network is only the channel which has been cut by the regular current of commerce and migrations, etc., flowing in the same direction. Doubtless if phenomena of a morphological kind were the only ones that displayed this rigidity, it might be thought that they constituted a separate species. But a legal rule is no less permanent an arrangement than an architectural style, and yet it is a "physiological" fact. A simple moral maxim is certainly more malleable, yet it is cast in forms much more rigid than a mere professional custom or fashion. Thus there exists a whole range of gradations which, without any break in continuity, join the most clearly delineated structural facts to those free currents of social life which are not yet caught in any definite mold. This therefore signifies that the differences between them concern only the degree to which they have become consolidated. Both are forms of life at varying stages of crystallization. It would undoubtedly be advantageous to reserve the term "morphological" for those social facts which relate to the social substratum, but only on condition that one is aware that they are of the same nature as the others. Our definition will therefore subsume all that has to be defined if it states:

A social fact is any way of acting, whether fixed or not, capable of exerting over the individual an external constraint;

or:

which is general over the whole of a given society whilst having an existence of its own, independent of its individual manifestations.[4]

Notes

1. Moreover, this is not to say that all constraint is normal. We shall return to this point later.
2. Suicides do not occur at any age, nor do they occur at all ages of life with the same frequency.
3. It can be seen how far removed this definition of the social fact is from that which serves as the basis for the ingenious system of Tarde. We must first state that our research has nowhere led us to corroboration of the preponderant influence that Tarde attributes to imitation in the genesis of collective facts. Moreover, from this definition, which is not a theory but a mere résumé of the immediate data observed, it seems clearly to follow that imitation does not always express, indeed never expresses, what is essential and characteristic in the social fact. Doubtless every social fact is imitated and has, as we have just shown, a tendency to become generalized, but this is because it is social, i.e. obligatory. Its capacity for expansion is not the cause but the consequence of its sociological character. If social facts were unique in bringing about this effect, imitation might serve, if not to explain them, at least to define them. But an individual state which impacts on others none the less remains individual. Moreover, one may speculate whether the term "imitation" is indeed appropriate to designate a proliferation which occurs through some coercive influence. In such a single term very different phenomena, which need to be distinguished, are confused.

4. This close affinity of life and structure, organ and function, can be readily established in sociology because there exists between these two extremes a whole series of intermediate stages, immediately observable, which reveal the link between them. Biology lacks this methodological resource. But one may believe legitimately that sociological inductions on this subject are applicable to biology and that, in organisms as in societies, between these two categories of facts only differences in degree exist.

CHAPTER II
Rules for the Observation of Social Facts

The first and most basic rule is *to consider social facts as things*.

I

At the moment when a new order of phenomena becomes the object of a science they are already represented in the mind, not only through sense perceptions, but also by some kind of crudely formed concepts. Before the first rudiments of physics and chemistry were known, men already possessed notions about physical and chemical phenomena which went beyond pure perception alone. Such, for example, are those to be found intermingled with all religions. This is because reflective thought precedes science, which merely employs it more methodically. Man cannot live among things without forming ideas about them according to which he regulates his behavior. But, because these notions are closer to us and more within our mental grasp than the realities to which they correspond, we naturally tend to substitute them for the realities, concentrating our speculations upon them. Instead of observing, describing and comparing things, we are content to reflect upon our ideas, analyzing and combining them. Instead of a science which deals with realities, we carry out no more than an ideological analysis. Certainly this analysis does not rule out all observation. We can appeal to the facts to corroborate these notions or the conclusions drawn from them. But then the facts intervene only secondarily, as examples or confirmatory proof. Thus they are not the subject matter of the science, which therefore proceeds from ideas to things, and not from things to ideas.

It is clear that this method cannot yield objective results. These notions or concepts—however they are designated—are of course not legitimate surrogates for things. The products of common experience, their main purpose is to attune our actions to the surrounding world; they are formed by and for experience. Now a representation can effectively perform this

29

function even if it is theoretically false. Several centuries ago Copernicus dispelled the illusions our senses experienced concerning the movements of the heavenly bodies, and yet it is still according to these illusions that we commonly regulate the distribution of our time. For an idea to stimulate the reaction that the nature of a thing demands, it need not faithfully express that nature. It is sufficient for it to make us perceive what is useful or disadvantageous about the thing, and in what ways it can render us service or disservice. But notions formed in this way can only present a roughly appropriate practicality, and then only in the general run of cases. How often are they both dangerous and inadequate! It is therefore not by elaborating upon them, however one treats them, that we will ever succeed in discovering the laws of reality. On the contrary, they are as a veil interposed between the things and ourselves, concealing them from us even more effectively because we believe it to be more transparent.

Such a science can only be a stunted one, for it lacks the subject matter on which to feed. It has hardly come into existence, one might say, before it vanishes, transmuted into an art. Allegedly its notions contain all that is essential to reality, but this is because they are confused with the reality itself. From then onward they appear to contain all that is needful for us not only to understand what is, but also to prescribe what should be done and the means of implementation, for what is good is in conformity with the nature of things. What goes against nature is bad, and the means of attaining the good and eluding the bad both derive from that same nature. Thus if we have already comprehended the reality from the first, to study it has no longer any practical interest. Since it is this interest which is the reason for our study, there is henceforth no purpose to it. Our reflective thought is thus induced to turn away from what is the true subject matter of the science, namely the present and the past, and in one fell swoop to proceed to the future. Instead of seeking to understand the facts already discovered and acquired, it immediately undertakes to reveal new ones, more in accord with the ends that men pursue. If men think they know what is the essence of matter, they immediately embark on the quest for the philosopher's stone. This encroachment of art upon science, which hinders the latter's development, is made easy also by the very circumstances which determine the awakening of scientific reflection. For, since this reflection comes into being only to satisfy vital needs, it is quite naturally directed toward practical matters. The needs which it is called upon to assuage are always pressing ones, and consequently urge it to arrive at conclusions. Remedies, not explanations, are required.

This procedure is so much in accordance with the natural inclination of our mind that it is even to be found in the beginnings of the physical sciences. It is what characterizes alchemy as distinct from chemistry, and astrology from astronomy. It is how Bacon characterizes the method followed by the scholars of his day—one which he fought against. Indeed the notions just discussed are those *notiones vulgares*, or *praenotiones*,[1] which he points out as being at the basis of all the sciences,[2] in which they take the place of facts.[3] It is these *idola* which, resembling ghost-like creatures, distort the true appearance of things, but which we nevertheless mistake for the things themselves. It is because this imagined world offers no resistance that the mind, feeling completely unchecked, gives rein to limitless ambitions, believing it possible to construct—or rather reconstruct—the world through its own power and according to its wishes.

If this has been true for the natural sciences, how much more had it to be true for sociology. Men did not wait on the coming of social science to have ideas about law, morality, the family, the state or society itself, for such ideas were indispensable to their lives. It is above all in sociology that these preconceptions, to employ again Bacon's expression, are capable of holding sway over the mind, substituting themselves for things. Indeed, social things are only realized by men: they are the product of human activity. Thus they appear to be nothing save the operationalizing of ideas, which may or may not be innate but which we carry within us, and their application to the various circumstances surrounding men's relationships with one another. The organization of the family, of contracts, or repression, of the state and of society seems therefore to be a simple development of the ideas we have about society, the state, justice, etc. Consequently these and similar facts seem to lack any reality save in and through the ideas which engender them and which, from then on, become the subject matter proper of sociology.

The apparent justification for this view derives from the fact that since the details of social life swamp the consciousness from all sides, it has not a sufficiently strong perception of the details to feel the reality behind them. Lacking ties that are firm enough or close enough to us, this all produces the impression upon us that it is clinging to nothing and floating in a vacuum, consisting of matter half unreal and infinitely malleable. This is why so many thinkers have seen in the social organization mere combinations which are artificial and to some degree arbitrary. But if the details and the special concrete forms elude us, at least we represent to ourselves in a rough, approximate way the most general aspects of collective existence. It is precisely these schematic, summary representations which constitute the prenotions that we employ in our normal way of life. Thus we cannot visualize their existence being called into question, since we see it at the same time as we see our own. Not only are they within us, but since they are the product of repeated experiences, they are invested with a kind of ascendancy and authority, by dint of repetition and the habit which results from it. We feel their resistance when we seek to free ourselves from them, and we cannot fail to regard as real something which pits itself against us. Thus everything conspires to make us see in them the true social reality.

And indeed up to now sociology has dealt more or less exclusively not with things, but with concepts. It is true that Comte proclaimed that social phenomena are natural facts, subject to natural laws. In so doing he implicitly recognized their character as things, for in nature there are only things. Yet when, leaving behind these general philosophical statements, he tries to apply his principle and deduce from it the science it contained, it is ideas which he too takes as the object of his study. Indeed, what constitutes the principal subject matter of his sociology is the progress over time of humanity. His starting point is the idea that the continuous evolution of the human species consists of an ever-growing perfection of human nature. The problem with which he deals is how to discover the sequence of this evolution. Yet, even supposing this evolution exists, its reality can only be established when the science has been worked out. Thus the evolution cannot be made the subject of research unless it is postulated as a conception of the mind, and not a thing. Indeed, this is so much a wholly subjective idea that this progress of humanity does not exist. What do exist, and what alone are presented to us for observation, are particular societies which are born, develop and die independently of one another. If indeed the most recent societies were a continuation of those which had preceded them, each superior type might be considered merely as the repetition of the type at the level immediately below it, with some addition. They could all then be placed end-on, so to speak, assimilating together all those at the same stage of development; the series thus formed might be considered representative of humanity. But the facts do not present themselves with such extreme simplicity. A people which takes the place of another is not merely a prolongation of the latter with some new features added. It is different, gaining some extra properties, but having lost others. It constitutes a new individuality, and all such distinct individualities, being heterogeneous, cannot be absorbed into the same continuous series, and above all not into one single series. The succession of societies cannot be represented by a geometrical line; on the contrary, it resembles a tree whose branches grow in divergent directions. Briefly, in his consideration of historical development, Comte has taken his own notion of it, which is one that does not differ greatly from that commonly held. It is true that, viewed from a distance, history does take on somewhat neatly this simple aspect of a series. One perceives only a succession of individuals all moving in the same direction, because they have the same human nature. Moreover, since it is inconceivable that social evolution can be anything other than the development of some human idea, it appears entirely natural to define it by the conception that men have of it. But if one proceeds down this path one not only remains in the realm of ideology, but assigns to sociology as its object a concept which has nothing peculiarly sociological about it.

Spencer discards this concept, but replaces it with another which is none the less formed in the same way. He makes societies, and not humanity, the object of his study, but immediately gives to societies a definition which causes the thing of which he speaks to disappear and puts in its place the preconception he has of them. Indeed he states as a self-evident proposition that "a society is formed only when, besides juxtaposition, there is co-operation"; it is solely in this way that the union of individuals becomes a society proper.[4] Then, starting from this principle, that co-operation is the essence of social life, he divides societies into two classes according to the nature of the predominant mode of co-operation. "There is," he states, "a spontaneous co-operation which grows up without thought during the pursuit of private ends; and there is a co-operation which, consciously devised, implies distinct recognition of public ends."[5] The first category he dubs industrial societies, the latter military societies. One may say of this distinction that it is the seminal idea for his sociology.

But this initial definition enunciates as a thing what is only a mental viewpoint. It is presented as the expression of a fact that is immediately apparent, one sufficiently ascertained by observation, since it is formulated from the very beginning of the science as an axiom. Yet from mere inspection it is impossible to know whether co-operation really is the mainspring of social life. Such an assertion is only scientifically justified if at first all the manifestations of collective life have been reviewed and it has been demonstrated that they are all various forms of co-operation. Thus once again a certain conception of social reality is substituted for that reality.[6] What is defined in this way is not society but Spencer's idea of it. If he feels no scruples in proceeding in this fashion it is because for him also society is only, and can be only, the realization of an idea, namely that very idea of co-operation by which he defines society.[7] It would be easy to show, in each of the particular problems that he tackles, that his method remains the same. Also, although he has an air of proceeding empirically, because the facts accumulated in his sociology are used to illustrate analyses of notions rather than to describe and explain things, they seem indeed to be there to serve as arguments. All that is really essential in his doctrine can be directly deduced from his definition of society and the different forms of co-operation. For if we have only the choice between co-operation tyrannically imposed and one that is free and spontaneous, it is plainly the latter which is the ideal toward which humanity does and ought to strive.

These common notions are not to be encountered only at the basis of the sciences, but are also to be found constantly as the arguments unravel. In our present state of knowledge we do not know exactly what the state is, nor sovereignty, political freedom, democracy, socialism, communism, etc. Thus our method should make us forswear any use of these concepts so long as they have not been scientifically worked out. Yet the words that express them recur continually in the discussions of sociologists. They are commonly used with assurance, as if they corresponded to things well known and well defined, while in fact they evoke in us only confused notions, an amalgam of vague impressions, prejudices and passions. Today we mock at the strange ratiocinations that the doctors of the Middle Ages constructed from their notions of heat and cold, humidity and dryness, etc. Yet we do not perceive that we continue to apply the selfsame method to an order of phenomena which is even less appropriate for it than any other, on account of its extreme complexity.

In the specialized branches of sociology this ideological character is even more marked.

It is particularly so in the case of ethics. It may indeed be asserted that there is not a single system which does not represent it as the simple development of an initial idea which enshrines it potentially in its entirety. Some believe that men possess this idea complete at birth; on the other hand, others believe that it has grown up at a varying rate in the course of history. But for both empiricists and rationalists this is all that is truly real about morality. As for detailed legal and moral rules, these would have, in a manner of speaking, no existence *per se*, being merely applications of the basic notion to the particular circumstances of living, and varying according to different cases. Hence the subject matter of morality cannot be this unreal system of precepts, but the idea from which the precepts derive and which is interpreted differently according to cases. Thus all the questions that ethics normally raises relate not to things but to ideas. We must know what constitutes the ideas of law and morality and not what is the nature of morality and law considered in their own right. Moralists have not yet even grasped the simple truth that, just as our representations of things perceived by the senses spring from those things themselves and express them more or less accurately, our representation of morality springs from observing the rules that function before our very eyes and perceives them systematically. Consequently it is these rules and not the cursory view we have of them which constitute the subject matter of science, just as the subject matter of physics consists of actual physical bodies and not the idea that ordinary people have of it. The outcome is that the basis of morality is taken to be what is only its summit, namely, the way in which it extends itself to the individual consciousness and makes its impact upon it. Nor is it only for the more general problems of science that this method is followed; it is not modified even for more specialized questions. From the essential ideas that he studies at the outset the moralist passes on to the examination of second-order ideas, such as family, country, responsibility, charity and justice—but it is always to ideas that his thinking is applied.

The same applies to political economy. John Stuart Mill states that its subject matter is the social facts which arise principally or exclusively with a view to the acquisition of wealth.[8] But, in order for the facts defined in this way to be submitted to the scrutiny of the scientist as things, at the very least it should be possible to indicate the means whereby those which satisfy this condition can be recognized. With a new science one is in no position to affirm that the facts exist, and even less to know what they are. In any kind of investigation it is only when the explanation of the facts is fairly well advanced that it is possible to establish that they have a goal and what that goal is. There is no problem more complex or less likely to be resolved at the very beginning. We therefore lack any prior assurance that a sphere of social activity exists where the desire for wealth really plays this predominant role. Consequently the subject matter of economics so conceived is made up not of realities which may be precisely pointed to, but merely of possible ones, pure conceptions of the mind. They are facts which the economist *conceives of* as relating to the purpose under consideration, and facts as he conceives them. If, for example, he embarks on a study of what he terms production, he believes it possible immediately to spell out and review the principal agencies which assist it. This means therefore that he has not ascertained their existence by studying on what conditions the thing that he is studying depends. If he had, he would have begun by setting out the operations from which he drew that conclusion. If, in summary terms, at the beginning of his researches he proceeds to make such a classification, it is because he has arrived at it by mere logical analysis. He starts from the idea of production and as he dissects it he finds that it logically entails ideas of natural forces, of work, of tools or capital and he then goes on to treat in the same way these ideas which he has derived.[9]

The most basic economic theory of all, that of value, has clearly been built up according to the same method. If value were studied as a fact having reality should be, the economist would show how the thing so designated could be identified; he would then classify its various kinds, testing by methodical inductions how these vary according to different causes, and finally comparing the various results in order to arrive at a general formulation. A theory could therefore only emerge when the science was fairly well advanced. Instead it is met with at the very beginning. To do this the economist contents himself with his own reflective thinking, evoking his idea of value, namely that of an object capable of being exchanged. He finds that this implies the ideas of utility and scarcity, etc., and it is from these fruits of his analysis that he constructs his definition. He doubtless backs it up with a few examples. But, reflecting on the countless facts which such a theory must explain, how can one concede the slightest validity of proof to the necessarily very few facts which are cited at random as they suggest themselves to him?

Thus in political economy, as in ethics, the role of scientific investigation is extremely limited, and that of art is preponderant. The theoretical part of ethics is reduced to a few discussions on the ideas of duty, goodness and right. But such abstract speculations do not strictly speaking constitute a science, since their purpose is not to determine what is, in fact, supreme moral law, but what ought to be. Likewise, what economists dwell on most in their researches is the problem of knowing, for example, whether society *should be* organized on individualistic or socialist lines; whether *it is better* for the state to intervene in industrial and commercial relations or abandon them entirely to private initiative; whether the monetary system *should be* based on monometallism or bimetallism, etc. Laws properly so called are very few; even those which by custom we call laws do not generally merit the term, but are merely maxims for action, or in reality practical precepts. For example, the celebrated law of supply and demand has never been established inductively as an expression of economic reality. Never has any experiment or methodical comparison been instituted to establish whether, *in fact*, it is according to this law that economic relations are regulated. All that could be done, and has been done, has been to demonstrate by dialectical argument that individuals should act in this way if they perceive what is in their best interest; any other course of action would be harmful to them, and if they followed it would indeed constitute an error of logic. It is logical that the most productive industries should be the most prized, and that those who hold goods most in demand and most scarce should sell them at the highest price. But this entirely logical necessity in no way resembles the one that the true laws of nature reveal. These express the relationships whereby facts are linked together in reality, and not the way in which it would be good for them to be linked.

What we state about this law can be repeated for all those that the orthodox school of economists term "natural" and which, moreover, are scarcely more than special cases of this first law. They may be said to be natural in the sense that they enunciate the means which are, or may appear to be, natural to employ in order to reach some assumed goal. But they should not be termed so if by a natural law is understood any inductively verified mode of existence of nature. All in all, they are mere counsels of practical wisdom. If it has been possible to present them to a more or less plausible extent as a clear expression of reality, it is because, rightly or wrongly, the assumption has been that these counsels were effectively those followed by most men and in the majority of cases.

Yet social phenomena are things and should be treated as such. To demonstrate this proposition one does not need to philosophize about their nature or to discuss the analogies they present with phenomena of a lower order of existence. Suffice to say that they are the sole *datum* afforded the sociologist. A thing is in effect all that is given, all that is offered, or rather imposing itself upon our observation. To treat phenomena as things is to treat them as *data*, and this constitutes the starting point for science. Social phenomena unquestionably display this characteristic. What is given is not the idea that men conceive of value, because that is unattainable; rather is it the values actually exchanged in economic transactions. It is also not some conception or other of the moral ideal; it is the sum total of rules that in effect determine behavior. It is not the idea of utility or wealth; it is all the details of economic organization. Social life may possibly be merely the development of certain notions, but even if this is assumed to be the case, these notions are not revealed to us immediately. They cannot therefore be attained directly, but only through the real phenomena that express them. We do not know *a priori* what ideas give rise to the various currents into which social life divides, nor whether they exist. It is only after we have traced the currents back to their source that we will know from whence they spring.

Social phenomena must therefore be considered in themselves, detached from the conscious beings who form their own mental representations of them. They must be studied from the outside, as external things, because it is in this guise that they present themselves to us. If this quality of externality proves to be only apparent, the illusion will be dissipated as the science progresses and we will see, so to speak, the external merge with the internal. But the outcome cannot be anticipated, and even if in the end social phenomena may not have all the features intrinsic to things, they must at first be dealt with as if they had. This rule is therefore applicable to the whole of social reality and there is no reason for any exceptions to be made. Even those phenomena which give the greatest appearance of being artificial in their arrangement should be considered from this viewpoint. *The conventional character of a practice or an institution should never be assumed in advance.* If, moreover, we are allowed to invoke personal experience, we believe we can state with confidence that by following this procedure one will often have the satisfaction of seeing the apparently most arbitrary facts, after more attentive observation, display features of constancy and regularity symptomatic of their objectivity.

In general, moreover, what has been previously stated about the distinctive features of the social fact gives us sufficient reassurance about the nature of this objectivity to demonstrate that it is not illusory. A thing is principally recognizable by virtue of not being capable of modification through a mere act of the will. This is not because it is intractable to all modification. But to effect change the will is not sufficient; it needs a degree of arduous effort because of the strength of the resistance it offers, which even then cannot always be overcome. We have seen that social facts possess this property of resistance. Far from their being a product of our will, they determine it from without. They are like molds into which we are forced to cast our actions. The necessity is often ineluctable. But even when we succeed in triumphing, the opposition we have encountered suffices to alert us that we are faced with something independent of ourselves. Thus in considering facts as things, we shall be merely conforming to their nature.

In the end, the reform that must be introduced into sociology is identical in every respect to that which has transformed psychology over the last thirty years. Just as Comte and Spencer declare that social facts are facts of nature, but nevertheless refuse to treat them as things, the different empirical schools had long recognized the natural character of psychological phenomena, while continuing to apply to them a purely ideological method. Indeed the empiricists, no less than their opponents, proceeded exclusively by introspection. But the facts observable in ourselves are too few, too fleeting and malleable, to be able to impose themselves upon the corresponding notions that habit has rooted in us and to prevail over them. Thus when these notions are not subject to some other control, no countervailing force exists; consequently they take the place of facts and constitute the subject matter of the science. Thus neither Locke nor Condillac considered physical phenomena objectively. It is not sensation they study, but a certain idea of it. This is why, although in certain respects they were its forerunners, scientific psychology arose only much later. It arose after it had been finally established that states of consciousness can and must be studied externally and not from the perspective of the individual consciousness which experiences them. This is the great revolution that has been accomplished in this field of study. All the special procedures and new methods which have enriched this science are only various expedients for realizing more fully this basic idea. Such an advance remains to be accomplished in sociology, which must pass from the subjective stage, beyond which it has hardly progressed, to the objective stage.

This transition, moreover, is less difficult to accomplish in sociology than in psychology. Psychical facts naturally appertain to states of the individual, from whom they do not even appear to be separable. Internal by definition, such states cannot seemingly be treated as external save by doing violence to their nature. Not only is an effort of abstraction necessary, but a whole gamut of procedures and artifices as well, for them to be considered successfully from the external viewpoint. Social facts, on the other hand, display much more naturally and immediately all the characteristics of a thing. Law is enshrined in legal codes, the events of daily life are registered in statistical figures and historical monuments, fashions are preserved in dress, taste in works of art. By their very nature social facts tend to form outside the consciousnesses of individuals, since they dominate them. To perceive them in their capacity as things it is therefore not necessary to engage in an ingenious distortion. From this viewpoint sociology has significant advantages over psychology which have hitherto not been perceived, and this should accelerate its development. Its facts are perhaps more difficult to interpret because they are more complex, but they are more readily accessible. Psychology, on the other hand, has difficulty not only in specifying its facts, but also in comprehending them. Thus one may legitimately believe that as soon as this principle of sociological method has been universally acknowledged and is put into practice, sociology will be seen to progress at a speed that its present slow rate of development would scarcely allow one to suppose, even making up the lead of psychology, which it owes solely to its prior historical place.[10]

II

But our predecessors' experience has shown us that, in order to realize in practice the truth just established, it is not enough to demonstrate it theoretically or even to absorb it oneself. The mind has such a natural disposition to fail to recognize it that inevitably we will relapse into past errors unless we submit ourselves to a rigorous discipline. We shall formulate the principal rules for this discipline, all of which are corollaries of the previous rule.

(1) The first of these corollaries is: *One must systematically discard all preconceptions.* Special proof of this rule is unnecessary: it follows from all that we have stated above. Moreover, it is the basis of all scientific method. Descartes' method of doubt is in essence only an application of it. If at the very moment of the foundation of science Descartes prescribed a rule for himself to question all the ideas he had previously accepted, it is because he wished to use only concepts which had been scientifically worked out, that is, constructed according to the method that he devised. All those of another origin had therefore to be rejected, at least for the time being. We have seen that Bacon's theory of the idols has the same significance. The two great doctrines, so often placed in contradiction to each other, agree on this essential point. Thus the sociologist, either when he decides upon the object of his research or in the course of his investigations, must resolutely deny himself the use of those concepts formed outside science and for needs entirely unscientific. He must free himself from those fallacious notions which hold sway over the mind of the ordinary person, shaking off, once and for all, the yoke of those empirical categories that long habit often makes tyrannical. If necessity sometimes forces him to resort to them, let him at least do so in full cognizance of the little value they possess, so as not to assign to them in the investigation a role which they are unfit to play.

What makes emancipation from such notions peculiarly difficult in sociology is that sentiment so often intervenes. We enthuse over our political and religious beliefs and moral practices very differently from the way we do over the objects of the physical world. Consequently this emotional quality is transmitted to the way in which we conceive and explain our beliefs. The ideas that we form about them are deeply felt, just as are their purposes, thereby taking on such authority that they brook no contradiction. Any opinion which is embarrassing is treated as hostile. For example, a proposition may not accord with our view of patriotism or personal dignity. It is therefore denied, whatever may be the proofs advanced. We cannot allow it to be true. It is rejected, and our strong emotions, seeking a justification for so doing, have no difficulty in suggesting reasons which we find readily conclusive. These notions may even be so prestigious that they will not tolerate scientific examination. The mere fact of subjecting them, as well as the phenomena they express, to cold, dry analysis is repugnant to certain minds. The sociologist who undertakes to study morality objectively as an external reality seems to such sensitive souls bereft of moral sense, just as the vivisectionist seems to the ordinary person devoid of normal feelings. Far from admitting that these sentiments are subject to science, it is believed that it is to them one should address oneself in order to construct the science of things to which they relate. "Woe," writes an eloquent historian of religions, "Woe to the scientist who approaches the things of God without having in the depths of his consciousness, in the innermost indestructible parts of his being, in which sleep the souls of his ancestors, an unknown sanctuary from which at times there arises the fragrance of incense, a verse of a psalm, a cry of sorrow or triumph that as a child, following his brothers' example, he raised to heaven, and which suddenly joins him once again in communion with the prophets of yore!"[11]

One cannot protest too strongly against this mystical doctrine which—like all mysticism, moreover—is in essence only a disguised empiricism, the negation of all science. Feelings relating to social things enjoy no pride of place over other sentiments, for they have no different origin. They too have been shaped through history. They are a product of human experience, albeit one confused and unorganized. They are not due to some transcendental precognition of reality, but are the result of all kinds of disordered impressions and emotions accumulated through chance circumstance, lacking systematic interpretation. Far from bringing enlightenment of a higher order than the rational, they are composed exclusively of states of mind which, it is true, are strong but also confused. To grant them such a predominant role is to ascribe to the lower faculties of the intelligence supremacy over superior ones and to condemn oneself more or less to a rhetorical logomachy. A science constituted in this way can only satisfy those minds who prefer to think with their sensibility rather than their understanding, who prefer the immediate and confused syntheses of sensation to the patient, illuminating analyses of the reason. Feeling is an object for scientific study, not the criterion of scientific truth. But there is no science which at its beginnings has not encountered similar resistances. There was a time when those feelings relating to the things of the physical world, since they also possessed a religious or moral character, opposed no less violently the establishment of the physical sciences. Thus one can believe that, rooted out from one science after another, this prejudice will finally disappear from sociology as well, its last refuge, and leave the field clear for the scientist.

(2)   But the above rule is entirely negative. It teaches the sociologist to escape from the dominance of commonly held notions and to direct his attention to the facts, but does not state how he is to grasp the facts in order to study them objectively.

Every scientific investigation concerns a specific group of phenomena which are subsumed under the same definition. The sociologist's first step must therefore be to define the things he treats, so that we may know—he as well—exactly what his subject matter is. This is the prime and absolutely indispensable condition of any proof or verification. A theory can only be checked if we know how to recognize the facts for which it must account. Moreover, since this initial definition determines the subject matter itself of the science, that subject matter will either consist of a thing or not, according to how this definition is formulated.

To be objective the definition clearly must express the phenomena as a function, not of an idea of the mind, but of their inherent properties. It must characterize them according to some integrating element in their nature and not according to whether they conform to some more or less ideal notion. When research is only just beginning and the facts have not yet been submitted to any analysis, their sole ascertainable characteristics are those sufficiently external to be immediately apparent. Those less apparent are doubtless more essential. Their explanatory value is greater, but they remain unknown at this stage of scientific knowledge and cannot be visualized save by substituting for reality some conception of the mind. Thus it is among the first group of visible characteristics that must be sought the elements for this basic definition. Yet it is clear that the definition will have to include, without exception or distinction, all the phenomena which equally manifest these same characteristics, for we have neither reason nor the means to discriminate between them. These properties, then, are all that we know of reality. Consequently they must determine absolutely how the facts should be classified. We possess no other criterion which can even partially invalidate the effect of this rule. Hence the following rule: *The subject matter of research must only include a group of phenomena defined beforehand by certain common external characteristics and all phenomena which correspond to this definition must be so included.* For example, we observe that certain actions exist which all possess the one external characteristic that, once they have taken place, they provoke on the part of society that special reaction known as punishment. We constitute them as a group *sui generis* and classify them under a single heading: any action that is punished is termed a crime and we make crime, so defined, the subject matter of a special science of criminology. Likewise we observe within all known societies the existence of a smaller society outwardly recognizable because it is formed for the most part of individuals linked by a blood relationship and joined to each other by legal ties. From the relevant facts we constitute a special group to which we assign a distinctive name: phenomena of domestic life. We term every aggregate of this kind a family and make the family, so defined, the subject matter of a specific investigation which has not yet received a special designation in sociological terminology. When we later pass on from the family in general to the different types of family, the same rule should be applied. For example, embarking upon a study of the clan, or the maternal or patriarchal family, we should begin by defining them according to the same method. The subject matter of each topic, whether general or specialized, should be constituted according to the same principle.

By proceeding in this way from the outset the sociologist is immediately grounded firmly in reality. Indeed, how the facts are classified does not depend on him, or on his own particular cast of mind, but on the nature of things. The criterion which determines whether they are to be grouped in a particular category can be demonstrated and generally accepted by everybody, and the observer's statements can be verified by others. It is true that a notion built up in this way does not always chime—or does not generally even chime at all—with the notion commonly held. For example, it is evident that acts relating to free-thinking or lapses in etiquette which are so regularly and severely punished in many societies, from the viewpoint of common sense are not regarded as crimes when people consider those societies. In the same way a clan is not a family in the usual sense of the word. But this is of no consequence, for it is not simply a question of how we can discover with a fair degree of accuracy the facts to which the words of common parlance refer and the ideas that they convey. What has to be done is to form fresh concepts *de novo*, ones appropriate to the needs of science and expressed by the use of a special terminology. It is certainly not true that the commonly held concept is useless to the scientist. It serves as a benchmark, indicating to him that somewhere there exists a cluster of phenomena bearing the same name and which consequently are likely to possess common characteristics. Moreover, since the common concept is never without some relationship to the phenomena, it occasionally points to the approximate direction in which they are to be discovered. But as the concept is only crudely formulated, it is quite natural for it not to coincide exactly with the scientific concept which it has been instrumental in instituting.[12]

However obvious and important this rule is, it is scarcely observed at present in sociology. Precisely because sociology deals with things which are constantly on our lips, such as the family, property, crime, etc., very often it appears useless to the sociologist initially to ascribe a rigorous definition to them. We are so accustomed to using these words, which recur constantly in the course of conversation, that it seems futile to delimit the meaning being given to them. We simply refer to the common notion of them, but this is very often ambiguous. This ambiguity causes us to classify under the same heading and with the same explanation things which are in reality very different. From this there arises endless confusion. Thus, for example, there are two kinds of monogamous unions: the ones that exist in fact, and those that exist legally. In the first kind the husband has only one wife, although legally he may have several; in the second kind polygamy is legally prohibited. *De facto* monogamy is met with in several animal species and certain societies at a lower stage of development, not sporadically, but indeed with the same degree of generality as if it had been imposed by law. When a tribe is scattered over a wide area the social bond is very loose and consequently individuals live isolated from each other. Hence every man naturally seeks a female mate, but only one, because in his isolated state it is difficult for him to secure several. Compulsory monogamy, on the other hand, is only observed in societies at the highest stage of development. These two kinds of conjugal union have therefore very different significance, and yet the same word serves to describe them both. We commonly say that certain animals are monogamous, although in their case there is nothing remotely resembling an obligation. Spencer, embarking on his study of marriage, uses the term monogamy, without defining it, in its usual and equivocal sense. Consequently for him the development of marriage appears to present an incomprehensible anomaly, since he thinks he can observe the higher form of sexual union from the very earliest stages of historical development, while it apparently tends to disappear in the intermediate period, only to reappear again later. He concludes from this that there is no consistent relationship between social progress in general and the progressive advance toward a perfect type of family life. An expedient definition would have obviated this error.[13]

In other cases great care is taken to define the subject matter of the research but instead of including in the definition and grouping under the same heading all phenomena possessing the same external properties, a selection is made. Certain phenomena, a kind of elite, are chosen as those considered to have the sole right to possess these characteristics. The others are held to have usurped these distinctive features and are disregarded. It is easy to envisage that, using this procedure, only a subjective and partial notion can be obtained. Such a process of elimination can in fact only be made according to a preconceived idea, since at the beginnings of a science no research would have been able to establish whether such a usurpation was real, even assuming it to be possible. The phenomena selected can only have been chosen because, more than the others, they conformed to the ideal conception that had already been formed of that kind of reality. For example, Garofalo, at the beginning of his *Criminologie*, demonstrates extremely well that the point of departure for that science should be "the sociological notion of crime."[14] Yet, in order to build up this notion, he does not compare indiscriminately all the actions which in different types of society have been repressed by regular punishment, but only certain of them, namely those which offend the normal and unchangeable elements in the moral sense. As for those moral sentiments which have disappeared as a result of evolution, for him they were apparently not grounded in the nature of things for the simple reason that they did not succeed in surviving. Consequently the acts which have been deemed criminal because they violated those sentiments seemed to him to have merited this label only through chance circumstances of a more or less pathological kind. But he proceeds to make this elimination by virtue of a very personal conception of morality. He starts from the idea that moral evolution, considered at the source or its close proximity, carries along with it all sorts of deposits and impurities which it then progressively eliminates; only today has it succeeded in ridding itself of all the extraneous elements which at the beginning troubled its course. But this principle is neither a self-evident axiom nor a demonstrated truth: it is only a hypothesis, which indeed nothing justifies. The variable elements of the moral sense are no less founded in the nature of things than those that are immutable; the variations through which the former elements have passed evidence the fact that the things themselves have varied. In zoology those forms peculiar to the lower species are not considered any less natural than those which recur at all levels on the scale of animal development. Similarly, those actions condemned as crimes by primitive societies, but which have since lost that label, are really criminal in relation to those societies just as much as those we continue to repress today. The former crimes correspond to the changing conditions of social life, the latter to unchanging conditions, but the first are no more artificial than the rest.

More can be added to this: even if these acts had wrongly assumed a criminal character, they nevertheless should not be drastically separated from the others. The pathological forms of a phenomenon are no different in nature from the normal ones, and consequently it is necessary to observe both kinds in order to determine what that nature is. Sickness is not opposed to health; they are two varieties of the same species and each throws light on the other. This is a rule long recognized and practiced both in biology and psychology, and one which the sociologist is no less under an obligation to respect. Unless one allows that the same phenomenon can be due first to one cause and then to another—which is to deny the principle of causality—the causes which imprint upon an action, albeit abnormally, the distinctive mark of a crime, cannot differ in kind from those which normally produce the same effect. They are distinguishable only in degree, or because they are not operating in the same set of circumstances. The abnormal crime therefore continues to be a crime and must consequently enter into the definition of crime. But what happens? Thus Garofalo takes for the *genus* what is only the species or merely a simple variation. The facts to which his formulation of criminality are applicable represent only a tiny minority among those which should be included. His formulation does not fit religious crimes, or crimes against etiquette, ceremonial or tradition, etc., which, although they have disappeared from our modern legal codes, on the contrary almost entirely fill the penal law of past societies.

The same error of method causes certain observers to deny to savages any kind of morality.[15] They start from the idea that our morality is *the* morality. But it is clear that it is either unknown among primitive peoples or exists only in a rudimentary state, so that this definition is an arbitrary one. If we apply our rule, all is changed. To decide whether a precept is a moral one or not we must investigate whether it presents the external mark of morality. This mark consists of a widespread, repressive sanction, that is to say a condemnation by public opinion which consists of avenging any violation of the precept. Whenever we are confronted with a fact that presents this characteristic we have no right to deny its moral character, for this is proof that it is of the same nature as other moral facts. Not only are rules of this kind encountered in more primitive forms of society, but in them they are more numerous than among civilized peoples. A large number of acts which today are left to the discretion of individuals were then imposed compulsorily. We perceive into what errors we may fall if we omit to define, or define incorrectly.

But, it will be claimed, to define phenomena by their visible characteristics, is this not to attribute to superficial properties a kind of preponderance over more fundamental qualities? Is this not to turn the logical order upside down, to ground things upon their apex and not their base? Thus when crime is defined by punishment almost inevitably one runs the risk of being accused of wanting to derive crime from punishment, or, to cite a well-known quotation, to see the source of shame in the scaffold rather than in the crime to be expiated. But the reproach is based upon a confusion. Since the definition, the rule for which we have just enunciated, is made at the beginnings of the science its purpose could not be to express the essence of reality; rather is it intended to equip us in order to arrive at this essence later. Its sole function is to establish the contact with things, and since these cannot be reached by the mind save from the outside, it is by their outward aspect that science expresses them. But it does not thereby explain them; it supplies only an initial framework necessary for our explanations. It is not of course punishment that causes crime, but it is through punishment that crime, in its external aspects, is revealed to us. And it is therefore punishment that must be our starting point if we wish to understand crime.

The objection referred to above would be well founded only if these external characteristics were at the same time merely accidental, that is, if they were not linked to the basic properties of things. In these conditions science, after having pointed out the characteristics, would indeed lack the means of proceeding further. It could not penetrate deeper into reality, since there would be no connection between the surface and the depths.

But, unless the principle of causality is only empty words, when clearly determined characteristics are to be found identically and without exception in all phenomena of a certain order, it is assuredly because they are closely linked to the nature of these phenomena and are joined indissolubly to them. If any given set of actions similarly presents the peculiarity of having a penal sanction attached to it, it is because there exists a close link between the punishment and the attributes constituting those actions. Consequently, however superficial these properties may be, provided they have been methodically observed, they show clearly to the scientist the path that he must follow in order to penetrate more deeply into the things under consideration. They are the prime, indispensable link in the sequence later to be unfolded by science in the course of its explanations.

Since it is through the senses that the external nature of things is revealed to us, we may therefore sum up as follows: in order to be objective science must start from sense-perceptions and not from concepts that have been formed independently from it. It is from observable data that it should derive directly the elements for its initial definition. Moreover, it is enough to call to mind what the task of scientific work is to understand that science cannot proceed otherwise. It needs concepts which express things adequately, as they are, and not as it is useful in practical living to conceive them. Concepts formed outside the sphere of science do not meet this criterion. It must therefore create new concepts and to do so must lay aside common notions and the words used to express them, returning to sense-perceptions, the essential basic material for all concepts. It is from sense experience that all general ideas arise, whether they be true or false, scientific or unscientific. The starting point for science or speculative knowledge cannot therefore be different from that for common or practical knowledge. It is only beyond this point, in the way in which this common subject matter is further elaborated, that divergences will begin to appear.

(3) But sense experience can easily be subjective. Thus it is a rule in the natural sciences to discard observable data which may be too personal to the observer, retaining exclusively those data which present a sufficient degree of objectivity. Thus the physicist substitutes for the vague impressions produced by temperature or electricity the visual representation afforded by the rise and fall of the thermometer or the voltmeter. The sociologist must needs observe the same precautions. The external characteristics whereby he defines the object of his research must be as objective as possible.

In principle it may be postulated that social facts are more liable to be objectively represented the more completely they are detached from the individual facts by which they are manifested.

A sense-perception is indeed more objective the more stable the object is to which it relates. This is because the condition for any objectivity is the existence of a constant, fixed vantage point to which the representation may be related and which allows all that is variable, hence subjective, to be eliminated. If the sole reference points given are themselves variable, continually fluctuating in relationship to one another, no common measure at all exists and we have no way of distinguishing between the part of those impressions which depends on what is external and that part which is colored by us. So long as social life has not succeeded in isolating itself from the particular events which embody it, in order that it may be formed separately, it is precisely this difficulty which remains. As these events do not take on the same appearance each time nor from one moment to another and as social life is inseparable from them, they communicate to it their own fluctuating character. Thus social life consists of free-ranging forces which are in a constant process of change and which the observer's scrutinizing gaze does not succeed in fixing mentally. The consequence is that this approach is not open to the scientist embarking upon a study of social reality. Yet we do know that social reality possesses the property of crystallizing without changing its nature. Apart from the individual acts to which they give rise, collective habits are expressed in definite forms such as legal or moral rules, popular sayings, or facts of social structure, etc. As these forms exist permanently and do not change with the various applications which are made of them, they constitute a fixed object, a constant standard which is always to hand for the observer, and which leaves no room for subjective impressions or personal observations. A legal rule is what it is and there are no two ways of perceiving it. Since, from another angle, these practices are no more than social life consolidated, it is legitimate, failing indications to the contrary,[16] to study that life through these practices.

Thus when the sociologist undertakes to investigate any order of social facts he must strive to consider them from a viewpoint where they present themselves in isolation from their individual manifestations. It is by virtue of this principle that we have studied elsewhere social solidarity, its various forms and their evolution, through the system of legal rules whereby they are expressed.[17] In the same way, if an attempt is made to distinguish and classify the different types of family according to the literary descriptions imparted by travelers and sometimes by historians, we run the risk of confusing the widely differing species and of linking types extremely dissimilar. If, on the other hand, we take as the basis of classification the legal constitution of the family, and more especially the right of succession, we have an objective criterion which, although not infallible, will nevertheless prevent many errors.[18] If we aim at a classification of different kinds of crime, the attempt must be made to reconstitute the various modes of living and the "professional" customs in vogue in the different worlds of crime. As many criminological types will be identified as there are organizational forms. To penetrate the customs and popular beliefs we will turn to the proverbs and sayings which express them. Doubtless by such a procedure we leave outside science for the time being the concrete data of collective life. Yet, however changeable that life may be, we have no right to postulate *a priori* its incomprehensibility. But in order to proceed methodically we must establish the prime bases of the science on a solid foundation, and not on shifting sand. We must approach the social domain from those positions where the foothold for scientific investigation is the greatest possible. Only later will it be feasible to carry our research further and by progressive approaches gradually capture that fleeting reality which the human mind will perhaps never grasp completely.

Notes

1. Bacon, *Novum Organum*, I, p. 26.
2. Ibid., I, p. 17.
3. Ibid., I, p. 36.
4. H. Spencer, *The Principles of Sociology*, II, p. 244 (London: Williams & Norgate, 1882).
5. Ibid., II, p. 245.
6. This is moreover a conception which is controversial (cf. *Division du travail social*, II, 2, ss. 4).
7. Spencer, op. cit., II, p. 244: "Cooperation, then, is at once that which cannot exist without a society, and that for which a society exists."
8. J.S. Mill, *A System of Logic*, vol. 2, book VI, ch. IX, p. 496 (London: Longmans, Green Reader & Dyer, 1872): "Political economy shows mankind as occupied solely in acquiring and consuming wealth."
9. This trait emerges from the very expressions used by economists. They continually talk of ideas, of the ideas of utility, savings, investment and cost. (Cf. C. Gide, *Principes de l'économie politique*, book III, ch. 1, ss. 1; ch. 2, ss. 1; ch. 3, ss. 1 [First edition, Paris, 1884].)
10. It is true that the greater complexity of social facts renders the science that relates to them more difficult. But, as compensation, precisely because sociology is the latest arrival on the scene, it is in a position to benefit from the progress realized by the lesser sciences and to learn from them. This use of previous experience cannot fail to hasten its development.
11. J. Darmsteter, *Les Prophètes d'Israël* (Paris, 1892), p. 9.
12. It is in practice always the common concept and the common term which are the point of departure. Among the things that in a confused fashion this term denotes, we seek to discover whether any exist which present common external characteristics. If there are any, and if the concept formed by grouping the facts brought together in this way coincides, if not entirely (which is rare) but at least for the most part, with the common concept, it will be possible to continue to designate the former by the same common term, retaining in the science the expression used in everyday parlance. But if the difference is too considerable, if the common notion mixes up a number of different notions, the creation of new and special terms becomes a necessity.

13. It is the same absence of definition which has sometimes caused it to be stated that democracy occurred both at the beginning and the end of history. The truth is that primitive and present-day democracy are very different from each other.

14. R. Garofalo, *Criminologie* (Paris, 1888), p. 2 (trans. by the author from the Italian).

15. J. Lubbock, *Origins of Civilization*, ch. VIII. More generally still, it is stated, no less inaccurately, that ancient religions are amoral or immoral. The truth is that they have their own morality. [Durkheim may have read Sir John Lubbock's work in translation. It was published in French translation by E. Barbier in 1873. Two further editions in French followed in 1877 and 1881.]

16. For example, one should have grounds to believe that, at a given moment, law no longer expressed the real state of social relationships for this substitution to be invalid.

17. Cf. *Division du travail social*, I, 1.

18. Cf. Durkheim, "Introduction à la sociologie de la famille," *Annales de la Faculté des Lettres de Bordeaux*, 1889.

CHAPTER III

Rules for the Distinction of the Normal from the Pathological

---

Observation conducted according to the preceding rules mixes up two orders of facts, very dissimilar in certain respects: those that are just as they ought to be, and those that ought to be different from what they are—normal phenomena and pathological phenomena. We have even seen that it is necessary to include both in the definition with which all research should begin. Yet if, in certain aspects, they are of the same nature, they nevertheless constitute two different varieties between which it is important to distinguish. Does science have the means available to make this distinction?

The question is of the utmost importance, for on its solution depends one's conception of the role that science, and above all the science of man, has to play. According to a theory whose exponents are recruited from the most varied schools of thought, science cannot instruct us in any way about what we ought to desire. It takes cognizance, they say, only of facts which all have the same value and the same utility; it observes, explains, but does not judge them; for it, there are none that are reprehensible. For science, good and evil do not exist. Whereas it can certainly tell us how causes produce their effects, it cannot tell us what ends should be pursued. To know not what is, but what is desirable, we must resort to the suggestions of the unconscious—sentiment, instinct, vital urge, etc.—by whatever name we call it. Science, says a writer already quoted, can well light up the world, but leaves a darkness in the human heart. The heart must create its own illumination. Thus science is stripped, or nearly, of all practical effectiveness and consequently of any real justification. For what good is it to strive after a knowledge of reality if the knowledge we acquire cannot serve us in our lives? Can we reply that by revealing to us the causes of phenomena knowledge offers us the means of producing the causes at will, and thereby achieving the ends our will pursues for reasons that go beyond science? But, from one point of view, every means is an end, for to set the means in motion it requires an act of the will, just as it does to achieve the end for which it prepares the way. There are

50

always several paths leading to a given goal, and a choice must therefore be made between them. Now if science cannot assist us in choosing the best goal, how can it indicate the best path to follow to arrive at the goal? Why should it commend to us the swiftest path in preference to the most economical one, the most certain rather than the most simple one, or vice versa? If it cannot guide us in the determination of our highest ends, it is no less powerless to determine those secondary and subordinate ends we call means.

It is true that the ideological method affords an avenue of escape from this mysticism, and indeed the desire to escape from it has in part been responsible for the persistence of this method. Its devotees were certainly too rationalist to agree that human conduct did not require the guidance of reflective thought. Yet they saw in the phenomena, considered by themselves independently of any subjective data, nothing to justify their classifying them according to their practical value. It therefore seemed that the sole means of judging them was to relate them to some overriding concept. Hence the use of notions to govern the collation of facts, rather than deriving notions from them, became indispensable for any rational sociology. But we know that, in these conditions, although practice has been reflected upon, such reflection is not scientific.

The solution to the problem just posed will nevertheless allow us to lay claim to the rights of reason without falling back into ideology. For societies, as for individuals, health is good and desirable; sickness, on the other hand, is bad and must be avoided. If therefore we find an objective criterion, inherent in the facts themselves, to allow us to distinguish scientifically health from sickness in the various orders of social phenomena, science will be in a position to throw light on practical matters while remaining true to its own method. Since at present science is incapable of directly affecting the individual, it can doubtless only furnish us with general guidelines which cannot be diversified appropriately for the particular individual unless he is approached through the senses. The state known as health, in so far as it is capable of definition, cannot apply exactly to any individual, since it can only be established for the most common circumstances, from which everyone deviates to some extent. None the less it is a valuable reference point to guide our actions. Because it must be adjusted later to fit each individual case, it does not follow that knowledge of it lacks all utility. Indeed, precisely the opposite is true, because it establishes the norm which must serve as a basis for all our practical reasoning. Under these conditions we are no longer justified in stating that thought is useless for action. Between science and art there is no longer a gulf, and one may pass from one to the other without any break in continuity. It is true that science can only concern itself with the facts through the mediation of art, but art is only the extension of science. We may even speculate whether the practical shortcomings of science must not continue to decrease as the laws it is establishing express ever more fully individual reality.

I

Pain is commonly regarded as the index of sickness. It is certain that in general a relationship exists between these two phenomena, although one lacking uniformity and precision. There are serious physical dispositions of a painless nature, whereas minor ailments of no importance, such as that resulting from a speck of coal-dust in the eye, cause real torment. In certain cases it is even the absence of pain, or indeed the presence of positive pleasure, which is the symptom of ill-health. There is a certain lack of vulnerability to pain which is pathological. In circumstances where a healthy man would be suffering, the neurasthenic would experience a sensation of enjoyment, the morbid nature of which is indisputable. Conversely, pain accompanies many conditions, such as hunger, tiredness and childbirth, which are purely physiological phenomena.

May we assert that health, consisting in the joyous development of vital energy, is recognizable when there is perfect adaptation of the organism to its environment, and on the other hand may we term sickness as all that which upsets that adaptation? But first—and we shall have to return to this point later—it is by no means demonstrated that every state of the organism corresponds to some external state. Furthermore, even if the criterion of adaptation were truly distinctive of a state of health, some other criterion would be needed for it to be recognizable. In any case we should need to be informed of the principle to decide whether one particular mode of adaptation is more "perfect" than another.

Is it according to the manner in which one mode rather than another affects our chances of survival? Health would be the state of the organism in which those chances were greatest, whereas sickness would be anything which reduced those chances. Unquestionably sickness has generally the effect of really weakening the organism. Yet sickness is not alone in being capable of producing this result. In certain lower species the reproductive functions inevitably entail death, and even in higher species carry risks with them. Yet this is normal. Old age and infancy are subject to the same effect, for both the old person and the infant are more vulnerable to the causes of destruction. But are they therefore sick persons, and must we admit that the healthy type is represented only by the adult? This would be singularly to restrict the domain of health and physiology. Moreover, if old age is already a sickness in itself, how does one distinguish between a healthy old person and a sick one? By the same reasoning menstruation would have to be classified under pathological phenomena, for by the troubles that it brings on, it increases for a woman the liability to illness.

Yet how can one term unhealthy a condition whose absence or premature disappearance constitutes without question a pathological phenomenon? We argue about this question as if in a healthy organism each element, so to speak, had a useful part to play, as if every internal state corresponded exactly to some external condition and consequently contributed to maintaining the vital equilibrium and reducing the chances of dying. On the contrary it may legitimately be presumed that certain anatomical or functional arrangements serve no direct purpose, but exist simply because they are, and cannot cease, given the general conditions of life. They cannot, however, be characterized as morbid, for sickness is eminently something avoidable which is not intrinsic to the normal constitution of a living creature. It may even be true that, instead of strengthening the organism, these arrangements lower its powers of resistance and consequently increase the risk of death.

On the other hand it is by no means sure that sickness always entails the consequence by which people have sought to define it. Do not a number of illnesses exist that are too slight for us to be able to attribute to them any perceptible effect upon the basic functions of the organism? Even among the gravest afflictions there are some whose effects are wholly innocuous, if we know how to combat them with the weapons at our command. The gastritis-prone individual who follows a good, hygienic way of living can live as long as the healthy man. Undoubtedly he is forced to take precautions, but are we not all subject to the same constraint, and can life be sustained otherwise? Each of us has his own hygiene to follow. That of the sick person differs considerably from that of his average contemporary, living in the same environment. But this may be seen to be the sole difference between them. Sickness does not always leave us at a loss, not knowing what to do, in an irremediable state of inadaptability; it merely obliges us to adapt ourselves differently from most of our fellows. Who is there to say that some sicknesses even exist which in the end are not useful to us? Smallpox, a vaccine of which we use to inoculate ourselves, is a true disease that we give ourselves voluntarily, yet it increases our chance of survival. There may be many other cases where the damage caused by the sickness is insignificant compared with the immunities that it confers upon us.

Finally and most importantly, this criterion is very often inapplicable. At the very most it can be established that the lowest mortality rate known is encountered in a particular group of individuals, but it cannot be demonstrated that an even lower rate might not be feasible. Who is to say that other conditions might not be envisaged which would have the effect of lowering it still further? The actual minimum is not therefore proof of perfect adaptation and is consequently not a reliable index of the state of health, to come back to the preceding definition. Moreover, a group with this characteristic is very difficult to constitute and to isolate from all other groups. Yet this would be necessary to be able to observe the bodily constitution of its members which is the alleged cause of their superiority. Conversely, in the case of a generally fatal illness it is evident that the probability of survival is lower, but the proof is signally more difficult to demonstrate in the case of an affliction which does not necessarily cause death. Indeed, there is only one objective way to prove that creatures placed in closely defined conditions have less chance of survival than others: this is to show that in fact the majority do not live as long. Now although in cases of purely individual sickness this can often be demonstrated, it is utterly impracticable in sociology. For here we have not the criterion of reference available to the biologist, namely, the figures of the average mortality rate. We do not even know how to determine approximately the moment when a society is born and when it dies. All these problems, which even in biology are far from being clearly resolved, still remain wrapped in mystery for the sociologist. Moreover, the events occurring in social life and which are repeated almost identically in all societies of the same type, are much too diverse to be able to determine to what extent any particular one has contributed to hastening a society's final demise. In the case of individuals, as there are very many, one can select those to be compared so that they present only the same one irregularity. This factor is thus isolated from all concomitant phenomena, so that one can study the nature of its influence upon the organism. If, for example, about a thousand rheumatism sufferers taken at random exhibit a mortality rate above the average, there are good grounds for imputing this outcome to a rheumatoidal tendency. But in sociology, since each social species accounts for only a small number of individuals, the field of comparison is too limited for groupings of this kind to afford valid proof.

Lacking this factual proof, there is no alternative to deductive reasoning, whose conclusions can have no value except as subjective presumptions. We will be able to demonstrate, not that a particular occurrence does in fact weaken the social organism, but that it *should* have that effect. To do this it will be shown that the occurrence cannot fail to entail a special consequence esteemed to be harmful to society, and on these grounds it will be declared pathological. But, granted that it does bring about this consequence, it can happen that its deleterious effects are compensated, even over-compensated, by advantages that are not perceived. Moreover, only one reason will justify our deeming it to be socially injurious: it must disturb the normal operation of the social functions. Such a proof presumes that the problem has already been solved. The proof is only possible if the nature of the normal state has been determined beforehand and consequently the signs whereby normality may be recognized are already known. Could one try to construct *a priori* the normal state from scratch? There is no need to show what such a construction would be worth. This is why it happens in sociology, as in history, that the same events are judged to be salutary or disastrous, according to the scholar's personal convictions. Thus it constantly happens that a theorist lacking religious belief identifies as a pathological phenomenon the vestiges of faith that survive among the general collapse of religious beliefs, while for the believer it is the very absence of belief which is the great social sickness. Likewise for the socialist, the present economic organization is a fact of social abnormality, whereas for the orthodox economist it is above all the socialist tendencies which are pathological. To support his view each finds syllogisms that he esteems well founded.

The common weakness in these definitions is the attempt to reach prematurely the essence of phenomena. Thus they assume that propositions have already been demonstrated which, whether true or false, can only be proved when the progress of science is sufficiently advanced. This is nevertheless a case where we should conform to the rule already established. Instead of claiming to determine at the outset the relationship of the normal state, and the contrary state, to the vital forces, we should simply look for some immediately perceptible outward sign, but an objective one, to enable us to distinguish these two orders of facts from each other.

Every sociological phenomenon, just as every biological phenomenon, although staying essentially unchanged, can assume a different form for each particular case. Among these forms exist two kinds. The first are common to the whole species. They are to be found, if not in all, at least in most individuals. If they are not replicated exactly in all the cases where they are observed, but vary from one person to another, their variations are confined within very narrow limits. On the other hand, other forms exist which are exceptional. These are encountered only in a minority of cases, but even when they occur, most frequently they do not last the whole lifetime of an individual. They are exceptions in time as they are in space.[1] We are therefore faced with two distinct types of phenomena which must be designated by different terms. Those facts which appear in the most common forms we shall call normal, and the rest morbid or pathological. Let us agree to designate as the average type the hypothetical being which might be constituted by assembling in one entity, as a kind of individual abstraction, the most frequently occurring characteristics of the species in their most frequent forms. We may then say that the normal type merges into the average type and that any deviation from that standard of healthiness is a morbid phenomenon. It is true that the average type cannot be delineated with the same distinctness as an individual type, since the attributes from which it is constituted are not absolutely fixed but are capable of variation. Yet it can unquestionably be constituted in this way since it is the immediate subject matter of science and blends with the generic type. The physiologist studies the functions of the average organism; the same is true of the sociologist. Once we know how to distinguish between the various social species—this question will be dealt with later—it is always possible to discover the most general form presented by a phenomenon in any given species.

It can be seen that a fact can be termed pathological only in relation to a given species. The conditions of health and sickness cannot be defined *in abstracto* or absolutely. This rule is not questioned in biology: it has never occurred to anybody to think that what is normal in a mollusk should be also for a vertebrate. Each species has its own state of health, because it has an average type peculiar to it, and the health of the lowest species is no less than that of the highest. The same principle is applicable to sociology, although it is often misunderstood. The habit, far too widespread, must be abandoned of judging an institution, a practice or a moral maxim as if they were good or bad in or by themselves for all social types without distinction.

Since the reference point for judging the state of health or sickness varies according to the species, it can vary also within the same species, if that happens to change. Thus from the purely biological viewpoint, what is normal for the savage is not always so for the civilized person and vice versa.[2] There is one order of variations above all which it is important to take into account because these occur regularly in all species: they are those which relate to age. Health for the old person is not the same as it is for the adult, just as the adult's is different from the child's. The same is likewise true of societies.[3] Thus a social fact can only be termed normal in a given species in relation to a particular phase, likewise determinate, of its development. Consequently, to know whether the term is merited for a social fact, it is not enough to observe the form in which it occurs in the majority of societies which belong to a species: we must also be careful to observe the societies at the corresponding phase of their evolution.

We may seem to have arrived merely at a definition of terms, for we have done no more than group phenomena according to their similarities and differences and label the groups formed in this way. Yet in reality the concepts so formed, while they possess the great merit of being identifiable because of characteristics which are objective and easily perceptible, are not far removed from the notion commonly held of sickness and health. In fact, does not everybody consider sickness to be an accident, doubtless bound up with the state of being alive, but one which is not produced normally? This is what the ancient philosophers meant when they declared that sickness does not derive from the nature of things but is the product of a kind of contingent state immanent in the organism. Such a conception is assuredly the negation of all science, for sickness is no more miraculous than health, which also inheres in the nature of creatures. Yet sickness is not grounded in their normal nature, bound up with their ordinary temperament or linked to the conditions of existence upon which they usually depend. Conversely the type of health is closely joined for everybody to the type of species. We cannot conceive incontrovertibly of a species which in itself and through its own basic constitution would be incurably sick. Health is the paramount norm and consequently cannot be in any way abnormal.

It is true that health is commonly understood as a state generally preferable to sickness. But this definition is contained in the one just stated. It is not without good reason that those characteristics which have come together to form the normal type have been able to generalize themselves throughout the species. This generalization is itself a fact requiring explanation and therefore necessitating a cause. It would be inexplicable if the most widespread forms of organization were not also—*at least in the aggregate*—the most advantageous. How could they have sustained themselves in such a wide variety of circumstances if they did not enable the individual better to resist the causes of destruction? On the other hand, if the other forms are rarer it is plainly because—*in the average number of cases*—those individuals displaying such forms have greater difficulty in surviving. The greater frequency of the former class is thus the proof of their superiority.[4]

II

This last observation even provides a means of verifying the results of the preceding method.

Since the generality which outwardly characterizes normal phenomena, once directly established by observation, is itself an explicable phenomenon, it demands explanation. Doubtless we can have the prior conviction that it is not without a cause, but it is better to know exactly what that cause is. The normality of the phenomenon will be less open to question if it is demonstrated that the external sign whereby it was revealed to us is not merely apparent but grounded in the nature of things—if, in short, we can convert this factual normality into one which exists by right. Moreover, the demonstration of this will not always consist in showing that the phenomenon is useful to the organism, although for reasons just stated this is most frequently the case. But, as previously remarked, an arrangement may happen to be normal without serving any useful purpose, simply because it inheres in the nature of a creature. Thus it would perhaps be useful for childbirth not to occasion such violent disturbances in the female organism, but this is impossible. Consequently the normality of a phenomenon can be explained only through it being bound up with the conditions of existence in the species under consideration, either as the mechanically essential effect of these conditions or as a means allowing the organism to adapt to these conditions.[5]

This proof is not merely useful as a check. We must not forget that the advantage of distinguishing the normal from the abnormal is principally to throw light upon practice. Now, in order to act in full knowledge of the facts, it is not sufficient to know what we should want, but why we should want it. Scientific propositions relating to the normal state will be more immediately applicable to individual cases when they are accompanied by the reasons for them, for then it will be more feasible to pick out those cases where it is appropriate to modify their application, and in what way.

Circumstances even exist where this verification is indispensable, because the first method, if it were applied in isolation, might lead to error. This is what occurs in transition periods when the whole species is in the process of evolving, without yet being stabilized in a new and definitive form. In that situation the only normal type extant at the time and grounded in the facts is one that relates to the past but no longer corresponds to the new conditions of existence. A fact can therefore persist through a whole species but no longer correspond to the requirements of the situation. It therefore has only the appearance of normality, and the generality it displays is deceptive; persisting only through the force of blind habit, it is no longer the sign that the phenomenon observed is closely linked to the general conditions of collective existence. Moreover, this difficulty is peculiar to sociology. It does not exist, in a manner of speaking, for the biologist. Only very rarely do animal species require to assume unexpected forms. The only normal modifications through which they pass are those which occur regularly in each individual, principally under the influence of age. Thus they are already known or knowable, since they have already taken place in a large number of cases. Consequently at every stage in the development of the animal, and even in periods of crisis, the normal state may be ascertained. This is also still true in sociology for those societies belonging to inferior species. This is because, since a number of them have already run their complete course, the law of their normal evolution has been, or at least can be, established. But in the case of the highest and most recent societies, by definition this law is unknown, since they have not been through their whole history. The sociologist may therefore be at a loss to know whether a phenomenon is normal, since he lacks any reference point.

He can get out of this difficulty by proceeding along the lines we have just laid down. Having established by observation that the fact is general, he will trace back the conditions which determined this general character in the past and then investigate whether these conditions still pertain in the present or, on the contrary, have changed. In the first case he will be justified in treating the phenomenon as normal; in the other eventuality he will deny it that characteristic. For instance, to know whether the present economic state of the peoples of Europe, with the lack of organization[6] that characterizes it, is normal or not, we must investigate what in the past gave rise to it. If the conditions are still those appertaining to our societies, it is because the situation is normal, despite the protest that it stirs up. If, on the other hand, it is linked to that old social structure which elsewhere we have termed segmentary[7] and which, after providing the essential skeletal framework of societies, is now increasingly dying out, we shall be forced to conclude that this now constitutes a morbid state, however universal it may be. It is by the same method that all such controversial questions of this nature will have to be resolved, such as those relating to ascertaining whether the weakening of religious belief and the development of state power are normal phenomena or not.[8]

Nevertheless this method should in no case be substituted for the previous one, nor even be the first one employed. Firstly it raises questions which require later discussion and which cannot be tackled save at an already fairly advanced stage of science. This is because, in short, it entails an almost comprehensive explanation of phenomena, since it presupposes that either their causes or their functions are determined. At the very beginning of our research it is important to be able to classify facts as normal or abnormal, except for a few exceptional cases, in order to assign physiology and pathology each to its proper domain. Next, it is in relation to the normal type that a fact must be found useful or necessary in order to be itself termed normal. Otherwise it could be demonstrated that sickness and health are indistinguishable, since the former necessarily derives from the organism suffering from it. It is only with the average organism that sickness does not sustain the same relationship. In the same way the application of a remedy, since it is useful to the sick organism, might pass for a normal phenomenon, although it is plainly abnormal, since only in abnormal circumstances does it possess this utility. This method can therefore only be used if the normal type has previously been constituted, which could only have occurred using a different procedure. Finally, and above all, if it is true that everything which is normal is useful without being necessary, it is untrue that everything which is useful is normal. We can indeed be certain that those states which have become generalized in the species are more useful than those which have continued to be exceptional. We cannot, however, be certain that they are the most useful that exist or can exist. We have no grounds for believing that all the possible combinations have been tried out in the course of the process; among those which have never been realized but are conceivable, there are perhaps some which are much more advantageous than those known to us. The notion of utility goes beyond that of the normal, and is to the normal what the genus is to the species. But it is impossible to deduce the greater from the lesser, the species from the genus, although we may discover the genus from the species, since it is contained within it. This is why, once the general nature of the phenomena has been ascertained, we may confirm the results of the first method by demonstrating how it is useful.[9] We can then formulate the three following rules:

1 *A social fact is normal for a given social type, viewed at a given phase of its development, when it occurs in the average society of that species, considered at the corresponding phase of its evolution.*
2 *The results of the preceding method can be verified by demonstrating that the general character of the phenomenon is related to the general conditions of collective life in the social type under consideration.*
3 *This verification is necessary when this fact relates to a social species which has not yet gone through its complete evolution.*

III

We are so accustomed to resolving glibly these difficult questions and to deciding rapidly, after cursory observation and by dint of syllogisms, whether a social fact is normal or not, that this procedure will perhaps be adjudged uselessly complicated. It seems unnecessary to have to go to such lengths to distinguish sickness from health. Do we not make these distinctions every day? This is true, but it remains to be seen whether we make them appositely. The difficulty of these problems is concealed because we see the biologist resolve them with comparative ease. Yet we forget that it is much easier for him than for the sociologist to see how each phenomenon affects the strength of the organism and thereby to determine its normal or abnormal character with an accuracy which is adequate for all practical purposes. In sociology the complexity and the much more changing nature of the facts constrain us to take many more precautions, as is proved by the conflicting judgments on the same phenomenon emitted by the different parties concerned. To show clearly how great this circumspection must be, we shall illustrate by a few examples to what errors we are exposed when we do not constrain ourselves in this way and in how different a light the most vital phenomena appear when they are dealt with methodically.

If there is a fact whose pathological nature appears indisputable, it is crime. All criminologists agree on this score. Although they explain this pathology differently, they none the less unanimously acknowledge it. However, the problem needs to be treated less summarily.

Let us in fact apply the rules previously laid down. Crime is not only observed in most societies of a particular species, but in all societies of all types. There is not one in which criminality does not exist, although it changes in form and the actions which are termed criminal are not the same everywhere. Yet everywhere and always there have been men who have conducted themselves in such a way as to bring down punishment upon their heads. If at least, as societies pass from lower to higher types, the crime rate (the relationship between the annual crime figures and population figures) tended to fall, we might believe that, although still remaining a normal phenomenon, crime tended to lose that character of normality. Yet there is no single ground for believing such a regression to be real. Many facts would rather seem to point to the existence of a movement in the opposite direction. From the beginning of the century statistics provide us with a means of following the progression of criminality. It has everywhere increased, and in France the increase is of the order of 300 percent. Thus there is no phenomenon which represents more incontrovertibly all the symptoms of normality, since it appears to be closely bound up with the conditions of all collective life. To make crime a social illness would be to concede that sickness is not something accidental, but on the contrary derives in certain cases from the fundamental constitution of the living creature. This would be to erase any distinction between the physiological and the pathological. It can certainly happen that crime itself has abnormal forms; this is what happens, for instance, when it reaches an excessively high level. There is no doubt that this excessiveness is pathological in nature. What is normal is simply that criminality exists, provided that for each social type it does not reach or go beyond a certain level which it is perhaps not impossible to fix in conformity with the previous rules.[10]

We are faced with a conclusion which is apparently somewhat paradoxical. Let us make no mistake: to classify crime among the phenomena of normal sociology is not merely to declare that it is an inevitable though regrettable phenomenon arising from the incorrigible wickedness of men; it is to assert that it is a factor in public health, an integrative element in any healthy society. At first sight this result is so surprising that it disconcerted even ourselves for a long time. However, once that first impression of surprise has been overcome it is not difficult to discover reasons to explain this normality and at the same time to confirm it.

In the first place, crime is normal because it is completely impossible for any society entirely free of it to exist.

Crime, as we have shown elsewhere, consists of an action which offends certain collective feelings which are especially strong and clear-cut. In any society, for actions regarded as criminal to cease, the feelings that they offend would need to be found in each individual consciousness without exception and in the degree of strength requisite to counteract the opposing feelings. Even supposing that this condition could effectively be fulfilled, crime would not thereby disappear; it would merely change in form, for the very cause which made the well-springs of criminality dry up would immediately open up new ones.

Indeed, for the collective feelings, which the penal law of a people at a particular moment in its history protects, to penetrate individual consciousnesses that had hitherto remained closed to them, or to assume greater authority—whereas previously they had not possessed enough— they would have to acquire an intensity greater than they had had up to then. The community as a whole must feel them more keenly, for they cannot draw from any other source the additional force which enables them to bear down upon individuals who formerly were the most refractory. For murderers to disappear, the horror of bloodshed must increase in those strata of society from which murderers are recruited; but for this to happen the abhorrence must increase throughout society. Moreover, the very absence of crime would contribute directly to bringing about that result, for a sentiment appears much more respectable when it is always and uniformly respected. But we overlook the fact that these strong states of the common consciousness cannot be reinforced in this way without the weaker states, the violation of which previously gave rise to mere breaches of convention, being reinforced at the same time, for the weaker states are no more than the extension and attenuated form of the stronger ones. Thus, for example, theft and mere misappropriation of property offend the same altruistic sentiment, the respect for other people's possessions. However, this sentiment is offended less strongly by the latter action than the former. Moreover, since the average consciousness does not have sufficient intensity of feeling to feel strongly about the lesser of these two offenses, the latter is the object of greater tolerance. This is why the misappropriator is merely censured, while the thief is punished. But if this sentiment grows stronger, to such a degree that it extinguishes in the consciousness the tendency to theft that men possess, they will become more sensitive to these lesions, which up to then had had only a marginal effect upon them. They will react with greater intensity against these lesser faults, which will become the object of severer condemnation, so that, from the mere moral errors that they were, some will pass into the category of crimes. For example, dishonest contracts or those fulfilled dishonestly, which only incur public censure or civil redress, will become crimes. Imagine a community of saints in an exemplary and perfect monastery. In it crime as such will be unknown, but faults that appear venial to the ordinary person will arouse the same scandal as does normal crime in ordinary consciences. If therefore that community has the power to judge and punish, it will term such acts criminal and deal with them as such. It is for the same reason that the completely honorable man judges his slightest moral failings with a severity that the mass of people reserves for acts that are truly criminal. In former times acts of violence against the person were more frequent than they are today because respect for individual dignity was weaker. As it has increased, such crimes have become less frequent, but many acts which offended against that sentiment have been incorporated into the penal code, which did not previously include them.[11]

In order to exhaust all the logically possible hypotheses, it will perhaps be asked why this unanimity should not cover all collective sentiments without exception, and why even the weakest sentiments should not evoke sufficient power to forestall any dissentient voice. The moral conscience of society would be found in its entirety in every individual, endowed with sufficient force to prevent the commission of any act offending against it, whether purely conventional failings or crimes. But such universal and absolute uniformity is utterly impossible, for the immediate physical environment in which each one of us is placed, our hereditary antecedents, the social influences upon which we depend, vary from one individual to another and consequently cause a diversity of consciences. It is impossible for everyone to be alike in this matter, by virtue of the fact that we each have our own organic constitution and occupy different areas in space. This is why, even among lower peoples where individual originality is very little developed, such originality does however exist. Thus, since there cannot be a society in which individuals do not diverge to some extent from the collective type, it is also inevitable that among these deviations some assume a criminal character. What confers upon them this character is not the intrinsic importance of the acts but the importance which the common consciousness ascribes to them. Thus if the latter is stronger and possesses sufficient authority to make these divergences very weak in absolute terms, it will also be more sensitive and exacting. By reacting against the slightest deviations with an energy which it elsewhere employs against those that are weightier, it endues them with the same gravity and will brand them as criminal.

Thus crime is necessary. It is linked to the basic conditions of social life, but on this very account is useful, for the conditions to which it is bound are themselves indispensable to the normal evolution of morality and law.

Indeed today we can no longer dispute the fact that not only do law and morality vary from one social type to another, but they even change within the same type if the conditions of collective existence are modified. Yet for these transformations to be made possible, the collective sentiments at the basis of morality should not prove unyielding to change, and consequently should be only moderately intense. If they were too strong, they would no longer be malleable. Any arrangement is indeed an obstacle to a new arrangement; this is even more the case the more deep-seated the original arrangement. The more strongly a structure is articulated, the more it resists modification; this is as true for functional as for anatomical patterns. If there were no crimes, this condition would not be fulfilled, for such a hypothesis presumes that collective sentiments would have attained a degree of intensity unparalleled in history. Nothing is good indefinitely and without limits. The authority which the moral consciousness enjoys must not be excessive, for otherwise no one would dare to attack it and it would petrify too easily into an immutable form. For it to evolve, individual originality must be allowed to manifest itself. But so that the originality of the idealist who dreams of transcending his era may display itself, that of the criminal, which falls short of the age, must also be possible. One does not go without the other.

Nor is this all. Beyond this indirect utility, crime itself may play a useful part in this evolution. Not only does it imply that the way to necessary changes remains open, but in certain cases it also directly prepares for these changes. Where crime exists, collective sentiments are not only in the state of plasticity necessary to assume a new form, but sometimes it even contributes to determining beforehand the shape they will take on. Indeed, how often is it only an anticipation of the morality to come, a progression toward what will be! According to Athenian law, Socrates was a criminal and his condemnation was entirely just. However, his crime— his independence of thought—was useful not only for humanity but for his country. It served to prepare a way for a new morality and a new faith, which the Athenians then needed because the traditions by which they had hitherto lived no longer corresponded to the conditions of their existence. Socrates' case is not an isolated one, for it recurs periodically in history. The freedom of thought that we at present enjoy could never have been asserted if the rules that forbade it had not been violated before they were solemnly abrogated. However, at the time the violation was a crime, since it was an offense against sentiments still keenly felt in the average consciousness. Yet this crime was useful since it was the prelude to changes which were daily becoming more necessary. Liberal philosophy has had as its precursors heretics of all kinds whom the secular arm rightly punished through the Middle Ages and has continued to do so almost up to the present day.

From this viewpoint the fundamental facts of criminology appear to us in an entirely new light. Contrary to current ideas, the criminal no longer appears as an utterly unsociable creature, a sort of parasitic element, a foreign, unassimilable body introduced into the bosom of society.[12] He plays a normal role in social life. For its part, crime must no longer be conceived of as an evil which cannot be circumscribed closely enough. Far from there being cause for congratulation when it drops too noticeably below the normal level, this apparent progress assuredly coincides with and is linked to some social disturbance. Thus the number of crimes of assault never falls as low as it does in times of scarcity.[13] Consequently, at the same time, and as a reaction, the theory of punishment is revised, or rather should be revised. If indeed crime is a sickness, punishment is the cure for it and cannot be conceived of otherwise; thus all the discussion aroused revolves around knowing what punishment should be to fulfill its role as a remedy. But if crime is in no way pathological, the object of punishment cannot be to cure it and its true function must be sought elsewhere.

Thus the rules previously enunciated are far from having as their sole purpose to satisfy a logical formalism which lacks any great utility. This is because, on the contrary, according to whether they are applied or not, the most essential social facts totally change their character. If the example quoted is particularly cogent—and this is why we thought we should dwell upon it—there are nevertheless many others which could usefully be cited. There is no society where it is not the rule that the punishment should fit the crime—and yet for the Italian school of thought this principle is a mere invention of legal theoreticians devoid of any solid basis.[14] For these criminologists the whole institution of punishment, as it has functioned up to the present among all known peoples, is a phenomenon which goes against nature. We have already seen that for Garofalo the criminality peculiar to the lower forms of society has nothing natural about it. For the socialists it is capitalist organization, despite its widespread nature, which constitutes a deviation from the normal state and is an organization brought about by violence and trickery. On the other hand for Spencer it is our administrative centralization and the extension of governmental power which are the radical vices of our societies, in spite of the fact that both have developed entirely regularly and universally over the course of history. The belief is that one is never obliged systematically to decide on the normal or abnormal character of social facts according to their degree of generality. It is always by a great display of dialectic that these questions are resolved.

However, by laying this criterion on one side, not only is one exposed to confusion and partial errors like those just discussed, but science itself becomes impossible. Indeed its immediate object is the study of the normal type, but if the most general facts can be pathological, it may well be that the normal type has never really existed. Hence what use is it to study facts? They can only confirm our prejudices and root us more deeply in our errors, since they spring from them. If punishment and responsibility, as they exist in history, are merely a product of ignorance and barbarism, what use is it to strive to know them in order to determine their normal forms? Thus the mind is led to turn away from a reality which from then on lacks interest for us, turning in upon itself to seek the materials necessary to reconstruct that reality. For sociology to deal with facts as things, the sociologist must feel a need to learn from them. The principal purpose of any science of life, whether individual or social, is in the end to define and explain the normal state and distinguish it from the abnormal. If normality does not inhere in the things themselves, if on the contrary it is a characteristic which we impose upon them externally or, for whatever reason, refuse to do so, this salutary state of dependence on things is lost. The mind complacently faces a reality that has not much to teach it. It is no longer contained by the subject matter to which it applies itself, since in some respects it determines that subject matter. The different rules that we have established up to now are therefore closely linked. For sociology really to be a science of things, the generality of phenomena must be taken as the criterion of their normality.

Moreover, our method has the advantage of regulating action at the same time as thought. If what is deemed desirable is not the object of observation, but can and must be determined by some sort of mental calculus, no limit, in a manner of speaking, can be laid down to the free inventions of the imagination in their search for the best. For how can one assign to perfection bounds that it cannot exceed? By definition it escapes all limitations. The goal of humanity thus recedes to infinity, discouraging not a few by its very remoteness, arousing and exciting others, on the other hand, who, so as to draw a little nearer to it, hasten their steps and throw themselves into revolutionary activity. This practical dilemma is avoided if what is desirable is declared to be what is healthy, and if the state of health is something definite, inherent in things, for at the same time the extent of our effort is given and defined. There is no longer need to pursue desperately an end which recedes as we move forward; we need only to work steadily and persistently to maintain the normal state, to re-establish it if it is disturbed, and to rediscover the conditions of normality if they happen to change. The duty of the statesman is no longer to propel societies violently toward an ideal which appears attractive to him. His role is rather that of the doctor: he forestalls the outbreak of sickness by maintaining good hygiene, or when it does break out, seeks to cure it.[15]

Notes

1. Through this we can distinguish the case of sickness from monstrosity. The second is an exception only in space; it is not met with in the average member of the species, but it lasts the whole lifetime of the individuals in which it is to be found. Yet it is clear that these two orders of facts differ only in degree and basically are of the same nature. The boundaries drawn between them are very imprecise, for sickness can also have a lasting character and abnormality can evolve. Thus in defining them we can hardly separate them rigidly. The distinction between them cannot be more categorical than that between the morphological and the physiological, since after all morbidity is abnormal in the physiological order just as monstrosity is in the anatomical order.

2. For example, the savage who had the reduced digestive tube and developed nervous system of the civilized healthy being would be considered sick in relationship to his environment.

3. This section of our argument is abridged, for we can only reiterate here regarding social facts in general what we have said elsewhere concerning the division of moral facts into the normal and abnormal (cf. *Division du travail social*, pp. 33–9).

4. It is true that Garofalo has attempted to distinguish the sick from the abnormal (*Criminologie*, pp. 109, 110). But the sole two arguments on which he relies to make this distinction are:

   1 The word "sickness" always signifies something which tends to the total or partial destruction of the organism. If there is not destruction, there

is a cure, but never stability, such as exists in several abnormalities. But we have just seen that the abnormal is also, in the average case, a threat to the living creature. It is true that this is not always so, but the dangers that sickness entails likewise exist only in average circumstances. As for the absence of stability allegedly distinctive of the morbid, this leaves out of account chronic illnesses and is to divide the study of monstrosities from that of the pathological. The monstrosities are permanent.

2   It is stated that the normal and abnormal vary according to different races, while the distinction between the physiological and the pathological is valid for the entire human race. On the contrary, we have shown that what is morbid for the savage is not so for the civilized person. The conditions of physical health vary according to different environments.

5. It is true that one may speculate whether, when a phenomenon derives necessarily from the general conditions of life, this very fact does not make it useful. We cannot deal with this philosophical question, although we touch upon it a little later.

6. Cf. on this point a note we published in the *Revue philosophique* (November 1893) on "La définition du socialisme."

7. Segmentary societies, particularly those which have a territorial basis, are ones whose essential components correspond to territorial divisions (cf. *Division du travail social*, pp. 189–210).

8. In certain cases one may proceed somewhat differently and demonstrate whether a fact whose normal character is suspect justifies this suspicion by showing whether it is closely linked to the previous development of the social type under consideration, and even to the totality of social evolution in general; or on the other hand whether it contradicts both. By this means we have been able to show that the present weakening of religious beliefs and, more generally, of collective sentiments toward collective objects, is utterly normal; we have proved that such weakening becomes increasingly marked as societies evolve toward our present type, and that this type, in turn, is more developed (cf. *Division du travail social*, pp. 73–182). But basically this method is only a special case of the preceding one. For if the normality of the phenomenon has been established in this way, it is because at the same time it has been linked to the most general conditions of our collective existence. Indeed, on the one hand, if this regression of religious consciousness is more apparent as the structure of our societies becomes more precisely determinate, it is because it does not depend on any accidental cause but on the very constitution of our social environment. Moreover, on the other hand, since the special characteristics of that constitution are certainly more developed today than formerly, it is entirely normal that the phenomena that depend upon it should themselves be more developed. This method differs only from the preceding one in that the conditions which explain and justify the general character of the phenomenon have been induced and not observed directly. We know that the phenomenon relates to the nature of the social environment without knowing by what, or how, it is connected.

9. But then it will be said that the realization of the normal type is not the highest objective that can be proposed and, in order to go beyond it, one

must also go beyond the bounds of science. We need not deal with this question here *ex professo*; let us merely reply: (1) that the question is purely theoretical because in fact the normal type, a state of health, is already somewhat difficult to determine and rarely enough attained for us to exercise our imagination to discover something better; (2) that these improvements, objectively more advantageous, are not for that reason objectively desirable. For if they do not correspond to any latent or actual tendency they would add nothing to happiness and, if they *do* correspond to some tendency, it is because the normal type has not been realized; and (3) finally, that, in order to improve the normal type, it must first be known. One cannot therefore in any case go beyond science except by first relying upon it.

10. From the fact that crime is a phenomenon of normal sociology it does not follow that the criminal is a person normally constituted from the biological and psychological viewpoints. The two questions are independent of each other. This independence will be better understood when we have shown later the difference which exists between psychical and sociological facts.

11. Calumny, insults, slander, deception, etc.

12. We have ourselves committed the error of speaking of the criminal in this way through not having applied our rule (cf. *Division du travail social*, pp. 395, 396).

13. But, although crime is a fact of normal sociology, it does not follow that we should not abhor it. Pain has likewise nothing desirable about it: the individual detests it just as society detests crime, and yet it is a normal physiological function. Not only does it necessarily derive from the very constitution of every living creature, but it plays a useful and irreplaceable role in life. Thus it would be a peculiar distortion to represent our thinking as an apologia for crime. We would not even have envisaged protesting against such an interpretation were we not aware of the strange accusations and misunderstandings to which one is exposed in undertaking to study moral facts objectively and to speak of them in language that is not commonly used.

14. Cf. Garofalo, *Criminologie*, pp. 299.

15. From the theory developed in this chapter it has sometimes been concluded that, in our view, the upward trend in criminality during the nineteenth century was a normal phenomenon. Nothing is farther from our thoughts. Several facts which we have pointed out in connexion with suicide (cf. *Le Suicide*, p. 420ff.) tend, on the contrary, to cause us to believe that this development has been, in general, pathological. However, it may be that a certain increase in certain forms of criminality would be normal, for every state of civilization has its own criminality. But on this matter one can only hypothesize.

CHAPTER IV

Rules for the Constitution of Social Types

Since a social fact can only be labeled normal or abnormal in relation to a given social species, what has been stated up to now implies that a branch of sociology must be devoted to the constitution and classification of these species.

This notion of social species has moreover the very great advantage of providing us with a middle ground between the two opposing conceptions of social life which for a long time have caused a division of opinion. I refer to the nominalism of the historians[1] and the extreme realism of the philosophers. For the historian, societies constitute so many individual types, heterogeneous and not comparable with one another. Each people has its own characteristics, its special constitution, its law, its morality and its economic organization, appropriate only to itself, and any generalization is almost impossible. For the philosopher, on the other hand, all these special groupings, which are called tribes, cities and nations, are only contingent and provisional aggregates without any individual reality. Only humanity is real, and it is from the general attributes of human nature that all social evolution derives. Consequently, for the historians history is only a sequence of events which are linked together but do not repeat themselves; for the philosophers these same events have value and interest only as an illustration of the general laws which are inscribed in the constitution of men and which hold sway over the course of historical development. For the former what is good for one society could not be applied to others. The conditions for the state of health vary from one people to another and cannot be theoretically determined; it is a matter of practice and experience of trial and error. For the philosophers these conditions can be calculated once and for all for the entire human race. It would therefore seem that social reality can only be the object of an abstract and vague philosophy or of purely descriptive monographs. But one escapes from this alternative once it is recognized that between the confused multitude of historical societies and the unique, although ideal, concept of humanity, there are intermediate entities: these are the social species. In the idea of species there are found joined both the unity that any truly scientific research requires and the diversity inherent in the facts, since the species is the same everywhere for all the individuals who comprise it, and yet, on the other hand, the species differ among themselves. It remains true that moral, judicial and economic institutions, etc. are infinitely variable, but the variations are not of such a nature as to be unamenable to scientific thought.

It is because Comte failed to recognize the existence of social species that he thought he could depict the progress of human societies as that of a single people "to which would be ideally related all the successive modifications observed among separate populations."[2] Indeed, if there exists only one single social species, individual societies can differ from each other only in degree, in the extent to which they display the constituent traits of that single species, and according to whether they express humanity more or less perfectly. If, on the contrary, social types exist which are qualitatively distinct from each other, it would be vain to seek to juxtapose them, since one cannot join them together exactly like the homogeneous segments that constitute a geometrical straight line. Thus historical development loses the ideal but simplistic unity attributed to it. It becomes fragmented, so to speak, into a myriad of sections, which, because each differs specifically from the rest, cannot be pieced together in a continuous fashion. The famous metaphor of Pascal, since taken up again by Comte, is hence devoid of truth.

But how should we set about constituting these species?

I

At first sight there seems no other way of proceeding than to study each society in detail, making of each as exact and complete a monograph as possible, then to compare these monographs with one another, to see how they agree or diverge, and finally, weighing the relative importance of these similarities and divergences, to classify peoples into similar or different groups. In support of this method we should note that it is the sole one acceptable for a science based on observation. In fact the species is only the summary of individuals; how then is it to be constituted, if we do not begin by describing each one and describing it in its entirety? Is it not the rule to pass to the general only after having observed the particular, and that particular completely? This is why on occasion some have wished to defer the study of sociology until the indefinitely distant time when history, in its study of particular societies, has arrived at results sufficiently objective and definite as to admit useful comparisons to be made.

But in reality this circumspection is only scientific in appearance. It is untrue that science can formulate laws only after having reviewed all the facts they express, or arrive at categories only after having described, in their totality, the individuals that they include. The true experimental method tends rather to substitute for common facts, which only give rise to proofs when they are very numerous and which consequently allow conclusions which are always suspect, *decisive* or *crucial* facts, as Bacon said,[3] which by themselves and regardless of their number, have scientific value and interest. It is particularly necessary to proceed in this fashion when one sets about constituting genera and species. This is because to attempt an inventory of all the characteristics peculiar to an individual is an insoluble problem. Every individual is an infinity, and infinity cannot be exhausted. Should we therefore stick to the most essential properties? If so, on what principle will we then make a selection? For this a criterion is required which is beyond the capacity of the individual and which consequently even the best monographs could not provide. Without carrying matters to this extreme of rigor, we can envisage that, the more numerous the characteristics to serve as the basis for a classification, the more difficult it will also be, in view of the different ways in which these characteristics combine together in particular cases, to present similarities and distinctions which are clear-cut enough to allow the constitution of definite groups and sub-groups.

Even were a classification possible using this method, it would present a major drawback in that it would not have the usefulness that was at first its rationale. Its main purpose should be to expedite the scientific task by substituting for an indefinite multiplicity of individuals a limited number of types. But this advantage is lost if these types can only be constituted after all individuals have been investigated and analyzed in their entirety. It can hardly facilitate the research if it does no more than summarize research already carried out. It will only be really useful if it allows us to classify characteristics other than those which serve as a basis for it, and if it furnishes us with a framework for future facts. Its role is to supply us with reference points to which we can add observations other than those which these reference points have already provided. But for this the classification must be made, not on the basis of a complete inventory of all individual characteristics, but according to a small number of them, carefully selected. Under these conditions it will not only serve to reduce to some order knowledge already discovered, but also to produce more. It will spare the observer from following up many lines of inquiry because it will serve as a guide. Thus once a classification has been established according to this principle, in order to know whether a fact is general throughout a particular species, it will be unnecessary to have observed all societies belonging to this species— the study of a few will suffice. In many cases even one observation well conducted will be enough, just as often an experiment efficiently carried out is sufficient to establish a law.

We must therefore select for our classification characteristics which are particularly essential. It is true that these cannot be known until the explanation of the facts is sufficiently advanced. These two operations of science are linked, depending upon each other for progress. However, without plunging too deeply into the study of the facts, it is not difficult to surmise in what area to look for the characteristic properties of social types. We know that societies are made up of a number of parts added on to each other. Since the nature of any composite necessarily depends upon the nature and number of the elements that go to make it up and the way in which these are combined, these characteristics are plainly those which we must take as our basis. It will be seen later that it is on them that the general facts of social life depend. Moreover, as they are of a morphological order, one might term that part of sociology whose task it is to constitute and classify social types *social morphology*.

The principle of this classification can be defined even more precisely. Indeed, it is known that the constituent parts of every society are themselves societies of a simpler kind. A people is produced by the combination of two or more peoples that have preceded it. If therefore we knew the simplest society that ever existed, in order to make our classification we should only have to follow the way in which these simple societies joined together and how these new composites also combined.

II

Spencer understood very well that the methodical classification of social types could have no other basis.

"We have seen," he stated, "that social evolution begins with small, simple aggregates, that it progresses by the clustering of these into larger aggregates, and that after consolidating such clusters are united with others like themselves into still larger aggregates. Our classification then must begin with the societies of the first or simplest order."[4]

Unfortunately, to put this principle into practice we should have to begin by defining precisely what is understood by a simple society. Now, not only does Spencer fail to give this definition, but he esteems it almost impossible to do so.[5] This is in fact because simplicity, as he understands it, consists essentially of a certain rudimentariness of organization. Now it is not easy to state precisely at what moment the social organization is crude enough to be termed simple; it is a matter of judgment. Thus the formula he gives for it is so vague that it can fit all sorts of societies. "Our only course," he affirms, "is to regard as a simple society, one which forms a single working whole unsubjected to any other end and of which the parts cooperate, with or without a regulating center, for certain public ends."[6] But there are a number of peoples which satisfy this condition.

The result is that he mixes somewhat at random under this same heading all the least civilized societies. With such a starting point one can perhaps imagine what the rest of his classification is like. Grouped together in the most astonishing confusion are societies of the most diverse character: the Homeric Greeks are placed alongside the fiefdoms of the tenth century and below the Bechuanas, the Zulus and the Fijians; the Athenian confederation alongside the fiefdoms of thirteenth-century France and below the Iroquois and the Araucanians.

The term "simplicity" can only have a precise meaning when it signifies a complete absence of any component elements. A simple society must therefore be understood as one which does not include others simpler than itself, which at present not only contains merely one single segment, but which presents no trace of any previous segmentation. The *horde*, as we have defined it elsewhere,[7] corresponds exactly to this definition. It is a social aggregate which does not include—and never has included—within it any other more elementary aggregate, but which can be split up directly into individuals. These do not form within the main group special sub-groups different from it, but are juxtaposed like atoms. One realizes that there can be no more simple society; it is the protoplasm of the social domain and consequently the natural basis for any classification.

It is true that there does not perhaps exist any historical society corresponding exactly to this description, but (as we have shown in the book already cited) we know of very many which have been formed directly and without any intermediary by a combination or hordes. When the horde thus becomes a social segment instead of being the whole society, it changes its name and becomes the clan, whilst retaining the same constituent features. Indeed the clan is a social aggregate which cannot be split up into any other more limited in size. Perhaps it will be remarked that generally, where it is still observable today, it comprises a number of individual families. But firstly, for reasons that we cannot expatiate upon here, we believe that the formation of these small family groups postdates the clan; and secondly, precisely speaking, these do not constitute social segments because they are not political divisions. Everywhere that it is met with, the clan constitutes the ultimate division of this kind. Consequently, even if we possessed no other facts on which to postulate the existence of the horde—and other facts exist which one day we shall have the opportunity to set out—the existence of the clan, that is to say of a society formed by the linking up of hordes, justifies our supposition that at first there were simpler societies which are reducible to the horde proper, thus making the latter the root source from which all social species have sprung.

Once this notion of the horde or single-segment society has been assumed—whether it is conceived of as an historical reality or as a scientific postulate—we possess the necessary support on which to construct the complete scale of social types. We can distinguish as many basic types as there exist ways in which hordes combine with one another to give birth to new societies, which in turn combine among themselves. We shall first encounter aggregates formed by a mere replication of hordes or clans (to give them their new name), without these clans being associated among themselves in such a way as to form intermediate groups within the total group which includes each and every one of them. They are merely juxtaposed like individuals within the horde. One finds examples of these societies, which might be termed *simple polysegments*, among certain Iroquois and Australian tribes. The *arch* or Kabyle tribe has the same character; it is a union of clans fixed in the form of villages. Very probably there was a moment in history when the Roman *curia* and the Athenian *phratry* was a society of this kind. Above them would be societies formed by the coming together of the societies of the former species, that is to say, *polysegmentary societies of simple composition*. Such is the character of the Iroquois confederation and that formed by the union of Kabyle tribes. The same is true originally of each of the three primitive tribes whose association later gave birth to the city state of Rome. Next one would find *polysegmentary societies of double composition*, which arise from the juxtaposition or fusion of several polysegmentary societies of simple composition. Such is the city, an aggregate of tribes which are themselves the aggregates of *curiae*, which in their turn break down into *gentes* or clans; such also is the Germanic tribe, with its count's districts which subdivide into their "hundreds," which in their turn have as their ultimate unit the clan, which has become a village.

We need not develop at greater length these few points, since there can be no question here of undertaking a classification of societies. It is too complex a problem to be dealt with incidentally in that way; on the contrary, it supposes a whole gamut of long and detailed investigations. We merely wished, through a few examples, to clarify the ideas and demonstrate how the principle behind the method should be applied. Even what has been expounded should not be considered as constituting a complete classification of lower societies. We have simplified matters somewhat, in the interests of greater clarity. Indeed, we have assumed that every higher type of society was formed by a combination of societies of the same type, that is, of the type immediately below. But it is not impossible for societies of different species, situated at different levels on the genealogical tree of social types, to combine in such a way as to form new species. At least one case of this is known: that of the Roman Empire, which included within it peoples of the most diverse kind.[8]

But once these types have been constituted, we need to distinguish different varieties in each one, according to whether the segmentary societies which serve to form a new society retain a certain individuality or, on the contrary, are absorbed in the total mass. It is understandable that social phenomena should vary not only according to the nature of their component elements, but according to the way in which they are combined. Above all they must be very different, according to whether each of the subgroups retains its own immediate life or whether they are all caught up in the general life, which varies according to their degree of concentration. Consequently we shall have to investigate whether, at any particular moment, a complete coalescence of the segments takes place. This will be discernible from the fact that the original component segments of a society will no longer affect its administrative and political organization. From this viewpoint the city state is sharply differentiated from the Germanic tribes. With the latter the organization based on the clan was maintained, although blurred in form, until the end of their history, while in Rome and Athens the *gentes* and the γένη ceased very early on to be political divisions and became private groupings.

Within the framework elaborated in this way one can seek to introduce new distinctions, according to secondary morphological traits. However, for reasons we shall give later, we scarcely believe it possible or useful to go beyond the general distinctions which have just been indicated. Furthermore, we need not enter into detail. It suffices to have postulated the principle of classification, which can be enunciated as follows:

> *We shall begin by classifying societies according to the degree of organization they manifest, taking as a base the perfectly simple society or the single-segment society. Within these classes different varieties will be distinguished, according to whether a complete coalescence of the initial segments takes place.*

III

These rules implicitly answer a question that the reader may have asked himself when we spoke of social species as if they existed, without having directly established their existence. The proof of existence is contained in the principle itself of the method which has just been expounded.

We have just seen that societies are only different combinations of one and the same original society. But the same element can only combine with others, and the combinations deriving from it can in their turn only do so in a limited number of ways. This is particularly the case when the constituent elements are very few, as with social segments. The scale of possible combinations is therefore finite, and consequently most of them, at the very least, must replicate themselves. Hence social species exist. Moreover, although it is still possible for certain of these combinations to occur only once, this does not prevent their being a species. Only we can say that in cases of this kind the species is made up of one individual entity.[9]

Thus there are social species for the same reason as there are biological ones. The latter are due to the fact that the organisms are only varied combinations of the same anatomical unity. However, from this viewpoint, there is a great difference between the two domains. With animals, a special factor, that of reproduction, imparts to specific characteristics a force of resistance that is lacking elsewhere. These specific characteristics, because they are common to a whole line of ancestors, are much more strongly rooted in the organism. They are therefore not easily whittled away by the action of particular individual environments but remain consistently uniform in spite of the diverse external circumstances. An inner force perpetuates them despite countervailing factors in favor of variation which may come from outside. This force is that of hereditary habits. This is why biological characteristics are clearly defined and can be precisely determined. In the social kingdom this internal force does not exist. Characteristics cannot be reinforced by the succeeding generation because they last only for a generation. This is because as a rule the societies that are produced are of a different species from those which generated them, because the latter, by combining, give rise to an entirely fresh organizational pattern. Only the act of colonization is comparable to reproduction by germination; even so, for the comparison to be exact, the group of colonizers should not mix with some other society of a different species or variety. The distinctive attributes of the species do not therefore receive reinforcement from heredity to enable them to resist individual variations. But they are modified and take on countless nuances through the action of circumstances. Thus, in seeking out these attributes, once all the variants which conceal them have been peeled away, we are often left with a rather indeterminate residue.

This indeterminate state is naturally increased the greater the complexity of the characteristics, for the more complex a thing, the more the possible number of combinations which can be formed by its constituent parts. The end result is that the specific type, beyond the most general and simple characteristics, is not so clearly delineated as in biology.[10]

Notes

1. I term it this because it has occurred frequently among historians, but I do not mean that it is to be found among all of them.
2. *Cours de philosophie positive*, IV, p. 263.
3. *Novum Organum*, II, ss. 36.
4. Spencer, *The Principles of Sociology*, vol. I, part. II, ch. X, p. 570.
5. Ibid., p. 570: "We cannot in all cases say with precision what constitutes a single society."
6. Ibid., 571.
7. *Division du travail social*, p. 189.
8. However, it is likely that in general the distance that separated societies composing it could not be too great; otherwise no social communality could exist between them.

9. Was this not the case with the Roman Empire, which indeed appears to have no parallel in history?
10. In writing this chapter for the first edition of this book we said nothing about the method which consists in classifying societies according to their state of civilization. At the time there did not exist classifications of that kind which would have been put forward by reputable sociologists, save that perhaps of Comte, which was very clearly archaic. Vierkandt ("Die Kulturtypen der Menschheit" in *Archiv f. Anthropogie*, 1898), A. Sutherland (*The Origin and Growth of the Moral Instinct*, 2 vols., London, 1898) and Steinmetz ("Classification des types sociaux," in *Année sociologique*, III, pp. 43–147) represent several attempts that since then have been made in this direction. Nevertheless we shall not stop to discuss them because they do not answer the problem posed in this chapter. One finds classified, not social species, but historical phases, something which is vastly different. From its origins France has passed through very different forms of civilization. It began by being agricultural, passing then to an industry of trades and small businesses, then to manufacturing, and finally to large-scale industry. One cannot admit that the same individual collectivity can change its species three or four times. A species must be defined by more permanent features. The economic or technological state, etc. presents phenomena which are too unstable and complex to provide a basis for classification. It is even extremely likely that the same industrial, scientific and artistic civilization is to be found in societies whose hereditary constitution is very different. Japan may borrow from us our arts, our industry and even our political organization, but it will not cease to belong to a different social species from that of France and Germany. It must be added that these attempts, although carried out by sociologists of worth, have given only results that are vague, disputable and of little utility.

CHAPTER V

Rules for the Explanation of Social Facts

The constitution of species is above all a means of grouping the facts so as to facilitate their interpretation, but social morphology is only one step toward the truly explanatory part of the science. What is the method appropriate for explanation?

I

Most sociologists believe they have accounted for phenomena once they have demonstrated the purpose they serve and the role they play. They reason as if phenomena existed solely for this role and had no determining cause save a clear or vague sense of the services they are called upon to render. This is why it is thought that all that is needful has been said to make them intelligible when it has been established that these services are real and that the social need they satisfy has been demonstrated. Thus Comte relates all the drive for progress of the human species to this basic tendency, "which directly impels man continually to improve his condition in all respects,"[1] whereas Spencer relates it to the need for greater happiness. It is by virtue of this principle that Spencer explains the formation of society as a function of the advantages which flow from co-operation, the institution of government by the utility which springs from regulating military co-operation,[2] and the transformations which the family has undergone from the need for a more perfect reconciliation of the interests of parents, children and society.

But this method confuses two very different questions. To demonstrate the utility of a fact does not explain its origins, nor how it is what it is. The uses which it serves presume the specific properties characteristic of it, but do not create it. Our need for things cannot cause them to be of a particular nature; consequently, that need cannot produce them out of nothing, conferring in this way existence upon them. They spring from causes of

78

another kind. The feeling we have regarding their utility can stimulate us to set these causes in motion and draw upon the effects they bring in their train, but it cannot conjure up these results out of nothing. This proposition is self-evident so long as only material or even psychological phenomena are being considered. It would also not be disputed in sociology if the social facts, because of their total lack of material substance, did not appear—wrongly, moreover—bereft of intrinsic reality. Since we view them as purely mental configurations, provided they are found to be useful, as soon as the idea of them occurs to us they seem to be self-generating. But since each fact is a force which prevails over the force of the individual and possesses its own nature, to bring a fact into existence it cannot suffice to have merely the desire or the will to engender it. Prior forces must exist, capable of producing this firmly established force, as well as natures capable of producing this special nature. Only under these conditions can facts be created. To revive the family spirit where it has grown weak, it is not enough for everybody to realize its advantages; we must set directly in operation those causes which alone can engender it. To endow a government with the authority it requires, it is not enough to feel the need for this. We must address ourselves to the sole sources from which all authority is derived: the establishment of traditions, a common spirit, etc. For this we must retrace our steps farther back along the chain of cause and effect until we find a point at which human action can effectively intervene.

What clearly demonstrates the duality of these two avenues of research is that a fact can exist without serving any purpose, either because it has never been used to further any vital goal or because, having once been of use, it has lost all utility but continues to exist merely through force of custom. There are even more instances of such survivals in society than in the human organism. There are even cases where a practice or a social institution changes its functions without for this reason changing its nature. The rule of *is pater est quem justae nuptiae declarant* has remained substantially the same in our legal code as it was in ancient Roman law. But while its purpose was to safeguard the property rights of the father over children born of his legitimate wife, it is much more the rights of the children that it protects today. The swearing of an oath began by being a kind of judicial ordeal before it became simply a solemn and impressive form of attestation. The religious dogmas of Christianity have not changed for centuries, but the role they play in our modern societies is no longer the same as in the Middle Ages. Thus words serve to express new ideas without their contexture changing. Moreover, it is a proposition true in sociology as in biology, that the organ is independent of its function, i.e. while staying the same it can serve different ends. Thus the causes which give rise to its existence are independent of the ends it serves.

Yet we do not mean that the tendencies, needs and desires of men never actively intervene in social evolution. On the contrary, it is certain that, according to the way they make an impact upon the conditions on which a fact depends, they can hasten or retard development. Yet, apart from the fact that they can never create something out of nothing, their intervention itself, regardless of its effects, can only occur by virtue of efficient causes. Indeed, a tendency cannot, even to this limited extent, contribute to the production of a new phenomenon unless it is itself new, whether constituted absolutely or arising from some transformation of a previous tendency. For unless we postulate a truly pre-established harmony, we could not admit that from his origins man carried within him in potential all the tendencies whose opportuneness would be felt as evolution progressed, each one ready to be awakened when the circumstances called for it. Furthermore, a tendency is also a thing; thus it cannot arise or be modified for the sole reason that we deem it useful. It is a force possessing its own nature. For that nature to come into existence or be changed, it is not enough for us to find advantage in this occurring. To effect such changes causes must come into play which require them physically.

For example, we have explained the constant development of the social division of labor by showing that it is necessary in order for man to sustain himself in the new conditions of existence in which he is placed as he advances in history. We have therefore attributed to the tendency which is somewhat improperly termed the instinct of self-preservation an important role in our explanation. But in the first place the tendency alone could not account for even the most rudimentary form of specialization. It can accomplish nothing if the conditions on which this phenomenon depends are not already realized, that is, if individual differences have not sufficiently increased through the progressive state of indetermination of the common consciousness and hereditary influences.[3] The division of labor must even have begun already to occur for its utility to be perceived and its need to be felt. The mere development of individual differences, implying a greater diversity of tastes and abilities, had necessarily to bring about this first consequence. Moreover, the instinct of self-preservation did not come by itself and without cause to fertilize this first germ of specialization. If it directed first itself and then us into this new path, it is because the course it followed and caused us to follow beforehand was as if blocked. This was because the greater intensity of the struggle for existence brought about by the greater concentration of societies rendered increasingly difficult the survival of those individuals who continued to devote themselves to more unspecialized tasks. Thus a change of direction was necessary. On the other hand if it turned itself, and for preference turned our activity, toward an ever-increasing division of labor, it was also because it was the path of least resistance. The other possible solutions were emigration, suicide or crime. Now, on average, the ties that bind us to our country, to life and to feeling for our fellows are stronger and more resistant sentiments than the habits which can deter us from narrower specialization. Thus these habits had inevitably to give ground as every advance occurred. Thus, since we are ready to allow for human needs in sociological explanations, we need not revert, even partially, to teleology. For these needs can have no influence over social evolution unless they themselves evolve, and the changes through which they pass can only be explained by causes which are in no way final.

What is even more convincing than the foregoing argument is the study of how social facts work out in practice. Where teleology rules, there rules also a fair margin of contingency, for there are no ends—and even fewer means—which necessarily influence all men, even supposing they are placed in the same circumstances. Given the same environment, each individual, according to his temperament, adapts himself to it in the way he pleases and which he prefers to all others. The one will seek to change it so that it better suits his needs; the other will prefer to change himself and to moderate his desires. Thus to arrive at the same goal, many different routes can be, and in reality are, followed. If then it were true that historical development occurred because of ends felt either clearly or obscurely, social facts would have to present an infinite diversity and all comparison would almost be impossible. But the opposite is true. Undoubtedly external events, the links between which constitute the superficial part of social life, vary from one people to another. Yet in this way each individual has his own history, although the bases of physical and social organization remain the same for all. If indeed one comes even a little into contact with social phenomena, one is on the contrary surprised at the outstanding regularity with which they recur in similar circumstances. Even the most trivial and apparently most puerile practices are repeated with the most astonishing uniformity. A marriage ceremony, seemingly purely symbolic, such as the abduction of the bride-to-be, is found to be identical everywhere that a certain type of family exists, which itself is linked to a whole political organization. The most bizarre customs, such as the *couvade*, the levirate, exogamy, etc. are to be observed in the most diverse peoples and are symptomatic of a certain social state. The right to make a will appears at a specific phase of history and, according to the severity of the restrictions which limit it, we can tell at what stage of social evolution we have arrived. It would be easy to multiply such examples. But the widespread character of collective forms would be inexplicable if final causes held in sociology the preponderance attributed to them.

Therefore when one undertakes to explain a social phenomenon the efficient cause which produces it and the function it fulfills must be investigated separately. We use the word "function" in preference to "end" or "goal" precisely because social phenomena generally do not exist for the usefulness of the results they produce. We must determine whether there is a correspondence between the fact being considered and the general needs of the social organism, and in what this correspondence consists, without seeking to know whether it was intentional or not. All such questions of intention are, moreover, too subjective to be dealt with scientifically.

Not only must these two kinds of problems be dissociated from each other, but it is generally appropriate to deal with the first kind before the second. This order of precedence corresponds to that of the facts. It is natural to seek the cause of a phenomenon before attempting to determine its effects. This method is all the more logical because the first question, once resolved, will often help to answer the second. Indeed, the solid link which joins cause to effect is of a reciprocal character which has not been sufficiently recognized. Undoubtedly the effect cannot exist without its cause, but the latter, in turn, requires its effect. It is from the cause that the effect derives its energy, but on occasion it also restores energy to the cause and consequently cannot disappear without the cause being affected.[4] For example, the social reaction which constitutes punishment is due to the intensity of the collective sentiments that crime offends. On the other hand it serves the useful function of maintaining those sentiments at the same level of intensity, for they could not fail to weaken if the offenses committed against them remained unpunished.[5] Likewise, as the social environment becomes more complex and unstable, traditions and accepted beliefs are shaken and take on a more indeterminate and flexible character, while faculties of reflection develop. These same faculties are indispensable for societies and individuals to adapt themselves to a more mobile and complex environment.[6] As men are obliged to work more intensively, the products of their labor become more numerous and better in quality; but this increase in abundance and quality of the products is necessary to compensate for the effort that this more considerable labor entails.[7] Thus, far from the cause of social phenomena consisting of a mental anticipation of the function they are called upon to fulfill, this function consists on the contrary, in a number of cases at least, in maintaining the pre-existent cause from which the phenomena derive. We will therefore discover more easily the function if the cause is already known.

If we must proceed only at a second stage to the determination of the function, it is none the less necessary for the complete explanation of the phenomenon. Indeed, if the utility of a fact is not what causes its existence, it must generally be useful to continue to survive. If it lacks utility, that very reason suffices to make it harmful, since in that case it requires effort but brings in no return. Thus if the general run of social phenomena had this parasitic character, the economy of the organism would be in deficit, and social life would be impossible. Consequently, to provide a satisfactory explanation of social life we need to show how the phenomena which are its substance come together to place society in harmony with itself and with the outside world. Undoubtedly the present formula which defines life as a correspondence between the internal and the external environments is only approximate. Yet in general it remains true; thus to explain a fact which is vital, it is not enough to show the cause on which it depends. We must also—at least in most cases—discover the part that it plays in the establishment of that general harmony.

II

Having distinguished between these two questions, we must determine the method whereby they must be resolved.

At the same time as being teleological, the method of explanation generally followed by sociologists is essentially psychological. The two tendencies are closely linked. Indeed, if society is only a system of means set up by men to achieve certain ends, these ends can only be individual, for before society existed there could only exist individuals. It is therefore from the individual that the ideas and needs which have determined the formation of societies emanate. If it is from him that everything comes, it is necessarily through him that everything must be explained. Moreover, in society there is nothing save individual consciousnesses, and it is consequently in these that is to be found the source of all social evolution. Thus sociological laws can only be a corollary of the more general laws of psychology. The ultimate explanation of collective life will consist in demonstrating how it derives from human nature in general, either by direct deduction from it without any preliminary observation, or by establishing links after having observed human nature.

These expressions are almost word for word those used by Auguste Comte to characterize his method. "Since the social phenomenon," he asserts, "conceived of in its totality, *is only basically a simple development of humanity without any creation of faculties at all*, as I have established above, the whole framework of effects that sociological observation can successively uncover will therefore necessarily be found, at least in embryo, in that primordial type which biology has constructed beforehand for sociology."[8] This is because, in his view, the dominant fact of social life is progress, and because progress furthermore depends on a factor exclusively psychical in kind: the tendency that impels man to develop his nature more and more. Social facts may even derive so immediately from human nature that, during the initial stages of history, they could be directly deduced from it without having recourse to observation.[9] It is true, as Comte concedes, that it is impossible to apply this deductive method to the more advanced phases of evolution. This impossibility is purely of a practical kind. It arises because the distance from the points of departure and arrival becomes too considerable for the human mind, which, if it undertook to traverse it without a guide, would run the risk of going astray.[10] But the relationship between the basic laws of human nature and the ultimate results of progress is none the less capable of analysis. The most complex forms of civilization are only a developed kind of psychical life. Thus, even if psychological theories cannot suffice as premises for sociological reasoning, they are the touchstone which alone permits us to test the validity of propositions inductively established. "No law of social succession," declares Comte, "which has been elaborated with all the authority possible by means of the historical method, should be finally accepted before it has been rationally linked, directly or indirectly, but always irrefutably, to the positivist theory of human nature."[11] Psychology will therefore always have the last word.

This is likewise the method followed by Spencer. Indeed, according to him, the two primary factors of social phenomena are the external environment and the physical and moral constitution of the individual.[12] Now the first factor can only influence society through the second one, which is thus the essential driving force for social evolution. Society arises to allow the individual to realize his own nature, and all the transformations through which it has passed have no other purpose than to make this act of self-realization easier and more complete. It is by virtue of this principle that, before proceeding to any research into social organization, Spencer thought it necessary to devote almost all the first volume of his *Principles of Sociology* to the study of primitive man from the physical, emotional and intellectual viewpoint. "The science of sociology," he states, "sets out with social units, conditioned as we have seen, constituted physically, emotionally and intellectually and possessed of certain early acquired notions and correlative feelings."[13] And it is in two of these sentiments, fear of the living and fear of the dead, that he finds the origin of political and religious government.[14] It is true that he admits that once it has been constituted, society reacts upon individuals.[15] But it does not follow that society has the power to engender directly the smallest social fact; from this viewpoint it has causal effectiveness only through the mediation of the changes that it brings about in the individual. Thus it is always from human nature, whether primitive or derived, that everything arises. Moreover, the influence which the body social exerts upon its members can have nothing specific about it, since political ends are nothing in themselves, but merely the summary expression of individual ends.[16] Social influence can therefore only be a kind of consequent effect of private activity upon itself. Above all, it is not possible to see of what it may consist in industrial societies whose purpose is precisely to deliver the individual over to his natural impulses by ridding him of all social constraint.

This principle is not only central to these great doctrines of general sociology, but also inspires a very great number of particular theories. Thus domestic organization is commonly explained by the feelings that parents have for their children and vice versa; the institution of marriage by the advantages that it offers husband and wife and their descendants; punishment by the anger engendered in the individual through any serious encroachment upon his interests. The whole of economic life, as conceived of and explained by economists, particularly those of the orthodox school, hangs in the end upon a purely individual factor, the desire for wealth. If we take morality, the basis of ethics is the duties of the individual toward himself. And in religion one can see a product of the impressions that the great forces of nature or certain outstanding personalities awaken in man, etc., etc.

But such a method is not applicable to sociological phenomena unless one distorts their nature. For proof of this we need only refer to the definition we have given. Since their essential characteristic is the power they possess to exert outside pressure on individual consciousnesses, this shows that they do not derive from these consciousnesses and that consequently sociology is not a corollary of psychology. This constraining power attests to the fact that they express a nature different from our own, since they only penetrate into us by force or at the very least by bearing down more or less heavily upon us. If social life were no more than an extension of the individual, we would not see it return to its origin and invade the individual consciousness so precipitately. The authority to which the individual bows when he acts, thinks or feels socially dominates him to such a degree because it is a product of forces which transcend him and for which he consequently cannot account. It is not from within himself that can come the external pressure which he undergoes; it is therefore not what is happening within himself which can explain it. It is true that we are not incapable of placing constraints upon ourselves; we can restrain our tendencies, our habits, even our instincts, and halt their development by an act of inhibition. But inhibitive movements must not be confused with those which make up social constraint. The process of inhibitive movements is centrifugal; but the latter are centripetal. The former are worked out in the individual consciousness and then tend to manifest themselves externally; the latter are at first external to the individual, whom they tend afterward to shape from the outside in their own image. Inhibition is, if one likes, the means by which social constraint produces its psychical effects, but is not itself that constraint.

Now, once the individual is ruled out, only society remains. It is therefore in the nature of society itself that we must seek the explanation of social life. We can conceive that, since it transcends infinitely the individual both in time and space, it is capable of imposing upon him the ways of acting and thinking that it has consecrated by its authority. This pressure, which is the distinctive sign of social facts, is that which all exert upon each individual.

But it will be argued that since the sole elements of which society is composed are individuals, the primary origin of sociological phenomena cannot be other than psychological. Reasoning in this way, we can just as easily establish that biological phenomena are explained analytically by inorganic phenomena. It is indeed certain that in the living cell there are only molecules of crude matter. But they are in association, and it is this association which is the cause of the new phenomena which characterize life, even the germ of which it is impossible to find in a single one of these associated elements. This is because the whole does not equal the sum of its parts; it is something different, whose properties differ from those displayed by the parts from which it is formed. Association is not, as has sometimes been believed, a phenomenon infertile in itself, which consists merely in juxtaposing externally facts already given and properties already constituted. On the contrary, is it not the source of all the successive innovations that have occurred in the course of the general evolution of things? What differences exist between the lower organisms and others, between the organized living creature and the mere protoplasm, between the latter and the inorganic molecules of which it is composed, if it is not differences in association? All these beings, in the last analysis, split up into elements of the same nature; but these elements are in one place juxtaposed, in another associated. Here they are associated in one way, there in another. We are even justified in wondering whether this law does not even extend to the mineral world, and whether the differences which separate inorganic bodies do not have the same origin.

By virtue of this principle, society is not the mere sum of individuals, but the system formed by their association represents a specific reality which has its own characteristics. Undoubtedly no collective entity can be produced if there are no individual consciousnesses: this is a necessary but not a sufficient condition. In addition, these consciousnesses must be associated and combined, but combined in a certain way. It is from this combination that social life arises and consequently it is this combination which explains it. By aggregating together, by interpenetrating, by fusing together, individuals give birth to a being, psychical if you will, but one which constitutes a psychical individuality of a new kind.[17] Thus it is in the nature of that individuality and not in that of its component elements that we must search for the proximate and determining causes of the facts produced in it. The group thinks, feels and acts entirely differently from the way its members would if they were isolated. If therefore we begin by studying these members separately, we will understand nothing about what is taking place in the group. In a word, there is between psychology and sociology the same break in continuity as there is between biology and the physical and chemical sciences. Consequently every time a social phenomenon is directly explained by a psychological phenomenon, we may rest assured that the explanation is false.

Some will perhaps argue that, although society, once formed, is the proximate cause of social phenomena, the causes which have determined its formation are of a psychological nature. They may concede that, when individuals are associated together, their association may give rise to a new life, but claim that this can only take place for individual reasons. But in reality, as far as one can go back in history, the fact of association is the most obligatory of all, because it is the origin of all other obligations. By reason of my birth, I am obligatorily attached to a given people. It may be said that later, once I am an adult, I acquiesce in this obligation by the mere fact that I continue to live in my own country. But what does that matter? Such acquiescence does not remove its imperative character. Pressure accepted and undergone with good grace does not cease to be pressure. Moreover, how far does such acceptance go? Firstly, it is forced, for in the vast majority of cases it is materially and morally impossible for us to shed our nationality; such a rejection is even generally declared to be apostasy. Next, the acceptance cannot relate to the past, when I was in no position to accept, but which nevertheless determines the present. I did not seek the education I received; yet this above all else roots me in my native soil. Lastly, the acceptance can have no moral value for the future, in so far as this is unknown. I do not even know all the duties which one day may be incumbent upon me in my capacity as a citizen. How then could I acquiesce in them in advance? Now, as we have shown, all that is obligatory has its origins outside the individual. Thus, provided one does not place oneself outside history, the fact of association is of the same character as the others and is consequently explicable in the same way. Furthermore, as all societies are born of other societies, with no break in continuity, we may be assured that in the whole course of social evolution there has not been a single time when individuals have really had to consult together to decide whether they would enter into collective life together, and into one sort of collective life rather than another. Such a question is only possible when we go back to the first origins of any society. But the treatment of historical facts cannot in any case be allowed to be affected by the (always) dubious solutions to such problems. We have therefore no need to discuss them.

Yet our thought would be singularly misinterpreted if the conclusion was drawn from the previous remarks that sociology, in our view, should or even could leave aside man and his faculties. On the contrary, it is clear that the general characteristics of human nature play their part in the work of elaboration from which social life results. But it is not these which produce it or give it its special form: they only make it possible. Collective representations, emotions and tendencies have not as their causes certain states of consciousness in individuals, but the conditions under which the body social as a whole exists. Doubtless these can be realized only if individual natures are not opposed to them. But these are simply the indeterminate matter which the social factor fashions and transforms. Their contribution is made up exclusively of very general states, vague and thus malleable predispositions which of themselves could not assume the definite and complex forms which characterize social phenomena, if other agents did not intervene.

What a gulf, for example, between the feelings that man experiences when confronted with forces superior to his own and the institution of religion with its beliefs and practices, so multifarious and complicated, and its material and moral organization! What an abyss between the psychical conditions of sympathy which two people of the same blood feel for each other,[18] and that hodgepodge of legal and moral rules which determine the structure of the family, personal relationships, and the relationship of things to persons, etc.! We have seen that even when society is reduced to an unorganized crowd, the collective sentiments which arise within it can not only be totally unlike, but even opposed to, the average sentiments of the individuals in it. How much greater still must be the gap when the pressure exerted upon the individual comes from a normal society, where, to the influence exerted by his contemporaries, is added that of previous generations and of tradition! A purely psychological explanation of social facts cannot therefore fail to miss completely all that is specific, i.e., social, about them.

What has blinkered the vision of many sociologists to the insufficiency of this method is the fact that, taking the effect for the cause, they have very often highlighted as causal conditions for social phenomena certain psychical states, relatively well defined and specific, but which in reality are the consequence of the phenomena. Thus it has been held that a certain religiosity is innate in man, as is a certain minimum of sexual jealousy, filial piety or fatherly affection, etc., and it is in these that explanations have been sought for religion, marriage and the family. But history shows that these inclinations, far from being inherent in human nature, are either completely absent under certain social conditions or vary so much from one society to another that the residue left after eliminating all these differences, and which alone can be considered of psychological origin, is reduced to something vague and schematic, infinitely removed from the facts which have to be explained. Thus these sentiments result from the collective organization and are far from being at the basis of it. It has not even been proved at all that the tendency to sociability was originally a congenital instinct of the human race. It is much more natural to see in it a product of social life which has slowly become organized in us, because it is an observable fact that animals are sociable or otherwise, depending on whether their environmental conditions force them to live in common or cause them to shun such a life. And even then we must add that a considerable gap remains between these well determined tendencies and social reality.

Furthermore, there is a means of isolating almost entirely the psychological factor, so as to be able to measure precisely the scope of its influence: this is by seeking to determine how race affects social evolution. Ethnic characteristics are of an organic and psychical order. Social life must therefore vary as they vary, if psychological phenomena have on society the causal effectiveness attributed to them. Now we know of no social phenomenon which is unquestionably dependent on race, although we certainly cannot ascribe to this proposition the value of a law. But we can at least assert that it is a constant fact in our practical experience. Yet the most diverse forms of organization are to be found in societies of the same race, while striking similarities are to be observed among societies of different races. The city state existed among the Phoenicians, as it did among the Romans and the Greeks; we also find it emerging among the Kabyles. The patriarchal family was almost as strongly developed among the Jews as among the Hindus, but it is not to be found among the Slavs, who are nevertheless of Aryan race. By contrast, the family type to be found among the Slavs exists also among the Arabs. The maternal family and the clan are observed everywhere. The precise nature of judicial proofs and nuptial ceremonies is no different among peoples most unlike from the ethnic viewpoint. If this is so, it is because the psychical contribution is too general to predetermine the course of social phenomena. Since it does not imply one social form rather than another, it cannot explain any such forms. It is true that there are a certain number of facts which it is customary to ascribe to the influence of race. Thus this, in particular, is how we explain why the development of literature and the arts was so rapid and intense in Athens, so slow and mediocre in Rome. But this interpretation of the facts, despite being the classic one, has never been systematically demonstrated. It seems to draw almost all its authority from tradition alone. We have not even reflected upon whether a sociological explanation of the same phenomena was not possible, yet we are convinced that this might be successfully attempted. In short, when we hastily attribute to aesthetic and inherited faculties the artistic nature of Athenian civilization, we are almost proceeding as did men in the Middle Ages, when fire was explained by phlogiston and the effects of opium by its soporific powers.

Finally, if social evolution really had its origin in the psychological makeup of man, one fails to see how this could have come about. For then we would have to admit that its driving force is some internal impulse within human nature. But what might such a motivation be? Would it be that kind of instinct of which Comte speaks, which impels man to realize increasingly his own nature? But this is to reply to one question by another, explaining progress by an innate tendency to progress, a truly metaphysical entity whose existence, moreover, has in no way been demonstrated. For the animal species, even those of the highest order, are not moved in any way by a need to progress, and even among human societies there are many which are content to remain stationary indefinitely. Might it be, as Spencer seems to believe, that there is a need for greater happiness, which forms of civilization of ever-increasing complexity might be destined to realize more and more completely? It would then be necessary to establish that happiness grows with civilization, and we have explained elsewhere all the difficulties to which such a hypothesis gives rise.[19] Moreover, there is something else: even if one or other of these postulates were conceded, historical development would not thereby become more intelligible; for the explanation which might emerge from it would be purely teleological. We have shown earlier that social facts, like all natural phenomena, are not explained when we have demonstrated that they serve a purpose. After proving conclusively that a succession of social organizations in history which have become increasingly more knowledgeable have resulted in the greater satisfaction of one or other of our fundamental desires, we would not thereby have made the source of these organizations more comprehensible. The fact that they were useful does not reveal to us what brought them into existence. We might even explain how we came to conceive them, by drawing up a blueprint of them beforehand, so as to envisage the services we might expect them to render—and this is already a difficult problem. But our aspirations, which would thereby become the purpose of such organizations, would have no power to conjure them up out of nothing. In short, if we admit that they are the necessary means to attain the object we have in mind, the question remains in its entirety: how, that is to say, from what, and in what manner, have these means been constituted?

Hence we arrive at the following rule: *The determining cause of a social fact must be sought among antecedent social facts and not among the states of the individual consciousness.* Moreover, we can easily conceive that all that has been stated above applies to the determination of the function as well as the cause of a social fact. Its function can only be social, which means that it consists in the production of socially useful effects. Undoubtedly it can and indeed does happen that it has repercussions which also serve the individual. But this happy result is not the immediate rationale for its existence. Thus we can complement the preceding proposition by stating: *The function of a social fact must always be sought in the relationship that it bears to some social end.*

It is because sociologists have often failed to acknowledge this rule and have considered sociological phenomena from too psychological a viewpoint that their theories appear to many minds too vague, too ethereal and too remote from the distinctive nature of the things which sociologists believe they are explaining. The historian, in particular, who has a close contact with social reality, cannot fail to feel strongly how these too general interpretations are incapable of being linked to the facts. In part, this has undoubtedly produced the mistrust that history has often manifested toward sociology. Assuredly this does not mean that the study of psychological facts is not indispensable to the sociologist. If collective life does not derive from individual life, the two are none the less closely related. If the latter cannot explain the former, it can at least render its explanation easier. Firstly, as we have shown, it is undeniably true that social facts are produced by an elaboration *sui generis* of psychological facts. But in addition this action is itself not dissimilar to that which occurs in each individual consciousness and which progressively transforms the primary elements (sensations, reflexes, instincts) of which the consciousness was originally made up. Not unreasonably has the claim been made that the self is itself a society, just as is the organism, although in a different way. For a long time psychologists have demonstrated the absolute importance of the factor of *association* in the explanation of mental activity. Thus a psychological education, even more than a biological one, constitutes a necessary preparation for the sociologist. But it can only be of service to him if, once he has acquired it, he frees himself from it, going beyond it by adding a specifically sociological education. He must give up making psychology in some way the focal point of his operations, the point of departure to which he must always return after his adventurous incursions into the social world. He must establish himself at the very heart of social facts in order to observe and confront them totally, without any mediating factor, while calling upon the science of the individual only for a general preparation and, if needs be, for useful suggestions.[20]

III

Since the facts of social morphology are of the same nature as physiological phenomena, they must be explained according to the rule we have just enunciated. However, the whole of the preceding discussion shows that in collective life and, consequently, in sociological explanations, they play a preponderant role.

If the determining condition for social phenomena consists, as we have demonstrated, in the very fact of association, the phenomena must vary with the forms of that association, i.e., according to how the constituent elements in a society are grouped. Furthermore, since the distinct entity formed by the union of elements of all kinds which enter into the composition of a society constitutes its inner environment, in the same way as the totality of anatomical elements, together with the manner in which they are arranged in space, constitutes the inner environment of organisms, we may state: *The primary origin of social processes of any importance must be sought in the constitution of the inner social environment.*

We may be even more precise. In fact, the elements which make up this environment are of two kinds: things and persons. Apart from the material objects incorporated in the society, among things must be included the products of previous social activity—the law and the customs that have been established, and literary and artistic monuments, etc. But it is plain that neither material nor non-material objects produce the impulsion that determines social transformations, because they both lack driving force. Undoubtedly there is need to take them into account in the explanations which we attempt. To some extent they exert an influence upon social evolution whose rapidity and direction vary according to their nature. But they possess no elements essential to set that evolution in motion. They are the matter to which the vital forces of society are applied, but they do not themselves release any vital forces. Thus the specifically human environment remains as the active factor.

The principal effort of the sociologist must therefore be directed toward discovering the different properties of that environment capable of exerting some influence upon the course of social phenomena. Up to now we have found two sets of characteristics which satisfy that condition admirably. These are: firstly, the number of social units or, as we have also termed it, the "volume" of the society; and secondly, the degree of concentration of the mass of people, or what we have called the "dynamic density." The latter must be understood not as the purely physical concentration of the aggregate population, which can have no effect if individuals—or rather groups of individuals—remain isolated by moral gaps, but the moral concentration of which physical concentration is only the auxiliary element, and almost invariably the consequence. Dynamic density can be defined, if the volume remains constant, as a function of the number of individuals who are effectively engaged not only in commercial but also moral relationships with each other, i.e., who not only exchange services or compete with one another, but live their life together in common. For, since purely economic relationships leave men separated from each other, these relationships can be very active without people necessarily participating in the same collective existence. Business ties which span the boundaries which separate peoples do not make those boundaries non-existent. The collective life can be affected only by the number of people who effectively co-operate in it. This is why what best expresses the dynamic density of a people is the degree to which the social segments coalesce. For if each partial aggregate forms a totality, a distinct individuality separated from the others by a barrier, it is because in general the activity of its members remains localized within it. If, on the other hand, these partial societies are entirely fused together, or tend to do so, within the total society, it is because the ambit of social life to this extent has been enlarged.

As for the material density—if this is understood as not only the number of inhabitants per unit of area, but also the development of the means of communication and transmission—this is *normally* in proportion to the dynamic density and, *in general*, can serve to measure it. For if the different elements in the population tend to draw more closely together, it is inevitable that they will establish channels to allow this to occur. Furthermore, relationships can be set up between remote points of the social mass only if distance does not represent an obstacle, which means, in fact, that it must be eliminated. However, there are exceptions,[21] and one would expose oneself to serious error if the moral concentration of a community were always judged according to the degree of physical concentration that it represented. Roads, railways, etc. can serve commercial exchanges better than they can serve the fusion of populations, of which they can give only a very imperfect indication. This is the case in England, where the physical density is greater than in France but where the coalescence of social segments is much less advanced, as is shown by the persistence of parochialism and regional life.

We have shown elsewhere how every increase in the volume and dynamic density of societies, by making social life more intense and widening the horizons of thought and action of each individual, profoundly modifies the basic conditions of collective life. Thus we need not refer again to the application we have already made of this principle. It suffices to add that the principle was useful to us in dealing not only with the still very general question which was the object of that study, but many other more specialized problems, and that we have therefore been able to verify its accuracy already by a fair number of experiments. However, we are far from believing that we have uncovered all the special features of the social environment which can play some part in the explanation of social facts. All we can say is that these are the sole features we have identified and that we have not been led to seek out others.

But the kind of preponderance we ascribe to the social environment, and more especially to the human environment, does not imply that this should be seen as a kind of ultimate, absolute fact beyond which there is no need to explore further. On the contrary, it is plain that its state at any moment in history itself depends on social causes, some of which are inherent in society itself, while others depend on the interaction occurring between that society and its neighbors. Moreover, science knows no first causes, in the absolute sense of the term. For science a fact is primary simply when it is general enough to explain a great number of other facts. Now the social environment is certainly a factor of this kind, for the changes which arise within it, whatever the causes, have repercussions on every part of the social organism and cannot fail to affect all its functions to some degree.

What has just been said about the general social environment can be repeated for the particular environments of the special groups which society includes. For example, depending on whether the family is large or small, or more or less turned in upon itself, domestic life will differ considerably. Likewise, if professional corporations reconstitute themselves so as to spread over a whole area, instead of remaining enclosed within the confines of a city, as they formerly were, their effect will be very different from what it was previously. More generally, professional life will differ widely according to whether the environment peculiar to each occupation is strongly developed or whether its bonds are loose, as is the case today. However, the effect of these special environments cannot have the same importance as the general environment, for they are subject to the latter's influence. Thus we must always return to the general environment. It is the pressure that it exerts upon these partial groups which causes their constitution to vary.

This conception of the social environment as the determining factor in collective evolution is of the greatest importance. For if it is discarded, sociology is powerless to establish any causal relationship.

Indeed, if this order of causes is set aside, there are no concomitant conditions on which social phenomena can depend. For if the external social environment—that which is formed by neighboring societies—is capable of exercising some influence, it is only upon the functions of attack and defense; moreover, it can only make its influence felt through the mediation of the internal social environment. The principal causes of historical development would not therefore be found among the *circumfusa* (external influences). They would all be found in the past. They would themselves form part of that development, constituting simply more remote phases of it. The contemporary events of social life would not derive from the present state of society, but from prior events and historical precedents, and sociological explanations would consist exclusively in linking the present to the past.

It is true that this may seem sufficient. Is it not commonly said that the purpose of history is precisely to link up events in their sequence? But it is impossible to conceive how the state which civilization has attained at any given time could be the determining cause of the state which follows. The stages through which humanity successively passes do not engender each other. We can well understand how the progress realized in a given era in the fields of law, economics and politics, etc., makes fresh progress possible, but how does the one predetermine the other? The progress realized is a point of departure which allows us to proceed further, but what stimulates us to further progress? We would have to concede that there was a certain inner tendency which impels humanity constantly to go beyond the results already achieved, either to realize itself more fully or to increase its happiness, and the purpose of sociology would be to rediscover the order in which this tendency has developed. But without alluding afresh to the difficulties which such a hypothesis implies, in any case a law to express this development could not be in any sense causal. A relationship of causality can in fact only be established between two given facts. But this tendency, presumed to be the cause of development, is not something that is given. It is only postulated as a mental construct according to the effects attributed to it. It is a kind of driving impulse which we imagine as underlying the movement which occurs, in order to account for it. But the efficient cause of a movement can only be another movement, not a potentiality of this kind. Thus all that we can arrive at experimentally is in point of fact a series of changes between which there exists no causal link. The antecedent state does not produce the subsequent one, but the relationship between them is exclusively chronological. In these conditions any scientific prediction is thus impossible. We can certainly say how things have succeeded each other up to the present, but not in what order they will follow subsequently, because the cause on which they supposedly depend is not scientifically determined, nor can it be so determined. It is true that normally it is accepted that evolution will proceed in the same direction as in the past, but this is a mere supposition. We have no assurance that the facts as they have hitherto manifested themselves are a sufficiently complete expression of this tendency. Thus we are unable to forecast the goal toward which they are moving in the light of the stages through which they have already successively passed. There is no reason to suppose that the direction this tendency follows even traces out a straight line.

This is why the number of causal relationships established by sociologists is so limited. Apart from a few exceptions, among whom Montesquieu is the most illustrious example, the former philosophy of history concentrated solely on discovering the general direction in which humanity was proceeding, without seeking to link the phases of that evolution to any concomitant condition. Despite the great services Comte has rendered to social philosophy, the terms in which he poses the sociological problem do not differ from those of his predecessors. Thus his celebrated law of the three stages has not the slightest causal relationship about it. Even if it were true, it is, and can only be, empirical. It is a summary review of the past history of the human race. It is purely arbitrary for Comte to consider the third stage to be the definitive stage of humanity. Who can say whether another will not arise in the future? Similarly, the law which dominates the sociology of Spencer appears to be no different in nature. Even if it were true that we at present seek our happiness in an industrial civilization, there is no assurance that, at a later era, we shall not seek it elsewhere. The generality and persistence of this method is due to the fact that very often the social environment has been perceived as a means whereby progress has been realized, and not the cause which determines it.

Furthermore, it is also in relationship to this same environment that must be measured the utilitarian value, or as we have stated it, the function of social phenomena. Among the changes caused by the environment, those are useful which are in harmony with the existing state of society, since the environment is the essential condition for collective existence. Again, from this viewpoint the conception we have just expounded is, we believe, fundamental, for it alone allows an explanation of how the useful character of social phenomena can vary without depending on arbitrary factors. If historical evolution is envisaged as being moved by a kind of *vis a tergo* (vital urge) which impels men forward, since a driving tendency can have only a single goal, there can exist only one reference point from which to calculate the utility or harmfulness of social phenomena. It follows that there exists, and can only exist, a single type of social organization which fits humanity perfectly, and the different societies of history are only successive approximations to that single model. It is unnecessary to show how such a simplistic view is today irreconcilable with the acknowledged variety and complexity of social forms. If on the other hand the suitability or unsuitability of institutions can only be established in relation to a given environment, since these environments are diverse, a diversity of reference points thus exists, and consequently a diversity of types which, whilst each being qualitatively distinct, are all equally grounded in the nature of the social environment.

The question just dealt with is therefore closely connected to the constitution of social types. If there are social species, it is because collective life depends above all on concomitant conditions which present a certain diversity. If, on the contrary, the main causes of social events were all in the past, every people would be no more than the extension of the one preceding it, and different societies would lose their individuality, becoming no more than various moments in time of one and the same development. On the other hand, since the constitution of the social environment results from the mode in which the social aggregates come together—and the two phrases are in the end synonymous—we have now the proof that there are no characteristics more essential than those we have assigned as the basis for sociological classification.

Finally, we should now realize better than before how unjust it would be to rely on the terms "external conditions" and "environment" to serve as an indictment of our method, and seek the sources of life outside what is already alive. On the contrary, the considerations just mentioned lead us back to the idea that the causes of social phenomena are internal to the society. It is much rather the theory which seeks to derive society from the individual that could be justly reproached with seeking to deduce the internal from the external (since it explains the social being by something other than itself) and the greater from the lesser (since it undertakes to deduce the whole from the part). Our own preceding principles in no way fail to acknowledge the spontaneous character of every living creature: thus, if they are applied to biology and psychology, it will have to be admitted that individual life as well develops wholly within the individual.

IV

From the set of rules which has just been established, there arises a certain conception of society and collective life.

Two opposing theories divide men on this question.

For some, such as Hobbes and Rousseau, there is a break in continuity between the individual and society. Man is therefore obdurate to the collective life and can only resign himself to it if forced to do so. Social ends are not simply the meeting point for individual ends; they are more likely to run counter to then. Thus, to induce the individual to pursue social ends, constraint must be exercised upon him, and it is in the institution and organization of this constraint that lies the supreme task of society. Yet because the individual is regarded as the sole and unique reality of the human kingdom, this organization, which is designed to constrain and contain him, can only be conceived of as artificial. The organization is not grounded in nature, since it is intended to inflict violence upon him by preventing him from producing anti-social consequences. It is an artifact, a machine wholly constructed by the hands of men and which, like all products of this kind, is only what it is because men have willed it so; an act of volition created it, another one can transform it. Neither Hobbes nor Rousseau appear to have noticed the complete contradiction that exists in admitting that the individual is himself the creator of a machine whose essential role is to exercise domination and constraint over him. Alternatively, it may have seemed to them that, in order to get rid of this contradiction, it was sufficient to conceal it from the eyes of its victims by the skillful device of the social contract.

It is from the opposing idea that the theoreticians of natural law and the economists, and more recently Spencer,[22] have drawn their inspiration. For them social life is essentially spontaneous and society is a natural thing. But, if they bestow this characteristic upon it, it is not because they acknowledge it has any specific nature, but because they find a basis for it in the nature of the individual. No more than the two thinkers already mentioned do they see in it a system of things which exists in itself, by virtue of causes peculiar to itself. But while Hobbes and Rousseau only conceived it as a conventional arrangement, with no link at all in reality, which, so to speak, is suspended in air, they in turn state its foundations to be the fundamental instincts of the human heart. Man is naturally inclined to political, domestic and religious life, and to commercial exchanges, etc., and it is from these natural inclinations that social organization is derived. Consequently, wherever it is normal, there is no need to impose it by force. Whenever it resorts to constraint it is because it is not what it ought to be, or because the circumstances are abnormal. In principle, if individual forces are left to develop untrammeled they will organize themselves socially.

Neither of these doctrines is one we share.

Doubtless we make constraint the characteristic trait of every social fact. Yet this constraint does not arise from some sort of artful machination destined to conceal from men the snares into which they have stumbled. It is simply due to the fact that the individual finds himself in the presence of a force which dominates him and to which he must bow. But this force is a natural one. It is not derived from some conventional arrangement which the human will has contrived, adding it on to what is real; it springs from the heart of reality itself; it is the necessary product of given causes. Thus to induce the individual to submit to it absolutely of his own free will, there is no need to resort to deception. It is sufficient to make him aware of his natural state of dependence and inferiority. Through religion he represents this state to himself by the senses or symbolically; through science he arrives at an adequate and precise notion of it. Because the superiority that society has over him is not merely physical, but intellectual and moral, it need fear no critical examination, provided this is fairly undertaken. Reflection which causes man to understand how much richer or more complex and permanent the social being is than the individual being, can only reveal to him reasons to make comprehensible the subordination which is required of him and the feelings of attachment and respect which habit has implanted within him.[23]

Thus only singularly superficial criticism could lay us open to the reproach that our conception of social constraint propagates anew the theories of Hobbes and Machiavelli. But if, contrary to these philosophers, we say that social life is natural, it is not because we find its origin in the nature of the individual; it is because it derives directly from the collective being which is, of itself, a nature *sui generis*; it is because it arises from that special process of elaboration which individual consciousnesses undergo through their association with each other and whence evolves a new form of existence.[24] If therefore we recognize with some authorities that social life presents itself to the individual under the form of constraint, we admit with others that it is a spontaneous product of reality. What logically joins these two elements, in appearance contradictory, is that the reality from which social life emanates goes beyond the individual. Thus these words, "constraint" and "spontaneity," do not have in our terminology the respective meanings that Hobbes gives to the former and Spencer to the latter.

To summarize: to most of the attempts that have been made to explain social facts rationally, the possible objection was either that they did away with any idea of social discipline, or that they only succeeded in maintaining it with the assistance of deceptive subterfuges. The rules we have set out would, on the other hand, allow a sociology to be constructed which would see in the spirit of discipline the essential condition for all collective life, while at the same time founding it on reason and truth.

Notes

1. Comte, *Cours de philosophie positive*, IV, p. 262.
2. Spencer, *Principles of Sociology*, vol. II, part V, ch. II, p. 247.
3. *Division du travail social*, II, chs. 3 and 4.

4. We would not wish to raise questions of general philosophy which would be inappropriate here. However, we note that, if more closely studied, this reciprocity of cause and effect could provide a means of reconciling scientific mechanism with the teleology implied by the existence and, above all, the persistence of life.
5. *Division du travail social*, II, ch. 2, and especially pp. 105ff.
6. Ibid., pp. 52–3.
7. Ibid., p. 301ff.
8. Comte, *Cours de philosophie positive*, IV, pp. 333–4.
9. Ibid., IV, p. 345.
10. Ibid., IV, p. 346.
11. Ibid., IV, p. 334.
12. Spencer, *Principles of Sociology*, vol. I, part I, ch. 2.
13. Ibid., vol. I, part I, ch. XXVII, p. 456. [Durkheim paraphrases. The exact quotation reads: "Setting out with social units as thus conditioned physically, emotionally and intellectually, and as thus possessed of certain early-acquired ideas and correlative feelings, the science of sociology has to give an account of all the phenomena that result from their combined actions."]
14. Ibid., p. 456.
15. Ibid., p. 15.
16. "Society exists for the benefit of its members; not its members for the benefit of society . . . the claims of the body politic are nothing in themselves, and become something only in so far as they embody the claims of its component individuals" (vol. I, part II, ch. II, pp. 479–80).
17. In this sense and for these reasons we can and must speak of a collective consciousness distinct from individual consciousnesses. To justify this distinction there is no need to hypostatize the collective consciousness; it is something special and must be designated by a special term, simply because the states which constitute it differ specifically from those which make up individual consciousnesses. This specificity arises because they are not formed from the same elements. Individual consciousnesses result from the nature of the organic and psychical being taken in isolation, collective consciousnesses from the combination of a plurality of beings of this kind. The results cannot therefore fail to be different, since the component parts differ to this extent. Our definition of the social fact, moreover, did no more than highlight, in a different way, this demarcation line.
18. Inasmuch as it may exist before all animal life. Cf. on this point, A. Espinas, *Des sociétés animales* (Paris, 1877), p. 474.
19. *Division du travail social*, II, ch. I.
20. Psychical phenomena can only have social consequences when they are so closely linked to social phenomena that the actions of both are necessarily intermingled. This is the case for certain socio-psychical phenomena. Thus a public official is a social force, but at the same time he is an individual. The result is that he can employ the social energy he commands in a way determined by his individual nature and thereby exert an influence on the constitution of society. This is what occurs with statesmen and, more generally, with men of genius. The latter, although they do not fulfill a social role, draw from the collective sentiments of which they are the object an authority

which is itself a social force, one which they can to a certain extent place at the service of their personal ideas. But it can be seen that such cases are due to individual chance and consequently cannot affect the characteristics which constitute the social species, which alone is the object of science. The limitation on the principle enunciated above is therefore not of great importance to the sociologist.

21. In our book, *De la Division du travail social*, we were wrong to emphasize unduly physical density as being the exact expression of dynamic density. However, the substitution of the former for the latter is absolutely justified for everything relating to the economic effects of dynamic density, for instance the division of labor as a purely economic fact.

22. The position of Comte on this subject is one of a pretty ambiguous eclecticism.

23. This is why all constraint is not normal. Only that constraint which corresponds to some social superiority, intellectual or moral, merits that designation. But that which one individual exercises over another because he is stronger or richer, above all if this wealth does not express his social worth, is abnormal and can only be maintained by violence.

24. Our theory is even more opposed to Hobbes than that of natural law. Indeed, for the supporters of this latter doctrine, collective life is only natural in so far as it can be deduced from the nature of the individual. Now only the most general forms of social organization can at a pinch be derived from that origin. As for the details of social organization, these are too far removed from the extreme generality of psychical properties to be capable of being linked to them. They therefore appear to the disciples of this school just as artificial as to their adversaries. For us, on the contrary, everything is natural, even the strangest arrangements, for everything is founded on the nature of society.

CHAPTER VI

Rules for the Demonstration of Sociological Proof

We have only one way of demonstrating that one phenomenon is the cause of another. This is to compare the cases where they are both simultaneously present or absent, so as to discover whether the variations they display in these different combinations of circumstances provide evidence that one depends upon the other. When the phenomena can be artificially produced at will by the observer, the method is that of experimentation proper. When, on the other hand, the production of facts is something beyond our power to command, and we can only bring them together as they have been spontaneously produced, the method used is one of indirect experimentation, or the comparative method.

We have seen that sociological explanation consists exclusively in establishing relationships of causality, that a phenomenon must be joined to its cause, or, on the contrary, a cause to its useful effects. Moreover, since social phenomena clearly rule out any control by the experimenter, the comparative method is the sole one suitable for sociology. It is true that Comte did not deem it to be adequate. He found it necessary to supplement it by what he termed the historical method, but the reason for this lies in his special conception of sociological laws. According to him, these should mainly express, not the definite relationships of causality, but the direction taken by human evolution generally. They cannot therefore be discovered with the aid of comparisons: for it to be possible to compare the different forms that a social phenomenon takes with different peoples, it must have been isolated from the time series to which it belongs. But if we begin by fragmenting human development in this way, we are faced with the impossible task of rediscovering the sequence. To arrive at it, it is more appropriate to proceed by broad syntheses rather than by analysis. It is necessary to juxtapose both sets of phenomena and join, in the same act of intuition, so to speak, the successive states of humanity so as to perceive "the continuous increase which occurs in every tendency, whether physical, intellectual, moral or political."[1] This is the justification for what

101

Comte calls the historical method, but which is consequently robbed of all purpose once the basic conception of Comtean sociology has been rejected.

It is true that John Stuart Mill declares that experimentation, even if indirect, is inapplicable to sociology. But what already suffices to divest his argument of most of its authority is that he applies it equally to biological phenomena and even to the most complex physical and chemical data.[2] But today we no longer need to demonstrate that chemistry and biology can only be experimental sciences. Thus there is no reason why his criticisms should be better founded in the case of sociology, for social phenomena are only distinguishable from the other phenomena by virtue of their greater complexity. The difference can indeed imply that the use of experimental reasoning in sociology offers more difficulty than in the other sciences, but one cannot see why it should be radically impossible.

Moreover, Mill's whole theory rests upon a postulate which is doubtless linked to the fundamental principles of his logic, but which is in contradiction with all the findings of science. He admits in fact that the same consequence does not always result from the same antecedent, but can be due now to one cause, now to another. This conception of the causal link, by removing from it all determining power, renders it almost inaccessible to scientific analysis, for it introduces such complications into the tangle of causes and effects that the mind is irredeemably confused. If an effect can derive from different causes, in order to know what determines it in a set of given circumstances, the experiment would have to take place in conditions of isolation which are unrealizable in practice, particularly in sociology.

But this alleged axiom of the plurality of causes is a negation of the principle of causality. Doubtless if one believes with Mill that cause and effect are absolutely heterogeneous and that there is between them no logical connection, there is nothing contradictory in admitting that an effect can follow sometimes from one cause, sometimes from another. If the relationship which joins C to A is purely chronological, it does not exclude another relationship of the same kind which, for example, would join C to B. But if, on the other hand, the causal link is at all intelligible, it could not then be to such an extent indeterminate. If it consists of a relationship which results from the nature of things, the same effect can only sustain this relationship with one single cause, for it can express only one single nature. Moreover, it is only the philosophers who have ever called into question the intelligibility of the causal relationship. For the scientist it is not problematic; it is assumed by the very method of science. How can one otherwise explain both the role of deduction, so important in experimental reasoning, and the basic principle of the proportionality between cause and effect? As for the cases that are cited in which it is claimed to observe a plurality of causes, in order for them to be proved it would have first to be established either that this plurality is not merely apparent, or that the outward unity of the effect did not conceal a real plurality. How many times has it happened that science has reduced to unity causes whose diversity, at first sight, appeared irreducible! John Stuart Mill gives an example of it when he recalls that, according to modern theories, the production of heat by friction, percussion or chemical action, etc., derives from one single, identical cause. Conversely, when he considers the question of effect, the scientist often distinguishes between what the layman confuses. In common parlance the word "fever" designates the same, single pathological entity. But for science there is a host of fevers, each specifically different, and the plurality of causes matches the plurality of effects. If, among all these different kinds of diseases there is, however, something all have in common, it is because these causes likewise possess certain characteristics in common.

It is even more important to exorcise this principle in sociology, because a number of sociologists are still under its influence, even though they raise no objection to the comparative method. Thus it is commonly stated that crime can equally be produced by the most diverse causes, and that this holds true for suicide, punishment, etc. If we practice in this spirit the experimental method, we shall collect together a considerable number of facts to no avail, because we shall never be able to obtain precise laws or clear-cut relationships of causality. We shall only be able to assign vaguely some ill-defined effect to a confused and amorphous group of antecedents. If therefore we wish to use the comparative method scientifically, i.e., in conformity with the principle of causality as it arises in science itself, we shall have to take as the basis of the comparisons established the following proposition: *To the same effect there always corresponds the same cause.* Thus, to revert to the examples cited above, if suicide depends on more than one cause it is because in reality there are several kinds of suicide. It is the same for crime. For punishment, on the other hand, if we have believed it also explicable by different causes, this is because we have not perceived the common element to be found in all its antecedents, by virtue of which they produce their common effect.[3]

II

However, if the various procedures of the comparative method are applicable to sociology, they do not all possess equal powers of proof.

The so-called method of "residues," in so far as it constitutes a form of experimental reasoning at all, is of no special utility in the study of social phenomena. Apart from the fact that it can only be useful in the fairly advanced sciences, since it assumes that a considerable number of laws are already known, social phenomena are far too complex to be able, in any given case, to eliminate the effect of all causes save one.

For the same reason the method of agreement and the method of difference are scarcely usable. They assume in fact that the cases compared either agree or differ only in one single point. Undoubtedly no science exists which has ever been able to set up experiments in which the strictly unique characteristic of an agreement or a difference could ever be irrefutably established. We can never be sure that we have not omitted to consider some antecedent which agrees with or differs from the consequent effect, at the same time and in the same manner as the sole known antecedent. However, the total elimination of every adventitious element is an ideal which can never really be achieved. Yet in fact the physical and chemical sciences, and even the biological sciences, approximate closely enough to it for the proof to be regarded in a great number of cases as adequate in practice. But it is not the same in sociology because of the too great complexity of the phenomena, and the impossibility of carrying out any artificial experiments. As an inventory could not be drawn up which would even come close to exhausting all the facts which coexist within a single society, or which have succeeded each other in the course of its history, we can never be assured, even very approximately, that two peoples match each other or differ from each other in every respect save one. The chances of one phenomenon eluding our attention are very much greater than those of not neglecting a single one of them. Consequently, such a method of proof can only yield conjectures which, viewed separately, are almost entirely devoid of any scientific character.

But the case of the method of concomitant variations is completely different. Indeed, for it to be used as proof it is not necessary for all the variations different from those we are comparing to have been rigorously excluded. The mere parallelism in values through which the two phenomena pass, provided that it has been established in an adequate number of sufficiently varied cases, is proof that a relationship exists between them. This method owes its validity to the fact that it arrives at the causal relationship, not externally as in the preceding methods, but from the inside, so to speak. It does not simply highlight for us two facts which accompany or exclude each other externally,[4] so that there is no direct proof that they are joined by some inner bond. On the contrary, the method shows us the facts connecting with each other in a continuous fashion, at least as regards their quantitative aspects. Now this connection alone suffices to demonstrate that they are not foreign to each other. The manner in which a phenomenon develops expresses its nature. For two developments to correspond there must also exist a correspondence between the natures that they reveal. Constant concomitance is therefore by itself a law, regardless of the state of the phenomena left out of the comparison. Thus to invalidate the method it is not sufficient to show that it is inoperative in a few particular applications of the methods of agreement or of difference; this would be to attribute to this kind of proof an authority which it cannot have in sociology. When two phenomena vary regularly together, this relationship must be maintained even when, in certain cases, one of these phenomena appears without the other. For it can happen that either the cause has been prevented from producing its effect by the influence of some opposing cause, or that it is present, but in a form different from that in which it has previously been observed. Doubtless we need to review the facts, as is said, and to examine them afresh, but we need not abandon immediately the results of a proof which has been regularly demonstrated.

It is true that the laws established through this procedure do not always present themselves at the outset in the form of causal relationships. Concomitance can occur, not because one of the phenomena is the cause of the other, but because they are both effects of the same cause, or indeed because there exists between them a third phenomenon, interposed but unnoticed, which is the effect of the first phenomenon and the cause of the second. The results to which this method leads therefore need to be interpreted. But what experimental method allows one to obtain in mechanical fashion a relationship of causality without the facts which it establishes requiring further mental elaboration? The sole essential is for this elaboration to be methodically carried out. The procedure is as follows. First we shall discover, with the help of deduction, how one of the two terms was capable of producing the other; then we shall attempt to verify the result of this induction with the aid of experiments, i.e., by making fresh comparisons. If the deduction proves possible and the verification is successful, we can therefore regard the proof as having been demonstrated. If, on the other hand, no direct link between these facts is perceived, particularly if the hypothesis that such a link exists contradicts laws already proved, we must set about finding a third phenomenon on which the two others equally depend or which may have served as an intermediary between the two. For example, it can be established absolutely certainly that the tendency to suicide varies according to education. But it is impossible to understand how education can lead to suicide; such an explanation contradicts the laws of psychology. Education, particularly if confined to elementary knowledge, reaches only the most superficial areas of our consciousness, whereas, on the contrary, the instinct of self-preservation is one of our basic tendencies. It could not therefore be appreciably affected by a phenomenon so remote and with such a feeble influence. Thus we are moved to ask whether both facts might not be the consequence of one single state. This common cause is the weakening of religious traditionalism, which reinforces at the same time the desire for knowledge and the tendency to suicide.

But another reason exists which makes the method of concomitant variations the supreme instrument for sociological research. Even when the circumstances are most favorable for them, the other methods cannot be employed usefully save when the number of facts to be compared is very large. If it is not possible to find two societies which resemble or differ from each other only in one single respect, at least it can be established that two facts very frequently go together or mutually exclude each other. But for this statement to have scientific value it must be validated a very great number of times; we would almost have to be assured that all the facts had been reviewed. But not only is such an exhaustive inventory impossible, but also the facts accumulated in this way can never be established with sufficient exactness, precisely because they are too numerous. Not only do we run the risk of omitting some which are essential and which contradict those already known, but we are also not sure that we know these latter, which are known, sufficiently well. Indeed, what has often discredited the reasoning of sociologists is that, because they have preferred to use the methods of agreement or difference—particularly the former—they have been more intent on accumulating documents than on criticizing and selecting from them. Thus they perpetually place the same reliance on the confused and cursory observations of travelers as on the more precise texts of history. Upon seeing such demonstrations of proof we cannot help reflecting that one single fact would suffice to invalidate them, and also that the facts themselves upon which the proofs have been established do not always inspire confidence.

The method of concomitant variations does not force us to make these incomplete enumerations or superficial observations. For it to yield results a few facts suffice. As soon as we have proved that in a certain number of cases two phenomena vary with each other, we may be certain that we are confronted with a law. Since they do not require to be numerous, the documents can be selected, and what is more, studied closely by the sociologist who makes use of them. Therefore he can, and consequently must, take as the chief material for his inductions societies whose beliefs, traditions, customs and law have been embodied in written and authentic records. Undoubtedly he will not disdain the information supplied by the ethnographer. (No facts can be disdained by the scientist.) But he will assign them to their appropriate place. Instead of making these data the nub of his researches, he will generally use them only to supplement those which he gleans from history, or at the very least he will try to confirm them by the latter. Thus he will not only be more discerning in limiting the scope of his comparisons, but he will conduct them more critically, for by the very fact that he will attach himself to a restricted order of phenomena he will be able to check them more carefully. Undoubtedly he does not have to do the work of the historians over again, but nor can he receive passively and unquestioningly the information which he uses.

It would be wrong to think that sociology is visibly in a state of inferiority as compared with the other sciences merely because it can hardly use more than one experimental process. This drawback is in fact compensated by the wealth of variations which are spontaneously available for the comparisons made by the sociologist, riches without example in any other domain of nature. The changes which take place in an organism in the course of its existence are not very numerous and are very limited; those which can be brought about artificially without destroying its life are themselves confined within narrow bounds. It is true that more important ones have occurred in the course of zoological evolution, but these have left few and only obscure vestiges behind, and it is even more difficult to discover the conditions which determined them. Social life, by contrast, is an uninterrupted series of transformations, parallel to other transformations in the conditions of collective existence. We have available not only information regarding those transformations which relate to a recent era, but information regarding a great number of those through which passed peoples now extinct has also come down to us. In spite of its gaps, the history of humanity is clear and complete in a way different from that of the animal species. Moreover, there exists a wealth of social phenomena which occur over the whole society, but which assume various forms according to regions, occupations, religious faiths, etc. Such are, for instance, crime, suicide, birth and marriage, savings, etc. From the diversity of these particular environments there result, for each of these new orders of facts, new series of variations beyond those which historical evolution has produced. If therefore the sociologist cannot use with equal effectiveness all the procedures of experimental research, the sole method which he must use to the virtual exclusion of all others can be very fruitful in his hands, for he has incomparable resources to which to apply it.

But it can only produce the appropriate results if it is practiced with rigor. Nothing is proved when, as happens so often, one is content to demonstrate by a greater or lesser number of examples that in isolated cases the facts have varied according to the hypothesis. From these sporadic and fragmentary correlations no general conclusion can be drawn. To illustrate an idea is not to prove it. What must be done is not to compare isolated variations, but series of variations, systematically constituted, whose terms are correlated with each other in as continuous a gradation as possible and which moreover cover an adequate range. For the variations of a phenomenon only allow a law to be induced if they express clearly the way in which the phenomenon develops in any given circumstances. For this to happen there must exist between the variations the same succession as exists between the various stages in a similar natural evolution. Moreover, the evolution which the variations represent must be sufficiently prolonged in length for the trend to be unquestionably apparent.

III

The manner in which such series must be formed will differ according to the different cases. The series can include facts taken either from a single, unique society (or from several societies of the same species), or from several distinct social species.

The first process can, in a pinch, be sufficient when we are dealing with facts of a very general nature about which we have statistical data which are fairly extensive and varied. For instance, by comparing the curve which expresses a suicide trend over a sufficiently extended period of time, with the variations which the same phenomenon exhibits according to provinces, classes, rural or urban environments, sex, age, civil status, etc., we can succeed in establishing real laws without enlarging the scope of our research beyond a single country. Nevertheless, it is always preferable to confirm the results by observations made of other peoples of the same species. Furthermore, we cannot content ourselves with such limited comparisons except when studying one of those social tendencies which are widely prevalent throughout the whole of society, although varying from one place to another. When, on the other hand, we are dealing with an institution, a legal or moral rule, or an organized custom which is the same and functions in the same manner over an entire country and which only changes over time, we cannot limit ourselves to the study of a single people. If we did so we would only have as material proof a mere pair of parallel curves, namely, the one which expresses the historical development of the phenomenon under consideration and that of its conjectured cause, but only in this single, unique society. Undoubtedly this mere parallelism, if it is constant, is already an important fact, but of itself would not constitute proof.

By taking into account several peoples of the same species, a more extensive field of comparison already becomes available. Firstly, we can confront the history of one people with that of the others and see whether, when each one is taken separately, the same phenomenon evolves over time as a function of the same conditions. Then comparisons can be set up between these various developments. For example, we can determine the form assumed by the particular fact in different societies at the moment when it reaches its highest point of development. However, as the societies are each distinctive entities although belonging to the same type, that form will not be the same everywhere; according to each case, its degree of definition will vary. Thus we shall have a new series of variations to compare with those forms which the presumed condition presents at the same moment in each of these societies. In this way, after we have followed the evolution of the patriarchal family through the history of Rome, Athens and Sparta, these cities can be classified according to the maximum degree of development which this family type attains in each. We can then see whether, in relation to the state of the social environment on which the type apparently depended in the first phase of the investigation, they can still be ranked in the same way.

But this method can hardly be sufficient by itself. This is because it is applicable only to phenomena which have arisen during the existence of the peoples under comparison. Yet a society does not create its organization by itself alone; it receives it in part ready-made from preceding societies. What is therefore transmitted to it is not any product of its historical development and consequently cannot be explained unless we go outside the confines of the species to which it belongs. Only the additions which are made to its original base and which transform it can be dealt with. But the higher the social scale, the less the importance of the characteristics acquired by each people as compared with those which have been handed down. This is moreover the condition of all progress. Thus the new elements we have introduced into domestic law, the law of property, and morality, from the beginning of our history, are relatively few and of small importance compared to those which the distant past has bequeathed to us. The innovations which occur in this way cannot therefore be understood unless we have first studied those more fundamental phenomena which are their roots, but which cannot be studied without the help of much broader comparisons. To be in a position to explain the present state of the family, marriage and property, etc., we must know the origins of each and what are the primal elements from which these institutions are composed. On these points the comparative history of the great European societies could not shed much light. We must go even further back.

Consequently, to account for a social institution belonging to a species already determined, we shall compare the different forms which it assumes not only among peoples of that species, but in all previous species. If, for instance, we are dealing with domestic organizations, we will first constitute the most rudimentary type that has ever existed, so as to follow step by step the way in which it has progressively grown more complex. This method, which might be termed "genetic," would yield at one stroke the analysis and the synthesis of the phenomenon. For, on the one hand, it would show us in dissociated state its component elements by the mere fact that it would reveal to us how one was successively added to the other. At the same time, thanks to the wide field of comparison, we would be much better placed to determine the conditions upon which their formation and association depend. *Consequently one cannot explain a social fact of any complexity save on condition that one follows its entire development throughout all social species.* Comparative sociology is not a special branch of sociology; it is sociology itself, in so far as it ceases to be purely descriptive and aspires to account for facts.

In the course of these extended comparisons, an error is often made which falsifies the results. Sometimes, in order to judge the direction in which social events are proceeding, one may simply have compared what occurs at the decline of each species with what occurs at the beginning of the succeeding one. Using this procedure, it was believed, for example, that one could state that the weakening of religious beliefs and of all traditionalism could only ever be a transitory phenomenon in the life of peoples, because it manifests itself only during the final phase of their existence and ceases as soon as a new stage of evolution takes over. In employing such a method one risks taking for the steady and necessary march of progress what is the effect of a completely different cause. In fact, the condition in which a young society finds itself is not simply the prolongation of that at which the societies it replaces had arrived at the end of their existence. It arises partly from that very state of youthfulness which stops the products of the experiences of the previous peoples from all becoming immediately assimilable and utilizable. Likewise, the child receives from his parents faculties and predispositions which come into play only much later in life. It is therefore possible—to continue the same example—that the return to traditionalism observed at the beginning of every people's history is due to the special conditions in which every young society is placed, and not to the fact that the waning of that phenomenon can never be anything but transitory. The comparison can therefore only serve as proof if we can eliminate this disturbing factor of the age of a society. To do this, *it will be sufficient to consider the societies which one is comparing at the same period of their development.* Thus in order to ascertain the direction in which a social phenomenon is evolving, one will compare what it is during the "youth" of every species with what the phenomenon becomes in the "youth" of the succeeding species. According to whether, from one of these stages to the next, it displays more, less or as much intensity, one will be able to state whether it is progressing, regressing or remaining static.

Notes

1. *Cours de philosophie positive,* IV, p. 328.
2. Cf. J.S. Mill, *System of Logic,* vol. II, book VI, ch. VII, p. 476.
3. *Division du travail social,* p. 87.
4. In the case of the method of difference, the absence of the cause excludes the presence of the effect.

Conclusion

To summarize, the characteristics of the sociological method are as follows:

Firstly, it is independent of all philosophy. Since sociology sprang from the great philosophical doctrines, it has been in the habit of relying on some system with which it has therefore identified itself. Thus it has been successively positivist, evolutionalist and spiritualist, when it should have contented itself with being just sociology. We should even hesitate to term it naturalistic, unless by this we mean only that it regards social facts as explicable naturally. In that case the epithet is somewhat useless, since it merely means that the sociologist is engaged in scientific work and is not a mystic. But we reject the word if it is assigned a doctrinal meaning relating to the essence of social things—if, for instance, it is meant that they are reducible to the other cosmic forces. Sociology has no need to take sides between the grand hypotheses which divide the metaphysicians. Nor has it to affirm free will rather than determinism. All that it asks to be granted it, is that the principle of causality should be applicable to social phenomena. Moreover, this principle is posed by it not as a rational necessity, but only as an empirical postulate, the product of a legitimate induction. Since the law of causality has been verified in the other domains of nature and has progressively extended its authority from the physical and chemical world to the biological world, and from the latter to the psychological world, one may justifiably grant that it is likewise true of the social world. Today it is possible to add that the research undertaken on the basis of this postulate tends to confirm this. But the question of knowing whether the nature of the causal link excludes all contingency is not thereby resolved.

Moreover, philosophy itself has every interest in seeing this emancipation of sociology. For, so long as the sociologist has not shed sufficiently the mantle of the philosopher, he will consider social matters only from their most general angle, that in which they most resemble the other things in the universe. Now if sociology, conceived of in this fashion, may serve to illustrate a philosophy with curious facts, it cannot enrich it with new vistas, since it would not point to anything new in the subject matter of philosophy. But in reality, if the basic facts of other fields of knowledge are to be found in the social domain, it is under special forms which cause us to understand its nature better because they are its highest expression. But, in order to perceive them in this light, we must abandon generalities and enter into the detailed examination of facts. Thus sociology, as it becomes more specialized, will provide additional original matter for philosophical reflection. Already what has been set out has been able to give some insight into how essential notions such as those of species, organ, function, health and sickness, cause and finality are displayed in an entirely novel light. Moreover, is it not sociology which is destined to highlight in all its aspects an idea which might well be at the basis not only of a psychology, but of an entire philosophy, the idea of association?

Face to face with practical doctrines, our method allows and commands the same independence. Sociology thus understood will be neither individualist, communist or socialist, in the sense commonly attributed to those words. On principle, it will ignore these theories, which it could not acknowledge to have any scientific value, since they tend not directly to express social facts but to reform them. At least, if sociology is interested in them, it is in so far as it sees in them social facts which may help it to understand social reality by clarifying the needs which operate in society. Nevertheless, this is not to say that sociology should profess no interest in practical questions. On the contrary, it has been seen that our constant preoccupation has been to guide it toward some practical outcome. It encounters these problems necessarily at the end of its investigations. But from the very fact that the problems do not manifest themselves until that moment and that, consequently, they arise out of facts and not from passions, it may be predicted that they will present themselves to the sociologist in completely different terms than to the masses. Moreover, the solutions, although incomplete, that sociology can provide to them will not chime exactly with those which attract the various interest groups. But the role of sociology, from this viewpoint, must consist precisely in liberating us from all parties. This will be done not so much by opposing one doctrine to other doctrines, but by causing those minds confronted with these questions to develop a special attitude, one that science alone can give through direct contact with things. Indeed, it alone can teach us to treat, with respect but without idolatry, historical institutions of whatever kind, by causing us to be aware, at one and the same time, of what is necessary and provisional about them, their strength of resistance and their infinite variability.

In the second place, our method is objective. It is wholly dominated by the idea that social facts are things and must be treated as such. Doubtless this principle is also found, in slightly different form, at the basis of the doctrines of Comte and Spencer. But these great thinkers formulated it theoretically rather than put it into practice. But for it not to remain a dead letter, it was not sufficient merely to publish it abroad; it had to be made the basis of an entire discipline, an idea that would take hold of the scholar at the very moment when he is entering upon the object of his research and which would accompany him step by step in all his operations. It was to establish that discipline that we have devoted our work. We have shown how the sociologist had to lay aside the preconceived notions that he held about the facts in order to confront the facts themselves; how he had to penetrate to them through their most objective characteristics; how he had to address himself to them in order to find a means of classifying them as healthy or pathological; how, finally, he had to be inspired by the same principle in seeking out explanations as in proving these explanations. For once we become aware that we are in the presence of things, we no longer dream of explaining them by calculations of utility or by reasoning of any kind. We understand too well the gulf that lies between such causes and such effects. A thing is a force which can only be engendered by another force. Thus, to account for social facts, we investigate the forces capable of producing them. Not only are the explanations different, but they are proved differently, or rather, it is only then that the need to prove them is felt. If sociological phenomena were mere objectivized systems of ideas, to explain them would consist of thinking them through again in their logical order and this explanation would be a proof in itself. At the most, there might be a need to confirm it by a few examples. On the contrary, only methodical experimentation can force things to yield up their secrets.

But if we consider social facts as things, it is as *social things*. The third feature which is characteristic of our method is that it is exclusively sociological. It has often seemed that these phenomena, because of their extreme complexity, were either intractable to science or could only become part of it if reduced to their elementary conditions, either psychical or organic, that is to say, divested of their proper nature. On the contrary, we have undertaken to establish that it is possible to deal with them scientifically without taking away any of their specific characteristics. We have even refused to relate the immateriality *sui generis* which characterizes them to the immateriality of psychological phenomena, which is moreover already very complex. We are thus all the more prohibited from assimilating them, as does the Italian school, into the general properties of organized matter.[1] We have demonstrated that a social fact cannot be explained except by another social fact and at the same time have shown how this sort of explanation is possible by indicating what within the inner social environment is the principal motivating force of collective evolution. Thus sociology is not the appendage of any other science; it is itself a distinct and autonomous science. The sense of the specific nature of social reality is even so essential to the sociologist that only a purely sociological culture can prepare him for the understanding of social facts.

We regard this progress of sociological culture as the most important of all the steps that remain to be taken in sociology. Undoubtedly when a science is in the process of being created one is indeed forced, in order to construct it, to refer to the sole models which exist, namely those of sciences already constructed. There is in them a treasure-house of ready-made experiences which it would be foolish not to exploit. However, a science cannot be considered definitively constituted until it has succeeded in establishing its own independent status. For it lacks any purpose unless its subject matter is an order of facts which other sciences do not study, since it is impossible for the same notions to fit identically things of a different nature.

Such appear to us to be the rules of sociological method.

This set of rules will perhaps appear needlessly complicated if compared to the procedures currently in use. All this apparatus of precautions can seem very laborious for a science which up to now has demanded hardly more than a general and philosophical culture of its devotees. It is indeed certain that the application of such a method cannot have the effect of stimulating further common curiosity about sociological matters. When, as a preliminary condition for initiation into sociology, people are asked to discard concepts which they are in the habit of applying to a particular order of things, to rethink these things with renewed effort, we cannot expect to enlist a numerous clientele. But this is not the goal toward which we strive. We believe, on the contrary, that the time has come for sociology to renounce worldly successes, so to speak, and take on the esoteric character which befits all science. Thus it will gain in dignity and authority what it will perhaps lose in popularity. For, so long as it remains embroiled in partisan struggles and is content to elaborate, with indeed more logic than commonly employed, common ideas, and in consequence presumes no special competence, it has no right to speak authoritatively enough to quell passions and dispel prejudices. Assuredly the time is still remote when it will be able effectively to play this role. Yet, from this very moment onward, we must work to place it in a position to fulfill this part.

Note

1. It is therefore improper to characterize our method as materialist.

Original Table of Contents

Introduction

The rudimentary state of methodology in the social sciences. The objective of the book.

Chapter I: What Is a Social Fact?

A social fact cannot be characterized by its generality within society. Distinctive features of a social fact: 1) its externality to the consciousness of individuals; 2) its coercive influence or potential coercive influence on the consciousness of individuals. Implementation of this definition to constituted practices and "social currents." Verification of this definition.

Other characterization of social facts: their independence of individual manifestations. Application of this definitional feature to constituted practices and "social currents." A social fact is general because it is collective, but it is far from being collective because it is general. This second definition is in fact another formulation of the first one.

Facts of morphological nature also present the same characteristics. General definition of the social fact.

Chapter II: Rules for the Observation of Social Facts

The basic rule: to consider social facts as things.

I.   Every discipline at its beginnings goes through an ideological phase during which it elaborates popular and practical notions instead of describing and explaining things. Reasons why this is all the more the case with sociology. Examples from Comte's and Spencer's sociology, and from the current state of the study of morals and of political economy showing that sociology is still in its ideological phase.

Reasons for overcoming this phase: 1) social facts must be treated as things because they are the immediate *data* of sociology, whereas

115

ideas, from which they are seen as arising, are not immediately given; 2) social facts have all the distinctive features of things.

The reform that must be introduced into sociology is analogous to that which has recently transformed psychology. Reasons to hope for rapid progress of sociology in the future.

II.   Immediate corollaries of the previous rule.

1) Sociology must systematically discard all preconceptions. The application of the rule is prevented by mysticism.
2) To grasp the facts in order to study them objectively, the sociologist must group them and define them on the basis of their common external characteristics. Relations of concepts thus formed with popular conceptions. Examples of errors caused by neglecting this rule or applying it wrongly: Spencer's theory of the evolution of marriage, Garofalo's definition of crime, the common error of those who deny to less advanced societies any kind of morality. External characteristics serving to provide an initial definition of phenomena do not constitute an obstacle to scientific explanations.
3) Furthermore, these external characteristics must be as objective as possible. The means to achieve that aim is to represent them as completely detached from the individual facts by which they are manifested.

Chapter III: Rules for the Distinction of the Normal from the Pathological

Theoretical and practical utility of this distinction. Science must have the means to make this distinction so that it can guide us in our conduct.

I.   Examination of the criteria commonly used: pain is not the index of illness because it can accompany health. It does not signify the diminution of our chances of survival because it is sometimes the outcome of normal events (aging, parturition, etc.) nor does it necessarily derive from illness. Furthermore, this last criterion is very often inapplicable, especially in sociology.

Illness differs from health as abnormality differs from normality. The average or specific (relative to a species) type. Variations relating to age must be taken into account in order to state whether a fact is normal or not.

This definition of the pathological coincides with the notion commonly held of illness: people consider the abonormal to be

Chapter V: **Rules for the Explanation of Social Facts**

I. The teleological character of explanations that are currently widely accepted. But the utility of a fact does not explain its existence. This approach confuses two distinct questions, as shown by the following examples: a fact that has lost all utility can continue to exist; it can change its function without changing its nature (the organ is independent of its function); and an institution can also serve multiple ends throughout its history. It is necessary to investigate the efficient causes of social phenomena. These causes are of considerable importance in the study of sociology, as shown by the generality of social practices, down to the most small-scale such practices.

Efficient causes have to be investigated independently of functions. It is generally appropriate to deal with the first problem before the second. Yet, the investigation of the second is useful.

II. Psychological character of the method generally followed by sociologists. This method misconceives the nature of social phenomena, since their very definition show that they are not reducible to psychological facts. Social facts can only be explained by social facts.

Explanation of why this is the case, even though society is solely composed of individuals (*individual consciousnesses*). This is because their association gives birth to a new entity which constitutes a new being and a new order of realities. There is between psychology and sociology a break in continuity analogous to that between biology and the physical and chemical sciences.

This argument also applies to the formation of society.

Positive relationship between psychological and social facts. The first are the indeterminate matter which the social factor fashions and transforms: examples.

What has blinkered the vision of many sociologists who ascribed a direct role to these facts in the genesis of social life is that they took states of consciousness that were nothing but transformed social facts for mere psychological facts.

Other examples proving this: 1) independence of social facts from ethnic factors, which are of an organico-psychical order; 2) social evolution is not explainable by means of merely psychological causes.

Statement of the rules concerning this topic. It is because these rules have not been acknowledged that sociological explanations have appeared too general and thus been discredited. Necessity of a properly sociological culture.

one experimental procedure does not mean that it is in a state of inferiority as compared with the other sciences. For this drawback is compensated by the wealth of variations which are spontaneously available for the comparisons made by the sociologist. What must be done is not to compare isolated variations, but series of variations, systemically constituted, whose terms are correlated with each other in as continuous a gradation as possible and which cover an adequate range.

III.   Different ways of forming these series. Cases where the facts can only be taken from one society. Cases where facts must be taken from different societies, yet belonging to the same species. Cases where different species must be compared. Why this case is the most widespread. Comparative sociology is not a special branch of sociology; it is sociology itself.

How to avoid errors often made in the course of these comparisons.

Conclusion

General characteristics of the sociological method:

1)   Its independence of all philosophy (philosophy itself has every interest in seeing this emancipation of sociology) and practical doctrines. Relations between sociology and these doctrines. How sociology liberates us from all parties.
2)   Its objectivity. Its method is wholly dominated by the idea that facts are things and must be treated as such.
3)   Its distinctively sociological character. Social facts can be explained without taking away any of their specific characteristics. Sociology is itself an autonomous science. The achievement of this autonomy is the most important of all the steps that remain to be taken in sociology.

Sociology will gain authority when practiced thus.

Subsequent Writings of Emile Durkheim on Sociology and Its Method

Marxism and Sociology:
The Materialist Conception of History (1897)*

The purpose of this book is to point out the principle of historical philosophy which is at the basis of Marxism, to subject it to a fresh analysis, not with a view to modifying it, but in order to make it clearer and more precise. The principle states that in the last analysis historical development depends upon economic causes. This is what has been called the dogma of economic materialism. As the book's author believes that its best formulation is to be found in the *Manifesto of the Communist Party*, it is that document which serves as the theme of his study. This study comprises two parts: the first expounds the origin of the doctrine, the second consists of a commentary upon it. An appendix contains the translation of the manifesto.

Normally the historian perceives only the most superficial part of social life. The individuals who are the enactors of history conceive a certain idea of the events in which they participate. In order to be able to understand their own behavior they imagine that they are pursuing some aim or another which appears to them to be desirable, and they conjure up reasons to prove to themselves and, if needs be, to prove to others that the aim is a worthy desideratum. It is these motives and reasons that the historian considers as having effectively been the determining causes of historical development. If, for instance, he succeeds in discovering the end that the men of the Reformation set out to attain, he believes that he has explained at the same time how the Reformation occurred. But these subjective explanations are worthless, for men never do perceive the true motives which cause them to act.

Even when our behavior is determined by private interest which, because it touches us more closely, is more easily perceptible, we discern only a very small part of the forces that impel us, and these are not the most important ones. For the ideas and reasons which develop in our consciousness and whose conflicts constitute our deliberations stem most frequently from organic states, from inherited tendencies and ingrained habits of which we are unaware. This is therefore even more true when we act under the influence of social causes which we fail to perceive even more because they are more remote and more complex. Luther was

---

* Review of Antonio Labriola, "Essais sur la conception materialiste de l'histoire," *Revue philosophique*, 44, 1897, pp. 645–51.

unaware that he was "a moment in the development of the Third Estate." He thought he was working for the glory of Christ and did not suspect that his ideas and actions were determined by a certain condition of society and that the relative situation of the social classes necessitated a transformation of the old religious beliefs: "All that which has happened in history is the work of man; but only very rarely was it the result of a critical choice or of a rational will" (p.149).

Thus if we wish to understand the real way in which facts are linked together, we must give up this ideological method. We must strip away that surface of ideas in order to penetrate to the deep things that they express more or less unreliably, the underlying forces from which they derive. In the author's words, "the historical facts must be extricated from those coverings which the facts themselves assume whilst they are evolving." The only rational and objective explanation of events consists in discovering in what way they really came about, and not the account of their genesis conceived by men who have been their instruments. It is this revolution in historical method which the materialist conception of history is alleged to have realized.

Indeed, if we proceed in this way we realize, according to Marx and his disciples, that social evolution has as its living source the state of technology at each moment of history, namely, "the conditions of the development of labor and the instruments appropriate to it" (p. 239). This is what constitutes the deep structure or, as our author has it, the economic infrastructure of society. Depending on whether production is agricultural or industrial, on whether the machines employed require to be concentrated in a small number of large undertakings, or, on the contrary, favor dispersion, etc., the relationships between the classes of producers are determined very differently. But it is on these relationships—the disturbances and contradictions of every kind which result from this organization—that all the rest depends. First of all, the state is a necessary consequence of the division of society into classes subordinated to one another, for the balance cannot be maintained between these economically unequal creatures save when it is imposed by violence and repression. This is the role of the state. It is a system of forces employed "to guarantee or perpetuate a mode of association whose foundation is a form of economic production" (p. 223). Thus its interests merge with those of the ruling classes. Likewise law is never anything save "the defense, whether customary, authoritarian or judicial, of a given interest" (p. 237); "it is merely the expression of interests that have carried the day" (p. 238) and consequently, "it comes down almost immediately to economics." Morality is the sum total of the inclinations and habits which social life, depending upon the manner in which it is organized, has developed in the conscience of individuals. Finally, even the products of art, science and religion are always related to determinate economic conditions.

The scientific interest of this viewpoint lies, it is said, in the effect it has of "naturalizing" history. It is "naturalized" by the mere circumstance that, in the explanation of social facts, there is substituted for those inconsistent ideals and phantasma of the imagination which up to now were made out to be the driving impulsion of progress, definite, real, resistant forces, that is to say the distribution of men into classes, which is itself linked to the state of economic techniques. But we must beware of confusing this naturalist sociology with what has been called political and social Darwinism. The latter consists merely in explaining the development of institutions by the principles and concepts which are sufficient for explaining zoological development. As animal life takes place in a purely physical environment which has not yet been modified by any labor, this simplistic philosophy is used to account for social evolution through causes which have nothing social about them, namely through the needs and appetites already to be found in the animal kingdom. According to Labriola, the theory which he defends is completely different. It seeks the motivating causes for historical development, not in the cosmic circumstances which may have affected the organism, but in the artificial environment which the labor of men in association has created from nothing and which has been added on to nature. It makes social phenomena depend, not on hunger, thirst, sexual desire, etc., but on the state at which human art has arrived and the ways of living which have resulted from it—in short, on the collective works of men. Doubtless in their origins men, like other animals, had no other field of action than the natural environment. But history has no need to go back as far as that hypothetical era, about which we cannot at the present time summon up any empirical representation. It only begins when there exists a supraphysical environment, however primitive it may be, for it is only then that social phenomena begin to appear. Nor has history to be concerned with the way, which is in any case indeterminable, that humanity has been led to raise itself from the realm of pure nature and constitute a new world. Consequently it can be said that the method of economic materialism is applicable to the whole of history.

From these abstract principles revolutionary socialism logically derives. Great changes have taken place in industrial techniques since a century ago; therefore changes of equal importance in social organization must result from them. Since everything concerning the nature and form of production is fundamental and substantive, the disturbance produced in this way is no limited social affliction which partial corrections in our collective economy can remedy. It is, of absolute necessity, a sickness *totius substantiae* which can only be cured by a radical transformation of society. All the old frameworks must be rent asunder, the entire substance of society must be set free so that it may be cast into new molds.

This is the summary of the work that Sorel, in the preface, not without reason, presents as an important contribution to socialist literature.

Doubtless the extreme diffuseness of the development of the theme, the evident defects in composition, certain excesses of language which are out of place in a scientific discussion, are regrettable. Yet it is, to our knowledge, one of the most rigorous attempts that has been made to bring back Marxist doctrine to its elementary concepts and to deepen them. The thought does not seek, as happens too often, to disguise itself by shades of meaning that are not clear-cut. It presses ahead, with a kind of vitality. The sole concern of the author is to see clearly the principle underlying beliefs whose logical consequences he resolutely accepts in advance. Thus this exposition of the system is remarkably appropriate for highlighting both its fertile insights and its weaknesses.

We believe it a fruitful idea that social life must be explained not by the conception of it formed by those who participate in it, but by the profound causes which escape their consciousness. We also think that these causes must be sought mainly in the way in which individuals associating together are formed in groups. It even seems to us, on this condition—but on this condition alone—that history may become a science and that sociology consequently may take on existence. For, in order for collective representations to become intelligible, they must truly spring from something and, since they cannot constitute a circle closed in upon itself, the source from which they derive must be found outside them. Either the collective consciousness is floating in a vacuum, as a kind of absolute incapable of being represented, or it is attached to the rest of the world by the intermediary of a substratum on which it consequently depends. On the other hand, of what else can this substratum be composed save the members of society, in the way that they are combined together in society? This postulate seems to us self-evident. Yet we see no reason to do as the author does and attach it to the socialist movement, from which it is entirely independent. For our part, we arrived at this postulate before we had learned of Marx, whose influence we have in no way undergone. In fact this conception is the logical outcome of the whole movement among historians and psychologists over the last fifty years. For a long while historians have perceived that social evolution has causes of which the actors in historical events are unaware. It is under the influence of these ideas that one tends to deny or limit the role played by great men, and that one seeks to discover, beneath literary or juridical movements, the expression of a collective thought that no one definite personality embodies in its entirety. At the same time, and above all, individual psychology has come to teach us that the consciousness of the individual very often merely reflects the underlying state of the organism. It also teaches us that the course of our representations is determined by causes concealed from their subject. From this it was natural to extend this notion to collective psychology. But it is impossible for us to perceive what share the sad conflict between the classes that we are witnessing at the present time may have had in the elaboration or development of this idea. Doubtless the latter came at an appropriate moment, when the conditions necessary for its appearance were present. It was not possible at any moment in time. But we must know what these conditions are. When Labriola asserts that the idea has arisen "by the widespread, conscious and continuous development of modern technology, by the inevitable suggestion of a new world about to be born," he enunciates as an evident fact a thesis which lacks any confirmation. Socialism has been able to use the idea to its advantage. But it has not produced it and, above all, the idea does not imply socialism.

It is true that if, as our author postulates, this objective conception of history was identical with the doctrine of economic materialism, since the latter has certainly socialist origins,[1] one might possibly believe that the former has been constituted under the same influence and is inspired with the same spirit. *But this confusion is devoid of all foundation and it is vital to get rid of it.* These two theories are in no ways interdependent, and their scientific value is singularly unequal. Just as it seems true to us that the causes of social phenomena must be sought outside individual representations, so does it seem false to us to bring them down, in the last resort, to the state of industrial technology and to make the economic factor the mainspring of progress.

Even without setting against economic materialism any definite fact, how can one fail to notice the inadequacy of the proofs on which it rests? Here is a law which lays claim to being the key to history. Yet, in order to demonstrate it, one is content to cite a few scattered and disjointed facts, which together make up no methodical series and whose interpretation is far from being settled: they postulate primitive communism, the struggles of patricians and plebs, of the third estate and the nobility, which are explained in economic terms. Even when to these rare documents, which are rapidly reviewed, have been added some examples adduced from English industrial history, the demonstration of so broad a generalization will have been unsuccessful. On this point Marxism is in disagreement with its own principle. It begins by stating that social life depends upon causes which escape consciousness and "reasoning reason." But then, in order to penetrate these causes, procedures must be employed which are at the very least as devious and complex as those employed by the natural sciences. Every kind of observation, experiment and laborious comparison must be used to discover separately some of these factors, and there can be no question at the present time of deriving any unitary representation from them. Yet, in a trice, all these mysteries are cleared up and a simple solution is given to these problems, which the human intelligence appeared not to be able to penetrate save with great difficulty. Will it be said that the objective conception, which we have just set out summarily, is no more proved in adequate fashion? Nothing is more sure. But also it does not

propose to assign a definite origin to social phenomena; it confines itself
to stating that there are causes to them. For, to say that they have objective causes has no other meaning, since collective representations cannot
have their ultimate causes within themselves. Thus it is merely a postulate
intended to guide research, and consequently always suspect, for in the
last resort it is experience which must decide. It is a rule of method, and
not a law from which one is justified in deducing important consequences,
whether theoretical or practical.

Not only is the Marxist hypothesis unproven, but it is contrary to facts
which appear established. Sociologists and historians tend increasingly
to come together in their common affirmation that religion is the most
primitive of all social phenomena. It is from it that have emerged, through
successive transformations, all the other manifestations of collective activity—law, morality, art, science, political forms, etc. In principle everything
is religious. Yet we know of no means of reducing religion to economics
nor of any attempt at really effecting this reduction. Up to now no one has
yet shown under what economic influences naturism emerged from totem-
ism, through what modifications in technology it became in one place the
abstract monotheism of Yahweh, and in another Greco-Latin polytheism.
Moreover we doubt strongly whether anyone will ever succeed in such an
undertaking. More generally, it is beyond dispute that, at the origin, the
economic factor is rudimentary, while, by contrast, religious life is rich
and pervasive. How therefore could the latter result from the former and,
on the contrary, is it not probable that the economy depends on religion
rather than vice versa?

Moreover, one should not push the above ideas to extremes where they
lose all validity. Psycho-physiology, after having pointed to the organic
substratum as the foundation of psychical life, has often committed the
error of denying all reality to the latter. From this arose the theory which
reduces consciousness to being a mere epiphenomenon. What has been lost
to sight is that if representations depend originally upon organic states,
once they are constituted, they are, by virtue of this, realities *sui generis*,
autonomous and capable of being causes in their turn, producing new
phenomena. Sociology must carefully guard against the same error. If the
different forms of collective activity also possess their own substratum
and if in the last instance they derive from it, once they exist they in turn
become original sources of influence, possessing an effectiveness of their
own, reacting upon the very causes upon which they depend. Thus we
are far from maintaining that the economic factor is an epiphenomenon:
once it exists it has an influence which is peculiar to it. It can partially
modify the very substratum from which it arises. But there is no ground
for confusing it, in some way, with that substratum, or for making something especially fundamental of it. Everything leads us to believe, on the
contrary, that it is secondary and derived. From this it follows that the

economic transformations that have occurred in the course of the century, the substitution of large- for small-scale industry, in no way require the over-toppling and entire renewal of the social order, and even that the malaise from which European societies may be suffering need not have these transformations as their cause.

Note

1. Although orthodox economics possesses also its materialism.

Sociology and the Social Sciences (1903)*

Sociology is commonly said to be the science of social facts, that is to say, the science of those phenomena which show the life of societies itself. Although this definition may pass as a truism no longer disputed by anybody, the object of the science is far from being determined by this alone. Indeed, those very facts which are ascribed as its subject matter are already studied by a host of specific disciplines, such as the history of religions, law and political institutions, and statistics and economics. We are therefore seemingly faced with this alternative: either sociology has the same subject matter as those sciences termed historical or social and is then merged with them, being no more than the generic term which serves to designate them as a whole; or it is a distinct science, possessing its own individual character. Yet to be so it must have a content specifically its own. Consequently, where is this to be found outside the phenomena with which the different social sciences deal?

The purpose of this paper is to show how this dilemma may be resolved. On the one hand we propose to establish that sociology is and can only be the system, the *corpus* of the social sciences. On the other hand we propose also to establish that grouping them all together under a common heading is no mere verbal operation, but implies and indeed indicates a radical alteration in the method and organization of these sciences. Yet we do not intend to set about such a demonstration using purely dialectical procedures. Our concern is not to analyze logically the content of an idea formulated beforehand. Such conceptual expositions are rightly held to be futile. Sociology exists, and has now already a history which reveals its nature. Thus there is no point in seeking to conjure it up from nothing, for it is possible to observe it. If it is useless to engage in abstract argument as to what the science should be, there is on the other hand real advantage to be gained from an awareness of what it is becoming as it develops, in accounting for the various elements from which it has emerged and for the part of each in the whole. This we shall attempt to do in the following pages.

---

* (With Paul Fauconnet) "Sociologie et sciences sociales," *Revue philosophique*, 55, 1903, pp. 465–97.

I

To reduce sociology to being merely the system of the social sciences seems at first to place one at odds with the founders of the new science and to break with the tradition they established. To mention only the greatest of them, it is absolutely certain that Auguste Comte never conceived sociology to be anything save a speculative, complete entity, closely linked to general philosophy, of which it is the crowning glory and pinnacle. It does not stand there in its own right, but because it alone can furnish the necessary principle for a complete systematization of experience. Thus not unreasonably it could be said in one sense not to be a special science, but "the sole science" and "the universal science," since the other sciences may be regarded as great sociological facts, and since the entirety of the facts we are given is subordinate to the supreme idea of humanity.[1] This is because the law of the three stages, which dominates the *Cours de philosophie positive* throughout, is essentially a sociological law. Moreover, since the demonstration of this law relies on philosophical considerations which relate to the conditions of knowledge, it follows that positive philosophy is wholly a sociology and Comtean sociology is itself a philosophy.

Not only did sociology display this character from the beginning, but it necessarily did so. It could only arise within the framework of a philosophy, for it was philosophical traditions that opposed its formation. The first of these obstacles was the religious or metaphysical dualism which made humanity a world apart, exempt, by some mysterious privilege, from that determinism whose presence the natural sciences affirm everywhere else in the universe. For the foundation of the new science to be made possible, the concept of natural laws had therefore to be enlarged to include human phenomena. So long as this prime condition remained unfulfilled, the application of reflective thinking to social facts could not engender a truly positive and progressive science. If the wise and penetrating observations which Aristotle and Bossuet, Montesquieu and Condorcet were able to make about the life of societies nevertheless did not constitute a sociology, it is because they lacked this fundamental principle. But such a principle could only spring from an advance in philosophical thinking. The dualist prejudice could only be dispelled by a bold assertion of the unity of nature, and this very assertion could only be the culmination of a more or less complete synthesis of the knowledge that the science had already accumulated. By providing for itself a conspectus of the work already accomplished, the human mind summoned up the necessary courage to advance it further. If the physicists, chemists and biologists are imbued with the positive spirit, it is because their sciences have for a long time been positive. Familiarity in the practice of the method used in the sciences, knowledge of the results obtained and of the laws that have been established, have sufficed to educate these scientists. But it took a philosopher, one who drew his positive faith from an encyclopedic culture, to perceive the positive character of a science not yet formed and to assert that a particular order of phenomena is subject to laws before those laws had been discovered. Moreover, he was able to reinforce that faith by sketching out in abridged form that science, without, however, his outline being separable from the general philosophy which had put the idea in his mind and which was confirmed by it.

From a further viewpoint, sociology and positive philosophy were implicit in each other. Indeed, the assertion of the unity of nature did not suffice for social facts to become the content of a new science. Materialistic monism likewise postulates that man is a part of nature, but by making human life, whether of individuals or of societies, a mere epiphenomenon of physical forces, it renders both sociology and psychology useless. On this view social phenomena, like individual representations, appear as if assimilated to their material substratum which, it is alleged, alone is susceptible to scientific investigation. For sociology to arise, it was therefore not enough to proclaim the unity of reality and knowledge: that unity had also to be affirmed by a philosophy which acknowledges the natural heterogeneity of things. It was not sufficient to establish that social facts are subject to laws. It had also to be made clear that they have their own laws, specific in nature, and comparable to physical or biological laws, without being directly reducible to the latter. Moreover, to discover those laws the mind had to be applied directly to the social realm considered by itself, without any kind of intermediary or surrogate, leaving all its complexity untouched. We know that for Comte the different fundamental sciences are irreducible to one another, although as a whole they form a homogeneous system. The unity of the positive method is no bar to their specificity. Thus, by the one fact that sociology was placed on an equal footing with the natural sciences, its own individuality was assured. But the principle which gave it this guarantee clearly assumed a broad comparison with the earlier sciences, their methods and results, a comparison which could not be undertaken save through an elaborate philosophical synthesis, such as that of positive philosophy.

Engendered within a philosophy, sheer necessity obliged sociology from the beginning to display the distinctive character of any philosophical discipline: a leaning toward general, overall views and, in contrast, a certain indifference to factual details and specialist investigations. Consequently it was natural for it to develop untrammeled by any special techniques, as an autonomous mode of speculation, capable of being self-sufficient. This stance was moreover justified by the state in which the sciences then were and by the spirit which infused them, one which on these essential points was radically opposed to that on which the new science proceeded. Not without reason does Comte reproach political economy in his day with not being a truly positive science, but with still being shot through with metaphysical philosophy, lingering over sterile discussions on the elementary notions of value, utility and production. Such discussions, he declares, recall "the strange debates of the medieval Schoolmen about the basic attributes of their pure, metaphysical entities."[2] Moreover, the general admission by economists of "the necessary isolation of their so-called science in relation to social philosophy in general" justifiably appeared to him to constitute "an involuntary recognition, decisive though indirect, of the scientific uselessness of that theory . . . For, by the very nature of the subject, in social studies as in all those relating to living objects, by force of necessity the various general aspects are interdependent and are rationally inseparable, to the point where they can only be clearly elucidated by reference to one another."[3] In fact it is certain that the notion of natural law as understood by Comte was unknown to economic science. Undoubtedly the economists freely used the word "law," but on their lips it possessed none of the meaning that it had in the sciences of nature. It did not connote relationships between facts, objectively observable among things, but purely logical connections between concepts formed in entirely ideological fashion. For the economist the task was not to discover what occurs in reality or investigate how stated effects derive from causes that are likewise stated, but mentally to combine purely formal notions such as value, utility, scarcity, supply and demand. The same charge could be leveled against the most current theories concerning law and morality— that of Montesquieu no less than of Kant.

For such diverse reasons, therefore, sociology could only achieve a consciousness of itself within the framework of philosophical thinking, remote from special disciplines and their influence. Indeed this characteristic sprang from causes too deep-seated to be entirely abandoned from the moment when the science began to be organized. Thus it is in no way surprising to discover that it recurs with Spencer, Comte's immediate successor. It is abundantly plain that Spencer worked on sociology as a philosopher, because he did not set out to study social facts in themselves and for their own sake, but in order to demonstrate how the hypothesis of evolution is verified in the social realm. But in so doing he was able to complement and correct in important respects the general conceptions of Comtean sociology. Although Comte had definitively integrated societies with nature, the excessive intellectualism which marked his doctrine was not easily reconcilable with that fundamental axiom of all sociology. If scientific evolution determines political, economic, moral and aesthetic evolution, a wide gulf separates sociological explanations from those employed in the other sciences of nature, so that it is difficult to avoid relapsing into ideology. By showing that under different forms the same law governs the social and the physical worlds, Spencer narrowed the gap between societies and the rest of the universe. He gave us a sense that, beneath the facts produced on the surface of the collective consciousness—facts which are interpreted as being the fruits of reflective thinking—obscure forces are at work which do not move men to act out of that sheer logical necessity which links together the successive phases of scientific development. On the other hand Comte did not admit that a large number of social types existed. According to him, only one society existed, the association of mankind in its totality; the various states represented only different moments in the history of that one society. Sociology was therefore placed in a peculiar position among all the sciences, since the object of study was an entity of a unique kind. Spencer disposed of this anomaly by showing that societies, like organisms, can be classified into genera and species and, whatever the merits of the classification he proposed, the principle at least was worthy of retention and has in fact survived. Although elaborated in philosophical terms, these two reforms thus represented invaluable gains for the science.

Yet if this way of understanding and developing sociology has at a given moment in time certainly been necessary and useful, that necessity and usefulness proved only temporary. To build itself up and even take its first steps forward, sociology needed to rely upon a philosophy. But to become truly itself, it was indispensable for it to assume a different character.

II

The very example of Comte can serve to prove this point, for, because of its philosophical character, the sociology he constructed was in no position to satisfy any of the conditions which he himself demanded for any positive science.

In fact, of the two divisions that he distinguished in sociology, the static and the dynamic, he really treated only the latter. From his viewpoint this was moreover the more important, for if, according to him, social facts exist distinct from purely individual phenomena, this is chiefly because a progressive evolution of humanity occurs. It is because the work of each generation survives it and is aggregated to that of succeeding generations. Progress is the paramount social fact. Thus social dynamism, as he expounded it, in no way presents "that continuity and that fecundity" which, as Comte himself observed, constitute "the least equivocal symptoms of all truly scientific conceptions,"[4] for he himself considered that he had finally explained social dynamism in broad terms. In fact, it is contained wholly in the law of the three stages. Once this law had been discovered it was impossible to see how it could be added to or extended, and even less so, how different laws might be discovered. The science was already complete almost before it had been founded. In fact those disciples of Comte who adhered closely to the substance of his doctrine could do no more than reproduce the propositions of their master, sometimes illustrating them with new examples, but without such purely formal variants ever constituting truly new discoveries. This explains the full stop to the development of the strictly Comtean school after Comte's death; the same formulae were religiously repeated without any progress being realized. This is because a science cannot live and develop when it is reduced to one single problem on which, at an ever-increasing distance in time, a great mind has placed its seal. For progress to be accomplished, the science must resolve itself into an increasingly large number of specific questions, so as to render possible co-operation between different minds and between successive generations. Only upon this condition will it have the collective, impersonal character without which there is no scientific research. But the philosophical and unitary conception which Comte imposed upon sociology ran counter to this division of labor. Thus his social dynamics are in the end only a philosophy of history, remarkable for its profundity and novel character, but constructed on the model of earlier philosophies. The task is to discern the law which controls "the necessary and continuous movement of humanity," which alone will allow insertion into the succession of historical events the unity and continuity which they lack. But Bossuet set himself no other task. The method varies, as does the solution, but the investigation is no different in kind.[5]

Yet, despite the lesson that could have been learned from the failure of such an attempt, sociology has remained for most of our contemporaries approximately what it was for Comte, as essentially philosophical speculation. Over the last twenty years we have seen a veritable flowering of sociological literature. Its production, once intermittent and sparse, has become continuous; new systems have been constructed and others are being constructed every day. But they are always, or almost always, systems in which the entire science is more or less undisguisedly reduced to a single problem. As with Comte and Spencer, the task is to discover the law which governs social evolution as a whole. For some it is the law of imitation, for others it is the law of adaptation, or the struggle for survival and, more particularly, the struggle between races. For yet another it is the influence of the physical environment, etc. Really, as we survey all these seekers after the supreme law, the cause which dominates all causes, the "key which opens all locks,"[6] we cannot help thinking of the alchemists of former days in their search for the philosopher's stone.[7]

Far from there having been any progress, rather has there been regression. For Comte, at least sociology was the complete science of social facts, encompassing the multifarious aspects of collective life. No category of phenomena was systematically excluded from it. If Comte refused to regard political economy as a sociological science, it is because in his day it was treated in a thoroughly unscientific spirit and because it mistook the true nature of social reality. But in no way did he intend to place economic facts beyond the pale of sociology. Consequently the way remained open for a further division of labor, for an increasing specialization in problems, as the domain of the science was extended and its complexity more fully grasped. The very opposite has occurred. The latest sociologists have gradually developed the idea that sociology is distinct from the social sciences, that there is a general social science which contrasts with these special disciplines, one with its own subject matter, its own special method, to which is reserved the name of sociology. Starting from the fact that the social sciences have been constituted outside the great philosophical syntheses which gave rise to the word sociology, it has been concluded from this that there must exist two kinds of investigations clearly different in kind, and efforts have been made to differentiate between them. While each science specializes in a determinate category of social phenomena, it has been stated that sociology has as its subject collective life in general. It is by virtue of this designation as a *general* social science that it constitutes a distinct and individual entity.

Yet, for it to be possible to set out and discuss with any precision the different attempts made in this direction, we must distinguish between the two different meanings ascribed by writers to this word "general."

In the first meaning, sociology is said to be *general* because it considers in all its complexity the social reality which the specific sciences have parceled up and dissected, being hived off from it. It is the concrete, synthetic science, while the others are analytical and abstract. To speak in the language of the logicians, the word *general* is here taken intentionally; it signifies that the subject under investigation is considered with all the characteristics appertaining to it and all the elements constituting it. Thus for John Stuart Mill general social science or sociology proper concerns the "states of society," as they succeed each other in the history of peoples. By the word "state" is understood "the simultaneous state of all the greater social facts or phenomena,"[8] and he gives as examples the level of education and of moral culture in the community and in each class, the state of industry and that of wealth and distribution, the normal occupations of the nation, its division into classes, the nature and strength of common beliefs, the nature of taste, the form of government, the most important laws and customs, etc. It is the sum of all these elements which constitutes the state of society, or to use another expression that Mill also employs, the state of civilization. Indeed, Mill postulates that these elements cannot combine in any way, but that there exist between them natural correlations through which they can only be associated with each other according to a determinate relationship. Sociology would have to deal with two kinds of problems: either it would determine what these correlations are, namely what uniformities coexist in the same state of society; or it would investigate how the successive states are linked, and what law governs this linkage. Anything beyond this is a matter for the particular social sciences. They would take as their starting point what for sociology is the ultimate stage: in a given state of society the social sciences would have to investigate what changes can be introduced into it by some determinate factor. Thus, for example, they would pose the question as to the effect that would be produced by the abolition of the corn laws (political economy), or the abolition of the monarchy and the introduction of universal suffrage (political science) on a given set of social conditions. From this standpoint sociology is so independent of the social sciences that it exercises over them a veritable supremacy, for it is sociology which provides them with their basic postulates, namely the states of society which serve as a basis for the deductions of specialists. Sociology, says Mill, is the means "by which the conclusions of the other and more special kind of inquiry must be limited and controlled."[9]

We shall not stop to demonstrate the untenable position of this conception of the social sciences. Mill plainly conceives them as being on the model of that abstract and deductive form of political economy which Comte already refused to rank among the positive sciences. How indeed may the appellation of positive science be given to an investigation whose object is not a set of established facts, grounded in reality, but one which is concerned solely with deduction from causes that are merely conjectured, of effects that may be merely possible? Regarding sociology proper, Mill's definition of it avoids that objection. The states within society with which it must deal indeed form part of that reality. But they are constituted from a conglomerate of such diverse phenomena that it is impossible for one and the same science to master subject matter of such great diversity. Indeed, within one state of society there enter elements made up of the religious system, the juridical, moral, economic, technical and scientific systems, etc. of a society at any given time. Each one of these systems in turn is a whole complex of institutions which themselves are each very complex. For instance, the religious system contains a host of dogmas, myths and rites, as well as the organization of the priesthood, etc. Likewise the juridical system comprises legal codes which are more or less numerous and voluminous, customs, a judicial organization, etc. Such a very heterogeneous entity could not be studied *en bloc* as if it were endowed with any objective unity. It is an infinite world of which one can have only a fragmented vision so long as one attempts to embrace it all at once and in its entirety, because to try to do so one must resign oneself to grasping it approximately and summarily—in other words, confusedly. So it is necessary for each part to be studied separately; each one is extensive enough to serve as the subject matter for an entire science. Thus that general and unique science to which was given the name of sociology breaks down into a multitude of branches which, although distinct, are interdependent. The relationships connecting the elements split up in this way, the influences and counter-influences which they exert upon one another, can only themselves be determined by dint of research which, although touching upon two or several fields, is none the less of a specialized nature. For example, it is for those scientists who deal with political economy or religion, and for them alone, to investigate the relationships between religious and economic phenomena.

But what is perhaps even more impossible is to undertake to explain these states of society by affiliating some of them to the others. For a state of society is not a kind of indivisible entity which engenders the next successive state, in the same way as it has been engendered by the preceding state. But each one of the systems and even each one of the institutions which serve to fashion it has its own individuality and is dependent on special conditions. It is not the whole which produces the whole, but the genesis of each part is distinct and requires to be established separately. Thus, to preserve the unified character of the research, Mill is forced to concede, following Comte's example, that in each state of society there is always one element which remains constant, dominating all the others and constituting the prime mover in the social evolution, "the central chain, to each successive link of which, the corresponding links of all the other progressions [are] . . . appended." This favored element is allegedly "the state of the speculative faculties of the human race; including the nature of the beliefs which by any means they have arrived at, concerning themselves and the world by which they are surrounded."[10] Thus the inextricable problem posed to the sociologist becomes singularly less complex: instead of the evolution of the states of society, considered in all their complexity, there is substituted solely the evolution of religions and of philosophy. It is unnecessary to show how arbitrary such a postulate is. There is nothing to justify our supposing that there is one social phenomenon which enjoys such a prerogative over all the others. Even presuming that in every social type there may be a system of opinions or practices which really does play a somewhat more predominant role, it is by no means proved that it is always the same one in every age and in every country. The influence of religious practices was once much more marked than that of ideas; the influence of the economic phenomenon has varied inversely. The conditions of social life have changed too much over the course of history for the same institutions always and everywhere to have retained the same importance. Thus in the zoological succession the pre-eminent function changes according to the species, and even the term "pre-eminent" possesses here only a somewhat vague and figurative meaning.

But the word "general" is taken in a very different sense, one that is almost the opposite, by a number of sociologists who term general social science, or sociology, the most abstract of all the social sciences, the one which, pushing analysis to its extreme, distances itself most from complex reality and delineates as its subject the simplest social relationships, those of which all the rest may be only different forms or combinations. It could be said that the word is used extensionally here; by "general" is understood here that which is indeterminate enough to be identified in all particular cases. It is in this way that Giddings has defined sociology. He finds no difficulty in acknowledging that the various aspects of social life are even now studied by the different economic, historical and political sciences. But, in his view, this is not the question for the sociologist. "Is society a whole? Is social activity continuous? Are there certain essential facts, causes or laws in society which are common to communities of all kinds, at all times, and which underlie and explain the more special social forms? If we must answer "yes," then these universal truths should be taught."[11] To establish and teach them would then be the proper task of sociology. For instance, political economy asks how wealth is produced in society and how it circulates; political science studies the organic condition of society once it has become a fully constituted state. But both sciences rely on a fact that they postulate without ever examining it: societies exist, and "human beings associate together." It is this fact which would serve as the subject matter of sociology. It would then have to investigate what constitutes human association in general, omitting the special forms that it can assume, and what are the factors on which its principal characteristics depend, the intellectual elements to which it gives rise. In short, it would be the science "of general principles"; it would consist in "an analysis of the general characteristics of social phenomena and a formulation of the general laws of social evolution."[12]

Certainly, if one merely meant to say that, once social sciences are sufficiently advanced, it would be opportune to compare the results obtained from each one of them so as to discern the most general relationships that they include, then the problem posed in this way would not be insoluble at all. Yet sociology so defined would not be different in nature from the other social sciences; it would range over the same field, save that it would embrace it on a loftier plane and as a whole. Far from constituting an autonomous science, on the contrary it would be most directly dependent on these various disciplines, from which it would have to draw all its subject matter, and it could only progress at the rate at which they themselves progressed. Thus there would be no grounds for making it a separate scientific entity, designated by a special term. But this is not at all the way that Giddings and, with him, a number of contemporary sociologists understand this general science of societies. Moreover, they could not do so, without being forced to acknowledge that sociology's hour is still far off, for these lofty generalizations will only be possible when the specific studies are more advanced than they are today. For these sociologists this synthesizing science, far from following in the train of the specific sciences, would on the contrary enjoy a real "logical primacy" over them. Instead of being their ultimate conclusion, it would provide their basic foundations. "Far from being merely the sum of the social sciences, it is rather their common basis. Its far-reaching principles are the postulates of special sciences."[13] It is political economy and the science of government, etc. which would need to rely on another science, for the study of the most complex forms of social life cannot usefully be undertaken unless one has already an adequate notion of its more elementary forms. Now it is said that sociology deals with these latter. Therefore it can and must be sufficient unto itself. The other social sciences presume its existence, but it presumes that no other science antedates it. It is through it that research and teaching must begin.[14]

Unfortunately these elementary forms exist nowhere in an isolated state, or even relatively isolated, so as to allow for their direct observation. Indeed, they must not be confused with primitive forms. The most rudimentary societies are still complex, although their complexity is confused. They contain within them, mingled together but none the less real, all the elements which in the course of evolution will become differentiated and develop. They are very special societies: they constitute particular types. Moreover, certainly neither Giddings nor other sociologists who have preceded or followed him down the same road have sought to restrict their research to these societies alone or to reduce sociology to mere comparative ethnography. Those forms which he calls elementary are, as we have seen, the most general forms; the two expressions are used interchangeably for each other. Now, whether we are dealing with social or physical phenomena, the general only exists in the particular. What is termed human association is not any specific society, but the sum total of characteristics to be found in all societies. These characteristics therefore never present themselves to the observer without being inextricably entangled with the distinctive characteristics of the various social types and even of the different collective individualities. Moreover, since to separate the former characteristics from the latter, one discards the method which would consist in first constituting special types and then sorting out by comparison what they possess in common, any criteria to effect that dissociation are lacking and one can only proceed judgmentally and according to personal impressions. Some facts are retained and others excluded because the first cluster *appear* essential and the second *appear* secondary, but without one being capable of advancing any objective reason for these preferences and exclusions. Thus when Giddings undertakes to analyze these primary and general elements, he starts by proposing as a self-evident axiom that they are all "conserved in its [society's] physical basis, the social population."[15] It is of course certain that population is an essential element in any society. But first there is a special science which studies the laws of population: this is demography, or more specifically what Mayr calls "demology." To distinguish himself from the demographer, must the sociologist adopt a special viewpoint? He will doubtless be obliged to study population by putting aside the various forms that it assumes according to the kind of society. But then there is not much more to be said about it. Thus Giddings is naturally obliged to go beyond these extreme generalities; he speaks of the distribution of population in different societies (uncivilized, half-civilized and civilized),[16] and of the different kinds of groupings (genetic, gregarious), etc.[17] How far does one follow him down this road and where is to be found the borderline between what is the sociologist's concern and what belongs to the other sciences? In book II, chapter III, under the heading "Social Composition" polyandrous and polygamic groupings, matronymical and patronymical tribes, and societies based on villages are discussed. This exposition contains a whole theory on the origins of the family. The subject matter assigned in this way to sociology therefore remains essentially indeterminate. It is the sociologist who determines it himself, arbitrarily, according to the extent of his knowledge and his personal tastes. What is more, in so determining it, he is obliged to encroach on the domain of the specific sciences. If he did not do so he would lack all content for his work. The questions with which he deals are no different in nature from those dealt with by the specialists, save that, since he cannot possess a universal competence, he is doomed to make imprecise and uncertain generalities, or even wholly inaccurate ones. Yet Giddings' treatise is one of the best, perhaps the best, of its kind. At least the author attempts to restrict his subject and study a limited number of elements in it. It would be much more difficult to say what Tarde, Gumplowicz, Ward and many others consider the precise subject of sociology, and how this science, which they however do distinguish from the other social sciences, is situated in relation to them. Here indeterminateness is elevated to a principle. Consequently sociology is no longer scientific. Nor is it any longer even that methodical philosophy which Comte attempted to institute. It is a very special mode of speculation, halfway between philosophy and literature, in which some very general, theoretical ideas are aired in connection with all kinds of problems.

Thus it is not by contrasting the words "general" and "special" that a clear-cut demarcation will ever be established between sociology and the specific social sciences. Therefore we might consider this distinction to be impossible had not an attempt been made recently by Simmel in Germany to establish it on an apparently different principle.

According to this writer, the distinction between these two kinds of investigation lies in the fact that the specific sciences study what takes place in society, and not the society itself. The phenomena with which they are concerned (religious, moral, juridical, etc.) occur within groups. But the groups within which they take place should be the subject of a different investigation, independent of those that have gone before, which is none other than sociology. Living in society, men pursue, under the protection of the society which they constitute, all sorts of varied ends, some religious, others economic, aesthetic, etc., and the specific sciences have as their explicit subject matter the special *processes* through which these ends are achieved. But these *processes* are not in themselves social, or at least only indirectly possess this character because they unfold in an environment which is itself properly a collective one. The corresponding sciences are therefore not truly sociological. In other words, in this *complexus* called society there are two kinds of elements which require to be very carefully distinguished from each other: there is the content, namely the various phenomena which occur between individuals in association together; and then there is the "container," namely the association itself within which these phenomena are observed. The association is the only expressly social thing, and sociology is the science of association *in abstracto*. "Sociology must seek its problems not in the matter of social life, but in its form . . . It is upon this abstract consideration of social forms that rests the right of sociology to exist, just as geometry owes its existence to the possibility of abstracting from material things their spatial shapes."

But how may this process of abstraction be accomplished? Since any human association is formed with particular ends in view, how may the association itself be isolated from the various ends that it serves, so as to determine the laws which govern it? "By comparing associations designed for very different goals and sifting out what they have in common. In this way all the differences presented by the special ends around which societies are constituted cancel each other out and the social form alone emerges. Thus a phenomenon such as the formation of party groups is noticeable in the artistic world as well as in political circles, in industry as in religion. If therefore one investigates what is to be discovered in all such cases despite the diversity of ends and interests, then the kinds that exist, and the laws which govern this particular mode of grouping, can be ascertained. The same method would allow one to study combination and subordination, the formation of hierarchies, the division of labor, competition, etc."[18]

Indeed, there can certainly be no question of denying to sociology the right to constitute itself by this method of residues. There exists no science which constitutes itself in any other way. Only the process of abstraction must be carried out methodically and things must be divided up according to their natural articulations. To classify facts into distinct categories, and above all to assign them to different sciences, they must not be of the same character nor be so mutually interlinked that one fact cannot be explained without another. To justify the definition of sociology proposed to us it is thus not enough to invoke the example of sciences which proceed by the method of abstraction. One must demonstrate that the kind of abstracting to which one resorts is indeed in conformity with the nature of things.

Yet by what right do we separate so drastically the "container" of society from its content? It is certainly absolutely true that not everything which occurs in society is social. But it is acknowledged that this does not hold good for everything not only produced in society *but by it*. To justify ruling out from sociology the various phenomena which constitute the very stuff of social life, we should therefore have to establish that they are not the work of the community, but that, having arisen from very different origins, they fill out and make use of the frameworks that society offers them. But it is difficult to perceive why the collective traditions and practices of religion, law, morality and political economy should be any less social than the external forms of the collectivity. On the contrary, no matter how little we come into contact with these facts, one cannot but feel present the hand of society, which organizes them and whose stamp they plainly bear. They are society itself, living and active, for a society is characterized by its law, morality and religion, etc. Thus we are in no way justified in placing them beyond the pale of sociology. Such a clear-cut opposition of what "contains" society and the content of society is indeed especially inconceivable, from Mr. Simmel's own viewpoint. If, with other sociologists, he were to admit that society as a body has its own peculiar mode of operation which is not to be confused with individual interactions, the forms of the association could be considered as the result *sui generis* of that operation. Consequently it would not be contradictory to allow for the possibility of their being studied divorced from the things to which they apply, since they would not be derived from them. But it so happens that Simmel rebuts this conception. For him society is not an active, productive cause.[19] It is merely the result of action and reaction between the parts, that is, between individuals. In other words, it is content which determines the nature of what contains it, it is the matter which produces the form. But then how would it be possible to understand anything about this form if that matter which constitutes its entire reality were abstracted from it?

Not only is there nothing methodical about such an abstraction, since its effect is to separate things which are essentially inseparable, but also what is abstracted in this way is completely indeterminate. At first sight one might think that by *social forms* or *forms of association* Simmel means the morphological aspect of societies, namely, their geographical basis, their population mass and density, the composition of secondary groups and their distribution over the area occupied by a society. Indeed this would certainly seem to be "what contains society," and using the term in this way would have a precise meaning. Yet if one refers to the examples that Simmel himself gives to illustrate his thinking it will be seen that for him the word has a totally different signification: the division of labor, competition, the condition of individual dependence on the group, imitation and opposition—these are in no way morphological phenomena. Finally, in so far as it is possible to clarify a concept which at bottom remains extremely ambiguous, it would seem that by social forms must simply be understood the most general types of relationships of all kinds established within a society. In certain respects they can be compared to molds whose very specific relationships reproduce the shape and consequently constitute the content. In this way the expressions employed would be explicable. But it can be seen that these are pure metaphors whose appropriateness is extremely questionable. In reality "what contains" and "what is contained" here do not exist, but are two aspects of social life, the one more general, the other more specific. Thus, in slightly different form, we come back to the conception which differentiates between sociology and the social sciences by the differing levels of generality of their object.

Yet we have seen the objections that this conception arouses; here they are even more compelling. As well as it being difficult to understand why facts of the same nature should be placed into different classifications and attributed to separate sciences for the sole reason that they are of unequal generality, no rule or objective criterion allows one to determine the degree of generality that a phenomenon must possess for it to be considered sociological. Must it be found in all societies, or only in some, in all spheres of social life, or only in a number? A form of organization observed in only a small number of peoples, such as the institution of caste, or which is peculiar to a single organ of society, such as the separation of the members of a church into the ordained and the laity—must such a form be ruled out of sociology, no matter how essential it may be? We have no means of answering these questions; it is the author's whim which decides. According to his predilections and way of seeing things, he enlarges or narrows the ambit of social facts. Although secret societies are peculiar to very clearly defined social strata, it is reckoned that "they raise a sociological problem," "provided that one holds a sufficiently broad idea of the forms of society."[20] Already political organization is a special form of social organization, an aristocracy itself, a special form of political organization, and yet aristocracy is held to be one of the subjects of sociology. Moreover, the sociologist demands the right to study, in addition to the general form of association, the determinations that it assumes "under the influence of the particular subject matter through which it realizes itself." By virtue of this the means are afforded of rolling back indefinitely the boundaries of the science so as to include, if so desired, even all that content which ought to have been carefully excluded from it. This is because the relationships in which it consists are determinations of those more general relationships known as forms, in the same way as the forms express what is most general in the particular determinations. But then, where does one call a halt? Thus, under the pretext of delimiting narrowly the field of research, this is abandoned to arbitrary judgment, to the entire circumstances of the individual temperament. Not only are its bounds fluctuating, but it is impossible to discern why they should be drawn at one point rather than another. Moreover, this extreme indeterminateness with which we reproach Simmel is not simply logically implicit and entirely inherent in his principles, but indeed does characterize all his work. The problems raised in it do not relate to determinate categories of facts: they are general themes for philosophical meditation.

Each study gives an overall view of society considered from a particular aspect. Society is studied now from the viewpoint of differentiation, now from that of its conservation.[21] Elsewhere it is treated from the viewpoint of the distribution of individuals into superiors and subordinates.[22] As the spirit moves him the questions with which he deals, because of their very imprecision, expand or contract. The most varied facts, the most disparate facts, are assembled. In such conditions it is therefore understandable that there can be no regular proof, for proof is only possible in so far as the scientist is dealing with a precise subject.

Thus, however conceived, to separate sociology from the social sciences is to separate it from reality, or at least to remove it farther from it. It reduces it to being no more than a formal, vague philosophy, and consequently deprives it of the distinctive characteristics of all positive science. And it is certainly to this unnatural separation that must be attributed the alarming state in which sociological studies are to be found today. Indeed, one cannot fail to recognize that, in spite of the relatively abundant output of studies, the impression is conveyed of marking time, and this cannot continue for long without the studies becoming discredited. The objective every sociologist sets himself is the construction of a complete theory of society. Now such macro-systems plainly may merely comprise the views of one mind, which, whatever interest they may otherwise have, at least all have a serious drawback: they depend too closely on the personality and temperament of the individual author to be easily detachable from him. Thus, since each thinker is confined within his own dogma, any division of labor, or indeed any continuity in research, becomes impossible, and consequently so does any progress. To succeed in progressively mastering so vast and complex a reality, the greatest number of researchers possible must at every moment have a share in the task; successive generations must even be capable of co-operating in it. Yet such co-operation is only possible if problems are distinguished within that undivided generality, thus becoming differentiated and specialized.

III

The lesson to be learned therefore from the present state of sociology is in no way that the Comtean conception of it was sterile, or that the idea of a positive science of societies, comparable to biology, should be abandoned. On the contrary, that idea still holds all its value today, and must be resolutely adhered to. Only, to prove fruitful, it must be applied to the appropriate subject matter, namely the totality, without exception, of social facts. There is no reason to isolate one aspect or another of it so as to make it especially the subject of a new science; in the same way, biology does not deal with one aspect of living phenomena rather than another. Sociology is nothing if it is not the science of societies considered concurrently in their organization, functioning and development. All that goes into the constitution or process of their development lies within the province of the sociologist. Such multitudinous phenomena can clearly only be studied through the medium of the limited number of special disciplines among which social facts are scattered. Since these disciplines are mutually complementary, sociology can only be the system of the sociological sciences.

Yet this is not to state that this is only a new label applied to a category of things existing for a long time, nor that Comte's reform was purely terminological. The term "sociology" sums up and implies a whole new set of ideas, namely that social facts are interdependent and above all must be treated as natural phenomena, subject to necessary laws. To state that the different social sciences must become special branches of sociology is thus to postulate that they must themselves be positive sciences, bathed in the spirit by which the other sciences of nature advance, inspired by the methods the latter use, yet retaining their own autonomy. But the social sciences arose outside the circle of natural sciences. Preceding in time the sociological idea, by this very fact they were not subject to its influence. To integrate them into sociology is thus not merely to impose a new generic name upon them, but to indicate that they must be turned toward a different direction. That notion of natural law—and Comte's great merit was that he extended it to the social realm in general—must be used to illuminate the detailed facts, permeating those specific areas of research from which it was originally missing, and yet into which it cannot penetrate without effecting their complete renovation. We believe this to be the present task of the sociologist and also the true way to continue the work of Comte and Spencer. It preserves their basic principle but imparts to it its complete value by the fact that it is no longer applied to a limited category of social phenomena which have been chosen more or less arbitrarily, but to the whole domain of social life.

Far from such an undertaking coming down merely to an enrichment of vocabulary, on first appearances fears might more legitimately be entertained that it would be too difficult to encompass save in the remote future. Indeed, given the original hostility between sociology and the so-called social sciences (history, political economy, etc.), it might appear that the latter cannot take on a sociological character without a veritable revolution, which would clear the board of everything that at present exists, and draw out from nothing a whole body of sciences which have as yet no existence. If this were to be the task of sociology it would be a singularly arduous one, the issue of which would be uncertain. Yet what renders that task easier and even gives grounds for the hope of speedy results, is the changes that have spontaneously occurred over the last fifty years in the key ideas which have inspired specialists in the social sciences.

They have begun to turn toward sociology of their own accord. Within this special group there has been carried out work of great importance, which, without being accomplished by sociologists proper, is assuredly destined to affect profoundly the future development of sociology. Awareness of this is important not only because this spontaneous development proves that progress is possible—and that, as we have demonstrated, is urgent—but because it allows us to understand better how this should and can be realized.

First of all, we need not expatiate on the great transformation that has occurred in historical method in the course of this century. Beyond the particular, the contingent events, the succession of which would seem to constitute the history of societies, historians have sought something more fundamental and permanent, which their research could grasp with greater assurance. This was found in institutions. Indeed institutions are to these external occurrences what for the individual are the nature and mode of functioning of the physical organs to the processes of all kinds which daily fill our life. Through this alone history ceases to be a narrative study and lays itself open to scientific analysis. The facts which have either been eliminated or relegated to the background are the least amenable of all collective manifestations to science, being essentially specific to each individual society at any given moment in its development. They present no analogy, as between societies or even within the same society. Wars, treaties, the intrigues of courts and assemblies, the actions of statesmen, are combinations of events which always lack any resemblance to one another. Thus they can only be narrated and, rightly or wrongly, appear to flow from no definite law. At least we can state with assurance that if these laws exist they are among the most difficult to discover. By contrast, institutions, although continuing to evolve, preserve their essential character over long periods of time, sometimes even over the entire existence of one society, for they express what is most deeply constitutional in any social organization. On the other hand, once the veneer of specific facts which concealed their internal structure had been stripped back, we could show that the structure, although varying to a greater or lesser degree from country to country, none the less presented striking similarities in different societies. Thus comparisons became possible and comparative history was born. Germanicists and Latin scholars such as Maurer and Wilda in Germany established concordances between the laws of the various Germanic peoples, between Teutons and Romans. By comparing classical texts dealing with the organization of Greek and Roman cities, Fustel de Coulanges succeeded in establishing in its essentials the abstract type of the city. With Sumner Maine, an even more extensive field of comparison included, as well as Greece and Italy, India, Ireland and the Slav nations, and unsuspected similarities emerged between peoples who up to then had been held to possess no traits in common.

Nothing testifies better to the importance of the scientific transformations just noted than the development undergone by political economy during the nineteenth century. Influenced by different ideas, moreover ill-defined, but which can be reduced to two main types, with German economists it lost some of the features which had enabled Comte to contrast it to sociology as being the prime type of an ideological construct. In order to establish the legitimacy of protectionism, and more generally of state economic influence, List reacted both against individualism and the cosmopolitan nature of liberal economics. His book, *The National System of Political Economy*, was based on the principle that between humanity and the individual stands the *nation*, with its language, literature, institutions, customs and past. Classical economics fashioned a world that does not exist, the *Güterwelt*, a world in isolation, everywhere uniform, in which the clash of purely individual forces would be resolved according to ineluctable economic laws. In reality individuals strive to accumulate wealth within widely differing societies; the nature of their effort changes, and their success is uneven, according to the characteristics of the society in which they work. The practical consequence of this principle is that the state, through the reforms it introduces and its external policy, affects individual economic behavior. The theoretical consequence is that economic laws vary from people to people and therefore that a *national economy*, based upon observation, must be substituted for an abstract one founded upon *a priori* suppositions. The concept of the *nation* is undoubtedly an obscure, mystical idea, and the very definition of a national economy rules out the possibility of truly scientific laws, since its object is conceived of as unique, thereby excluding comparisons. List had nevertheless made an important advance by introducing into economic speculation the idea that society is a real being, and that the manifestations of its own life comprise relationships interacting with economic phenomena.

Socialism *of the chair*, also seeking to impart a theoretical foundation to its political conception of the state's role, has taken up and perfected List's idea. To state that individual economic activity depends upon social phenomena is insufficient; we must add that it is only by a process of abstracting that we can talk of individual economic activity. What is real is the *Volkswirtschaft*, the economic activity of society, which has its own ends for economics, just as for morality or jurisprudence. It is this *Volkswirtschaft* which is the immediate subject of economic science, which is essentially concerned with societal interests and only consequentially with those of the individual. Here political economy, if it still maintains its normative rather than speculative character, is at least clearly conceived as being a social science, whose subject matter is social phenomena in their own right, of the same nature as juridical institutions and customs, already acknowledged to be joined by bonds of interdependence.

Another advance, indissolubly linked to the above, was accomplished at the same time. The historical mind is directed toward all those special characteristics which mark off one society and one era from another: hence the concept of a *national economy* was to find in history arguments against the universalist theories of the school of classical economists. From its origins List invokes the historical method. Moreover Roscher, the founder of the historical school, does not divorce the study of economic facts from that of juridical ones in particular, nor from social facts in general: language, religion, art, science, law, the state and the economy are various facets of a whole which consists in the national life. However, this school has had an original influence on the evolution of political economy. It has adopted an attitude more distinctly speculative. Without ever having entirely abandoned the idea of historical research as a means of judging the value of a given political action in any given political circumstances, it has interested itself in facts remote both in space and time, attempting to study them solely with a view to understanding them. To some extent it has introduced comparisons into economic history; among its more recent exponents, Schmoller has formulated clearly the idea that economic laws are inductive; another, Bücher, has sketched out a classification of *economic systems*, thus constituting abstract types to which, by their economic organization, all peoples, past and present, might belong. Both—particularly Bücher—are no longer content to study historical societies but are already demanding from ethnography information regarding the economic constitution of more primitive societies.

However, what constitutes the great innovation of the century, even more than this renewal of history and economics, is the appearance of an entire array of new disciplines which, by the very nature of the problems they set, were led from the outset to establish principles and to practice methods hitherto unknown.

Firstly, there are the two related sciences, anthropology or ethnography on the one hand, and the science or history of civilizations on the other. From the dawn of the century Humboldt, relying upon facts already gathered together, had been able to proclaim as a fundamental axiom the unity of the human mind. This implied the potentiality for comparing the various historical artifacts of human activity. This postulate once accepted, in order to establish the unity of the different civilizations of man, it naturally led to their study and classification, at the same time as those of races and languages. This was the task of Klemm in Germany, with his *Kulturgeschichte*, and of Prichard in England, with his *Natural History of Man*. The building up of the archaeology of pre-history strikingly confirmed that the human race in very ancient times must have everywhere had to pass through a condition akin to that in which have remained the savages whom we can observe today; this likewise contributed to enlarging the scope of these studies and to reinforcing their methods. No longer was it solely the unity of the human spirit which was thus demonstrated; it was also the relatively identical nature of human evolution. After the impulsion was given, ethnographical studies multiplied, focusing attention on the remarkable similarities between the most diverse peoples. This was already emerging from the incomplete but nevertheless encyclopedic studies of Schoolcraft[23] and Bancroft.[24] But above all it was highlighted in the great work of Waitz and Gerland,[25] which synthesized the ethnographical and anthropological labors of a whole era.

However, these syntheses were almost exclusively descriptive. The first essay in explanatory systematization was attempted in the field of juridical phenomena. Discoveries relating to the history of the family largely brought this about. However disputable were the theories of Bachofen, Morgan, MacLennan, etc. in certain respects, they proved from the evidence the existence of forms of the family very different from those known up to then, as well as their generality. A not unimportant fact was the remarkable identity between kinship designations in Australia with the Red Indians in North America. The resemblances between the Iroquois clans and the Roman *gentes*, although exaggerated by Morgan, were none the less not entirely fictitious. Similarities of the same kind were confirmed in relation to the laws regarding crime and property. Thus a school of comparative law was founded whose task was precisely to distinguish concordances, classify them systematically, and seek to explain them. This was the school of *ethnological jurisprudence* or *juridical ethnology*, of which Hermann Post may be considered the founder and to which are likewise linked the names of Kohler, Bernhoeft, and even Steinmetz.

The study of religions underwent an almost identical revolution. With the assistance of comparative grammar, Max Müller had founded a "comparative mythology," but this comparative study long remained limited only to the historical religions of the Aryan peoples. Under the influence of ethnography and anthropology (or ethnology, as the English term it), the field of comparison was broadened. Numerous scientists— Mannhardt in Germany, Tylor, Lang, Robertson Smith, Frazer and Sidney Hartland in England, and Wilken in Holland—assembled a large number of facts which tended to demonstrate the uniformity of religious beliefs and practices over the whole of humanity. Armed with the theory of *survival*, the same writers annexed at a stroke for the comparative science of religions the whole body of facts relating to *folklore* or *Volkskunde* which the Germans had observed, recorded and compared since the beginning of the century, and which thereby took on a new significance. The agricultural customs of our countries, magical practices, ideas concerning the dead, tales and legends, all appeared to be the residue of ancient cults and beliefs. Thus the religions of the most highly cultured societies and those of the lowest tribes were linked, each serving to explain the other.

What emerged from all these investigations was the fact that social phenomena could no longer be deemed the product of fortuitous combinations, arbitrary acts of the will, or local and chance circumstances. Their generality attests to their essential dependence on general causes which, everywhere that they are present, produce their effects. These effects are always the same, endowed with a degree of necessity equal to that of other natural causes. Ethnological jurisprudence, asserts Post, "has discovered in the juridical life of all natural peoples widespread parallels which cannot be ascribed to purely chance occurrences but must be considered as general manifestations of human nature. This discovery confirms one of the most basic propositions of modern ethnology, namely, that it is not we who think, but the world which thinks in us."[26] Moreover, historical analysis itself, which has become increasingly more penetrating, has finally acknowledged the impersonal character of the forces which dominate history. Beneath what was once held to be the preponderant influence of princes, statesmen, legislators and men of genius of every kind, was discovered that of the masses, which was much more decisive. It was realized that legislation is only the codification of popular morals and customs, a legislation which cannot survive unless it takes root in the minds of peoples. Furthermore, it was realized that the morals, customs and spirit of peoples are in no way things which can be created at will, but are the work of the peoples themselves. One has even gone so far as to attribute an important role to societies in a field which might not unreasonably be regarded as more especially reserved to individuals, namely, that of art and literature. Literary monuments such as the Bible, the Homeric poems and other great national epics were ascribed to an obscure and indeterminate multitude of anonymous collaborators. Yet if peoples have their own ways of thinking and feeling, this mental life can become an object of scientific study, just as that of individuals. Thus a new science arose in Germany whose purpose was to study the outcomes of this special psychological activity: *Völkerpsychologie*, or the psychology of peoples, was founded by Lazarus and Steinthal. Although the results obtained by these researchers may be esteemed to be somewhat meager, the attempt in itself was nevertheless a significant fact.[27]

Finally, a science which was only just beginning to emerge when the *Cours de philosophie positive* was being written, but one which has undergone extensive development over the last thirty years, started to make an important contribution to these conceptions: this was statistics. In fact statistics demonstrates the existence of these general and impersonal forces by measuring them. As soon as it was established that every people has its own birth-rate, marriage rate, crime rate, etc., which can be computed numerically, and which remain constant so long as the circumstances are unchanged, but which vary from one people to another, it became apparent that these different categories of acts relating to births, marriages, crimes, suicides, etc. do not depend only upon individual capriciousness but express permanent and well-defined social states whose intensity can be measured. The stuff of social life, in what seemed to be its most fluctuating aspect, thus took on a consistency and stability which naturally called for scientific investigation. Where for a long time there had been perceived only isolated actions, lacking any links, there was found to be a system of definite laws. This was already expressed in the title of the book in which Quételet expounded the basic principles of the statistics of morality: *Du système social et des lois qui le régissent.*

IV

However hasty and incomplete this outline may be, the fact emerges that from now on the sociological idea is no longer entirely and exclusively the monopoly of sociologists alone. It is clearly evident that the various scientific ventures we have just discussed lead increasingly toward the same conception. Whether implicitly or explicitly, they all rest on the principle that social phenomena obey certain laws and that these laws can be determined. The specialization that sociology needs in order to become a truly positive science does not constitute a kind of massive task without historical antecedents. On the contrary, it is the natural sequel to a whole movement. There need be no question of inventing and creating *de novo* some discipline or another not yet known. For the most part it will suffice to develop a certain number of existing disciplines in the direction toward which they are spontaneously tending.

Yet however real this spontaneous evolution may be, what still remains to be done is considerable. Preparation for the necessary work has been made, but the work has not been completed. Because the specialist scientists have a closer acquaintance with the facts, they have a stronger sense of the diversity and complexity of things, and are consequently less inclined to be content with simplistic formulas and facile explanations. On the other hand, as they have not first surveyed overall the ground to be explored, they proceed somewhat at random, without being fully aware of the goal to be attained nor of the closeness of the links which bind them to one another and make them fellow-workers in the same task. The upshot is that on many points they do not form a conception of their science which is truly adequate for its subject.

First, because these various disciplines have been constituted in isolation and almost in ignorance of each other, the manner in which they have divided up the social domain is not always in accordance with the nature of things. Thus, for example, geography and "demology" (the science of population) have until recently remained strangers to each other, and only now are beginning to become intermeshed. Yet both study the same object, namely the material substratum of society. For what else essentially constitutes the body social if it is not the social space, together with the population that occupies that space? Two orders of facts are here inextricably linked. How the density of a society varies depends on whether it is spread over a larger or smaller area, the configuration of its territory, the number and direction of flow of its watercourses, the location of its mountain ranges, etc. On the other hand, the external forms of social groups have varied over time and it is normally the historian who studies such variations. For example, the origin and development of rural and urban groupings is a question which is usually held to fall in the domain of the historian. Yet in order to understand thoroughly the nature and present functioning of these groupings, which is a matter dealt with by the demographer, it is indispensable to know their origins and the conditions under which they arose. Thus a whole gamut of historical studies exists which are inseparable from demography and consequently also from social geography. Now it is not merely in order that science should be a well-ordered affair that there is an advantage in drawing such fragmentary investigations out of their isolated state. For, as they are drawn together, new problems arise which otherwise would remain undetected. Ratzel's attempt has clearly demonstrated this, because its characteristic feature is precisely the sociological idea which was its premise. Since this geographer was at the same time an ethnographer and an historian, he could, for instance, perceive that the various forms which the frontiers between peoples have variously assumed might be classified into a certain number of different types, for which he later sought to determine the conditions. Thus it would be beneficial to bring together in one single science all the different research which relates to the material substratum of society. Elsewhere[28] we have suggested that this science should be termed *social morphology*. Conversely, it would be easy to show that other disciplines whose relationship with each other is only indirectly maintained are so jumbled together as to form an amalgam devoid of any unity. Who could say with precision of what consists the *Kulturgeschichte* of the Germans, their *Völkerpsychologie* or their *Volkskunde*? How could such heteroclite research, made up of such disparate elements, employ a method that had any precision? For the kind of method, since it stands always in a direct relationship to its subject, can be no more determinate than its subject.

But this same state of fragmentation has yet another consequence, perhaps of a more general nature: it prevents these various sciences from being social in anything but name. Indeed for this term not to be more than an empty epithet, their basic principle should be that all the phenomena they treat are social, that is, manifestations of one and the same reality, which is society. Those phenomena alone which possess this character should be noted by the observer; the explanation of them should consist in demonstrating how they depend upon the nature of societies and the special way in which this is expressed. Either directly or indirectly, they should always be related to that nature. So long as the specialists remain locked within their respective specialities, they cannot communicate in the light of this key idea. As each one studies only a portion of the whole, but which he takes for the whole itself, an adequate notion of that whole—society—escapes him. They state that the phenomena which they treat are social, because they are patently produced within associations of human beings. But very rarely is society considered to be the determining cause of the facts for which it is the arena. For instance, we have mentioned the progress that the science of religions has made, yet it is still utterly exceptional for religious systems to be considered as conditional upon determinate social systems. Religious beliefs and practices are invariably presented to us as the outcome of sentiments arising and developing within the individual consciousness, whose expression alone, because it is external, assumes social forms. It is the impressions left on the mind by the spectacle of the great cosmic forces, by the experience of sleep and death, which probably constituted the raw material of religion. Juridical anthropology, for its part, has declared that law is a social function and has chiefly sought to link it to certain general attributes of human nature. From the similarities which juridical institutions present in different societies, the scientists of this school have seen proof that a juridical consciousness exists in humanity. It is this prime, basic consciousness that they have set out to discover. Post, for instance, expressly presents us with "the legal systems of different peoples of the earth as the form assumed by the universal juridical consciousness of humanity as it has been imprinted on each separate collective mind."[29] This is to admit *a posteriori* a natural law which preceded the formation of societies—one implied, at least logically, in the moral consciousness of every human being. On this view social factors can no longer be invoked save to demonstrate how this primitive, universal and basic nucleus is differentiated in detail according to the various individual nationalities. As for political economy, we know how its general propositions, which it dubbed laws, remained for a very long time independent of conditions of time and place, hence therefore of all social conditions. It is true that recently, thanks to Bücher and Schmoller, economic science has been directed into a different path, because of the devising of economic types. But such attempts are isolated ones and moreover the method is still very uncertain. With Schmoller in particular are to be found, mingled in a somewhat confused eclecticism, procedures and inspirations of very diverse origins.

Even the principle of interdependence of social facts, although fairly readily admitted in theory, is far from being put into practice effectively. The moralist still studies moral phenomena as if they were separable from the juridical phenomena of which they are nevertheless a mere variation. Very rarely do jurists, for their part, realize that law is meaningless if it is detached from religion, which has given it its main distinguishing marks, and of which it is partially only a derivation. Conversely, historians of religion generally feel no need to relate the religious beliefs and practices of peoples to the political organization. This is true when a specialist has successfully perceived that the facts with which he is dealing are in solidarity with other collective manifestations. In order to determine the nature of this solidarity he is forced to elaborate once more, from his own standpoint, and incorporate into his research, all those specific sciences the help of which he requires. This is what Schmoller did in his *Grundriss der allgemeinen Volkswirtschaftslehre*. This work represents a whole sociology seen from the economic viewpoint. One realizes just how fragile must be such a synthesis of heterogeneous studies so summarily carried out, studies which demand a corresponding heterogeneity of special expertise. Only the spontaneous cooperation between all these specific sciences can impart to each one even a rough idea of the relation that each one sustains with the others.

Thus, although they tend increasingly to turn in the direction of sociology, in many respects this orientation still remains indecisive and unconscious. To work to make it more precise, to underline it, to make it more a conscious one is, we believe, the urgent problem for sociology. The sociological idea must penetrate more deeply these various technological disciplines. The latter may well be aspiring toward it spontaneously, but are groping their way forward in slow, embarrassed fashion. If this condition is fulfilled, Comte's conception will cease to be a mere intellectual vision and will become reality. For the unity of the social domain cannot find a fitting expression in a few general philosophical formulas infinitely removed from the facts and the detailed data of research. Such an idea can only have as its mechanism a body of distinct but interdependent sciences, with each possessing a sense of that solidarity. Moreover we can predict that these sciences, once they are organized, will repay philosophy with interest what they have borrowed from it. For from the relationships established between them will arise common doctrines which will constitute the soul of the organism so constituted and will become the subject of a renewed, rejuvenated social philosophy, one which will be positive and progressive, like the very sciences whose crowning glory it will be.

Notes

1. L. Lévy-Bruhl, *La philosophie d'Auguste Comte*, p. 403.
2. A. Comte, *Cours de philosophie positive*, IV, p. 215.
3. Ibid., p. 216.
4. Ibid., IV, p. 214.
5. *Social statics* consists of a very small number of theories which, all in all, remind one of the *political* philosophy of preceding centuries regarding the

family, the nature of the social bond, and that of government. Doubtless valuable information is to be found in them. Yet not only are most of the types of groups—clans, classes, castes, corporations, cities, towns, etc.—not considered, but the family, the basic social unit, is also conceived of as being invariable. The idea of a classification of the various kinds of domestic organization, which implies that of various correlations between the family and larger organizations, did not occur to Comte. Thus there were no data to give rise to discoveries, and the theory of the family was summarily dealt with.

6. The phrase is that of Tarde (*Lois de l'imitation*, p. v), who cites as his authority a philosopher, who appears to be Taine. But whoever the author, it seems to us to be only marginally scientific. We do not believe that there is a science for which a key of this kind exists. The locks must be laboriously opened, even forced, one after the other.

7. This way of conceiving sociology is so ingrained that sometimes the works of sociologists are interpreted as if they could not be conceived of in any other way. Thus we have been reproached for wanting to reduce everything to the division of labor, because we have written a book on the subject, or wishing to explain everything by collective constraint, whereas we have only seen in the coercive nature of institutions a means, perhaps not even the sole one, of defining social facts so as to determine the field of study.

8. John Stuart Mill, *Logic*, book VI, ch. X, ss. 2. The distinction between the two meanings of the word "general" has been nicely drawn by Belot in his Introduction to the sixth book of the French translation (1897), p. lxxv.

9. Ibid., book VI, ch. X, ss. 1.

10. Ibid., book VI, ch. X, ss. 7.

11. F. H. Giddings, *The Principles of Sociology*, New York, 1896, pp. 32–3.

12. Ibid., p. 33.

13. Ibid., loc. cit.

14. Giddings goes so far as to state that the social sciences are differentiated from sociology, just as the latter is from psychology and as psychology itself is from biology. Ibid., pp. 25–6.

15. Giddings, *The Principles of Sociology*, p. 79.

16. Ibid., pp. 82–7.

17. Ibid., p. 89.

18. G. Simmel, "Comment les formes sociologiques se maintiennent," *Année sociologique*, I, p. 72. Cf. by the same author, *Über soziale Differenzierung*, Leipzig, 1890, pp. 10–20, and "Le problème de la sociologie," *Revue de métaphysique*. Yr. 2, p. 497.

19. In the author's thinking there is a contradiction which seems to us insoluble. According to him sociology must include all that is produced by *society*. This seems to imply a certain efficacy on the part of the collectivity. On the other hand, he denies this efficacy to it: for him it is only a product. In the end the social forms of which he speaks have no reality in themselves, being only the pattern of underlying individual interactions, merely independent in appearance (cf. *Année sociologique*, 1, p. 74 and *Über soziale differenzierung*, p. 13). How therefore can be assigned to distinctive sciences things which are only different and independent in a superficial and mistaken view?

20. "Le problème de la sociologie," *Revue de métaphysique*, pp. 501–2, note. All the quotations which follow are drawn from the same passage.

21. "Comment les formes sociales se maintiennent."

22. "Superiority and subordination," *American Journal of Sociology*, 1896.

23. *History, Conditions and Prospects of the Indian Tribes of the United States*, 1851.

24. H.H. Bancroft, *The Native Races of the Pacific States of North America*.

25. T. Waitz and G. Gerland, *Anthropologie der Naturvölker*, 1858–72.

26. Post, *Grundriss der ethnologischen Jurisprudenz*, I, p. 4.

27. Care must be taken not to confuse the *Völkerpsychologie* of the Germans with what in France and Italy is frequently called social psychology. The latter term serves to designate in France somewhat indeterminate studies which deal with crowd psychology and also generalities of all kinds. Sometimes the word is taken as being synonymous with sociology. *Völkerpsychologie*, on the other hand, is a study whose subject matter is definite: it aims to investigate the laws of collective thought through its objective manifestations, in particular mythology and language (cf. Wundt's very recent work, *Völkerpsychologie*).

28. Cf. *Année sociologique*, vol. 2ff., 6th section.

29. "*Erscheinen dann die Rechte alter Völker der Erde als der vom Volksgeiste erzeugte Niederschlag des allgemeinen menschlichen Rechtsbewusstseins,*" *Grundriss der ethnologischen Jurisprudenz*, I, p. 4.

Debate on the Relationship Between Ethnology and Sociology (1907)*

René Worms states that, "according to the etymology, ethnology is simply the description of peoples; sociology is the science of societies. The former only assembles the materials; the latter, with the materials, builds structures. The former analyzes, the latter synthesizes. Moreover, ethnology studies only barbaric and savage societies; sociology is interested, at least as much, in civilized societies. Ethnography can only be linked to the present, for one can only describe what one has seen; sociology also takes into account the past. From all this it may be concluded that sociology borrows from ethnography a part of the facts that it elaborates, but only a part. Only, is that part the most important? There is some reason to doubt it.

"Ethnography rendered great services to sociology when the latter was formed. Thus investigations concerning the family among more civilized peoples have brought to light a multitude of forms of unions (androgamy, marriage by classes, etc.) the study of which has been particularly profitable to sociology, broadening current ideas concerning domestic organization. But today it may be that there is rather more to be gained by examining the great civilized societies of the West of the present day.

"Not only is knowledge of them of more practical use to us than knowledge of any other, but scientifically they are of greater significance because, being more complex, such societies afford richer material for research.

"Their very history, the study of preceding social forms in the same regions, is perhaps of greater importance than the description of backward tribes still extant, for it reveals both more perfect types and ones more capable of attaining perfection. Ethnographical data are not therefore the main source of information for present-day sociology."

The chairman thanks René Worms and points out that he had not come to speak himself about the problem posed in the program, but since Worms invites him to express his views, he thinks it would be churlish to refuse to do so.

"It is quite plain that sociology is not to be confused with ethnography. But for him [Durkheim] it appears impossible to restrict ethnography to being a mere descriptive study. Hardly any ethnographical works exist

* Extract from *Bulletin du Comité des travaux historiques et scientifiques. Section des sciences économiques et sociales*, 1907, pp. 199–201.

which are not explanatory as well as descriptive. If sociology goes beyond ethnography, on the other hand ethnography is a sociological science. The word 'ethnography' has moreover no definite accepted meaning. It is said to be a description whose subject is uncivilized societies; but the expression is then extremely vague, because there is no human society which does not have its civilization. We have here one of those scientific frameworks which, because they have been built up empirically, are destined to be transformed in the future, as and when the different branches of sociology become more conscious of themselves and their solid links with each other."

Finally Durkheim thinks that he must add that, in his view, the usefulness of these studies does not seem destined to grow less in the future. "The so-called lower societies have a very special interest for the sociologist: all the social forms which are observable as distinct and organized in more complex societies are to be found there in a state of interpenetration which highlights better their unity. Moreover, the functioning of more advanced societies can only be understood when we are informed about the organization of less developed societies."

Debate on Explanation in History and Sociology (1908)*

DURKHEIM: I feel a little embarrassed in replying to Seignobos's paper, for I am not very sure whether I have mastered his thought. Before setting out to him my objections I would like to know whether or not he admits the reality of the unconscious. I cannot see clearly what view he takes on that point.

SEIGNOBOS: I think that, among known phenomena, there are certainly some (for example, physiological phenomena such as the digestion) which have a spontaneous character and which undeniably exert a causal influence, but one of which we are ignorant.

DURKHEIM: In his exposition Seignobos seemed to oppose history to sociology, as if we had there two disciplines using different methods. In reality, so far as I know there is no sociology worthy of the name which does not possess a historical character. So if it were established that history cannot admit the reality of the unconscious, sociology could not say otherwise. Here there are not two methods and two opposing conceptions. What is true for history will be true for sociology. Only what must be examined carefully is whether history really does allow us to enunciate the conclusion at which Seignobos arrived: the unconscious, is it the unknown and the unknowable? Seignobos claims that this is the thesis of historians in general; but I believe that there are many who would refute that assertion. Let me mention in particular Fustel de Coulanges.

SEIGNOBOS: Fustel de Coulanges abominated the very notion of the "collective consciousness."

DURKHEIM: But at this moment we are not talking about the collective consciousness. These are two completely different problems. We can imagine the conscious and the unconscious in history without bringing in the notion of collective consciousness. The two questions are in no way related to each other. The unconscious can be unconscious in relation to the individual consciousness and yet none the less be perfectly real. So let us distinguish the two problems: the ideas of Fustel de Coulanges about the collective consciousness are completely irrelevant here. The question is to know whether in history we can really acknowledge causes other than conscious causes, those which men themselves attribute to events and to actions of which they are the agents.

---

* Extract from *Bulletin de la Société française de philosophie*, 1908, pp. 229–45.

SEIGNOBOS: But I have never said there were no other causes. I said that the conscious causes were those which we can reach most easily.

DURKHEIM: You said that the sole causes that the historian can determine with any degree of certainty are those revealed in the documents by participants or witnesses. Why are these to be privileged? On the contrary, I think that they are the most suspect of the causes.

SEIGNOBOS: But at least the witnesses or the participants saw the events, and that counts for a great deal.

DURKHEIM: We are not talking about events, but the inner motives which may have determined those events. How are these to be known? Two procedures are possible. Either we will seek to find out these motives objectively by some experimental method. Neither the witnesses nor the participants have been able to do that. Or we will seek to arrive at them by an inward-looking method, by introspection. That is the only method that witnesses and participants can apply to themselves. So it is the introspective method which you are introducing into history and that in an unrestricted fashion. But everybody knows how full the consciousness is of illusions.

For a very long time now there has no longer been any psychologist who believes that by introspection he can arrive at the deep causes. Every causal relationship is unconscious, it must be inferred after the event. By introspection we only arrive at the facts, never the causes. How then can the participants, who are mixed up with the acts themselves, how then would they be able to account for these causes? They are in the most awkward conditions in which to discover them precisely. And if this is true for individual psychical facts, how much more so is it for social events whose causes elude even more plainly the consciousness of the individual.

These causes, pointed to by the participants, far from having any kind of importance, must generally be held to be very suspect hypotheses. For my part I am aware of no case in which the participants perceived the causes accurately. To explain phenomena such as religious prohibitions, such as the *patria potestas* of the Romans, would you accept as well founded the reasons for them given by the Roman legal experts?

How can facts of this nature be explained unless by an experimental method which proceeds slowly and objectively? What can individual consciousness indeed know about the causes of facts so considerable and so complex?

SEIGNOBOS: We are not talking about the same facts. I am speaking simply about events, historical facts which have occurred only once.

DURKHEIM: But what would be said about a biologist who considered his science as merely a story about the events of the human body, without studying the functions of that organism? What is more, you yourself have spoken about religions, customs and institutions.

SEIGNOBOS: I have spoken about them as second-order phenomena that the historian arrives at, but concerning which he already feels much more ill at ease.

DURKHEIM: But you can understand absolutely nothing about events as such, about facts, developments and changes, you cannot understand what you call first-order phenomena, unless above all you know the religions and institutions which are the skeleton of society.

SEIGNOBOS: That's as may be.

DURKHEIM: At least you acknowledge that, as regards institutions, beliefs and customs, the conscious motives of the participants no longer enjoy the privileged place that you ascribe to them as regards events?

SEIGNOBOS: I am not saying here that the participants' hypotheses are worthless, I am saying that there must be a lot more critical thought before these motives are allowed, for there again it is the conscious motives that we touch upon first.

DURKHEIM: So, in any case, what the historian really arrives at are the conscious causes? And everything else remains a closed book to him?

SEIGNOBOS: Not entirely a closed book, but more so than what is conscious.

DURKHEIM: So the causes which are most immediately available to the historian are the inner motives, such as they appear to the participants? Why do they enjoy this singular privileged position?

SEIGNOBOS: But that's very simple: because the participants and the witnesses afford us an explanation of the conscious acts. Undoubtedly they can be mistaken, and we must criticize their explanations. But despite everything they had the means of knowing something—one which we don't.

DURKHEIM: If we have no other means of knowing, we must give up history. If we look upon history as you do, those who do not engage in it can comfort themselves and even rejoice that they do not do so.

SEIGNOBOS: There is indeed no security or certainty in history if we claim to fathom causes. This is proved by the fact that explanations of phenomena are always different and never agree.

DURKHEIM: Your method leads to the ultimate degree of nihilism. So why then give such a large place to the teaching of history? It would mean a lot of time wasted to achieve such singularly poor results.

SEIGNOBOS: Excuse me: the function of history is to remind those who forget it of the interdependence and continual reaction occurring between various successions of facts which we tend naturally to separate into watertight compartments. And, in this way it can have a strong influence on the orientation of the mind. It demonstrates that isolated or discrete phenomena cannot ever exist.

DURKHEIM: Yet all those who engage in the study of the past know full well that the immediately perceptible motives and apparent causes are by far the least important. We must penetrate much more deeply into reality in order to understand it. Or otherwise, if there is no possibility of arriving at other causes, we must state frankly that we cannot arrive at any real cause. It is true that you distinguish between, and seem to oppose, the *cause* and the *law*. But what is a cause which is not a law? Every causal relationship is a law.

SEIGNOBOS: Not at all. There are events which have occurred only once and yet whose cause can be determined.

DURKHEIM: As soon as I have established a relationship between two terms, A and B, I have a law. We do not define a law by the generality of the cases in which it is manifest. In fact it is not necessary for the relationship to recur more or less frequently; it is sufficient for it to be of a kind capable of recurring. Logicians recognize that a law can be established on the basis of one well-conducted experiment. Once the law is established, the facts may or may not recur, but that has no theoretical importance. Certain phenomena, such as those relating to human biological monstrosities, are instructive precisely because they are unique or exceptional. So I do not see how a causal relationship cannot be established which is not a law. If I know that A is the cause of B, I know that A will always be the cause of B. The bond that joins them is confirmed as a real one regardless of time and place.

SEIGNOBOS: Yet there is nobody who doubts that Marat was stabbed. A blow from a knife can bring about someone's death. That is a cause, and I don't see any laws behind that happening.

DURKHEIM: Everybody will say that Marat died from a knife wound, unless the over-heated bath before the dagger-stabbing is found to have effected his death. In any case, it is not because the stabbing came before his death that it is seen as the cause of death. It is by virtue of the general law that a stab by a knife determines death if it reaches an essential organ. The stab is only a cause if it has *produced* this result. If another cause had produced death, the stabbing would not be held to be the cause. On this point the scientist and popular opinion are absolutely in agreement.

But I go back to the techniques for searching out causes. Is there really no other method of discovering causes save by recourse to the clues provided by witnesses or participants? Why when we are faced with human and social phenomena should we be placed in conditions more unfavorable than when faced with phenomena of nature? Why should we not, there too, seek out the causes and the laws from the outside? I exclude sociology, which is still too young a science to serve as an example. But there is psychology which has existed for a long time. In psychology one seeks to study the unconscious, and is successful without in so doing building constructs in the sky.

SEIGNOBOS: The methods of observation are very much better.

DURKHEIM: If in any field the introspective method ever seemed indispensable, it is for the very study of the individual consciousness. For, by definition, here what are studied are internal phenomena. And yet, in spite of the difficulties, the psychological study of the unconscious and the objective study of the conscious are possible and do come off. Why should either be impossible for social and historical phenomena?

SEIGNOBOS: Is it really possible to study the unconscious in psychology? I am completely unaware that it is, and I think that no certain conclusion on the matter has been reached. But in any case the psychologist has at his command research procedures which are not available to us. Firstly, he is working on human subjects, by which is meant complete facts and not fragments randomly preserved. He can observe cataleptics—and particularly the insane. The psychologist sees events unfold before him. In history, on the contrary, the very elements are missing, and we have only the reflection of events perceived and related by others. We are obliged to work on second-hand materials, since by definition we only know about things what others who have seen them tell us about them.

DURKHEIM: The work will be more difficult and complex, that's all; the procedures remain the same.

SEIGNOBOS: Not if the very elements are not available to us.

DURKHEIM: Then we must give up trying to study history. If the historical data are in any way accessible, they are comparable, and the objective method must be applied. Otherwise, history no longer exists.

SEIGNOBOS: I beg your pardon: we have available some data which are sufficient to allow us to establish relationships of cause and effect, but which do not allow us to determine and explain the unconscious.

DURKHEIM: But here we are not talking about the unconscious. That's not the difficulty. What we are dealing with is knowledge of causes, and I maintain that we cannot, in order to know the cause of an event or an institution, limit ourselves in any way to questioning solely the actors in that event and to asking for their view.

SEIGNOBOS: That's an exaggeration. There are cases in which the witnesses are not mistaken. Thus they saw clearly that William of Orange left for England because he no longer feared the armies of Louis XIV.

DURKHEIM: I am not saying that these interpretations are bereft of any interest. When a sick person believes he has a temperature, his view, whether it is right or wrong, is an interesting fact that the doctor must take into consideration. Likewise here. But your example proves already that there is another method which is possible. For how would you choose between those cases where the witnesses are telling the truth and those where they are mistaken, if you have no other criterion than having recourse to witnesses? The doctor consults the sick person, he must begin there, but the person's answer must only be one fact among other facts, and all these facts require methodically to be elaborated, without any one of them being able to provide us directly and immediately with the real cause. Whatever the value of the information contained in the documents, they must be criticized and organized methodically and not merely recorded. But you see how much the question you have put is an ambiguous one. For the moment we are not discussing the conscious or the unconscious but come back to the problem which occupied us last year: the knowledge of causes in history. You have mixed up in that question some reflections upon the unconscious which are completely unrelated to it. It may be a truism, but that does not concern the problem of the unconscious in any way.

SEIGNOBOS: What I asked myself was: precisely what is the irreducible part of the unconscious in what is historically unknown?

DURKHEIM: But the two questions are completely unrelated. On this point I will go even further than you. You seem to identify the conscious and the known, as if what is made clear by the consciousness of the individual participant were more readily knowable than the rest. In reality, what is conscious is also very obscure. So I will say that the conscious and the unconscious are equally obscure and that, in both cases, the question of the method to be followed in order to arrive at a knowledge of causes is posed in identical terms.

SEIGNOBOS: And yet there are conscious phenomena which are not unknown. Take the case of languages.

DURKHEIM: Clearly words are known, but what meaning is placed behind the words? There is nothing more difficult to discover.

What we must look for is a means of comparing historical data, and establishing series of phenomena which vary on parallel lines; it is by these methodical comparisons that it is possible to discover causes. And I think we can succeed in doing so. You are really forgetting that over the last fifty years we have made a lot of progress in comparative history: that is a whole positive achievement that you seem totally to fail to recognize.

SEIGNOBOS: But also systems fall apart every twenty years.

DURKHEIM: If you want to show that science is always in a perpetual state of evolution. I think that we are in agreement on that point. Everybody admits that science progresses slowly and never establishes more than probabilities. But as soon as there are in history a certain number of positive data, as soon as you deem those data sufficient to provide the threads of an historical account, why should they be insufficient when one needs to institute a methodical comparison? Nowhere are ready-made causes to be found; it must always be the mind that uncovers them, and to do so one must proceed methodically. Why, because historical documents must be minutely criticized, because they are brief, incomplete, fragmentary, should one conclude that a science of history is impossible? But, if we look closely, the gap between the phenomena of life and what occurs in biology is no less great than the gap between social life and what occurs in the practice of history. This is the position in every science.

SEIGNOBOS: On the contrary, what is retained in the documents is infinitesimal if we think about the host of past events. In biology we are dealing with concrete entities; in history we have only fragments of events.

DURKHEIM: What is to prevent you from comparing the fragments? You yourself acknowledge their solid links, since you group them according to ages and build up from them a picture of the past.

SEIGNOBOS: We have the vague impression that several series of phenomena change at the same time, but . . .

DURKHEIM: When I find that, in a number of well observed and well studied cases, a particular kind of family organization is linked to a particular kind of social organization, why should you prevent my establishing a relationship between these two series of phenomena?

SEIGNOBOS: Because we are almost never dealing with sufficiently analogous phenomena to allow of a comparison.

DURKHEIM: But after all they are facts; I find them so, and you know how often one finds striking similarities between institutions of different peoples.

SEIGNOBOS: Such peoples are always very profoundly different.

DURKHEIM: But when, in studying marriage, I find, at very different points on the globe, identical formalities and ceremonies comparable in every respect, when I find that men and women live together in the same way, do you think that there is nothing worthwhile to compare? What do you therefore conclude from all that?

SEIGNOBOS: Nothing. I do not know the cause of these similarities.

LACOMBE: Seignobos seems to forget that the documents, consulted in themselves and in isolation, would never succeed in authenticating the facts. On the contrary, it is the generality and the resemblances between the facts which authenticate the documents. Without a comparison, there can be no certainty. Let us suppose that you have one single document, apparently authentic, but which tells of a fact of which there is no other example in history. You will probably doubt the fact, and rightly so.

SEIGNOBOS: But comparison in history in the end is reduced to *analogy*; there are never complete similarities.

LACOMBE: What does that matter? Without comparison, there is no certainty. And on the other hand, it is comparison which forms the basis of our criticism and which makes it certain. When I am confronted with certain motives that historians attribute to the Ancients, I am inclined to be doubtful, because, in the men that are described to me, I do not recognize the humanity that I know. You see that comparison is always valuable.

SEIGNOBOS: Quite so! It is in fact according to vague analogies with the present that one judges and criticizes most often past phenomena, because to find really exact analogies between two series of the past and to compare them happens only rarely. For the historian, to compare means above all to juxtapose what he finds with the present time in which he is living.

LALANDE: Up to this point we have only tackled the first question, that of the knowledge of causes and the unknown in history. There remains to be examined the second question, that of knowing under what forms we must represent what, in historical causes, escapes the consciousness of the individual. This is what Seignobos was intending in the last part of his note when he asked: "Must we bring into play a cause *sui generis* . . . , the pressure exerted by the body social in the form of tradition and collective organization. This would lead one to admit the existence of a species of particular phenomena, different from individual human facts. Should we attribute common characteristics whose cause escapes us to a *Volksgeist* or *Sozialpsyche* distinct from individuals?"

DURKHEIM: That question does not seem to me to come into the one with which we are dealing. Doubtless Seignobos appears to believe that the collective consciousness has been dreamed up as a way of explaining the unconscious in history. That is inexact. Firstly, one can admit that the unconscious exists, and yet deny any collective consciousness; the unconscious can be entirely individual. Then, if there is a collective consciousness, it must include conscious facts and account for them, as well as unconscious facts. For, after all, since it is a consciousness (provided we suppose it exists), it must indeed be conscious in some respects.

SEIGNOBOS: How then? I would indeed like to know where is located the place where the collectivity thinks consciously.

DURKHEIM: I have no need to tackle here the question of the collective consciousness, which goes far beyond the subject with which we are dealing. All I would say is that, if we admit the existence of a collective consciousness, we have not dreamed it up with the aim of explaining the unconscious. We thought we had discovered certain characteristic phenomena absolutely different from phenomena of individual psychology and it is by this route that we have been led to the hypothesis that you are attacking here—I hardly know why.

LALANDE: Yet it does seem that the two questions are linked: the solution of the first can depend on the solution to the second. If it is true that there exists a collective social mind, does that not rule out the method which consists in seeking the explanation of historical facts in the motives of the participants and in the consciousness they have of them? The only legitimate method would then be, as Durkheim thinks, to site oneself at an objective viewpoint, to compare series and arrive at laws by discovering that events repeat themselves.

DURKHEIM: I have not come here to expound my own method but to discuss the one Seignobos is proposing to us. But I would like to know for what reason he denies us the right to establish comparisons between historical facts.

SEIGNOBOS: In the positive sciences the elements are analogous and are precisely known, they are homogeneous and exact, so that one can then compare series of phenomena (well-defined chemical substances). In history, on the other hand, what we are comparing are quite simply things that are called or have been called the same, and such an identity of designation may be a purely verbal one. That is why I say that psychological phenomena are not comparable to one another. On the contrary, when by chance we are dealing with physical or physiological phenomena, comparison becomes possible. Thus the family can doubtless be studied more easily than other phenomena.

DURKHEIM: I must confess that I experience astonishment when I hear enunciated as self-evident a proposition which seems to me to be contradicted by all that I know about it. The starting point of domestic evolution is in no way physical. The greater part of family phenomena, as they have come down to us, do not seem to flow from the act of procreation. Procreation is not the central and constituting act for the family. The family is often a grouping of people who are not even united by the ties of blood (the element of blood relationship is often very small).

SEIGNOBOS: But that is precisely why we no longer call such a grouping a family. Historically a family is made up of elements related by blood.

BLOCH: But take the γενος in Greece. It has not been at all proved that it was made up of elements related by blood, nor that it owed its origins to consanguinity.

LACOMBE: The essential fact which classes you as a member of the family is the fact of *co-operation*. When the son leaves the father, when he no longer co-operates with him, he is no longer in the family, he even loses his right to inherit. On the contrary, he who has been received and allowed to co-operate, by this very fact enters the family. So, in the Middle Ages, when a man with no blood relationship shared hearth and board, he became a co-inheritor.

SEIGNOBOS: This discussion shows, better than I would have been able to do, the entire difficulty we have in agreeing in history, even about the most common and apparently the most clear ideas. For, after all, who can prove to me that the Greek γένοη can be assimilated to the family in the sense that we understand the word?

BLOCH: You say that it is not proved. But, if the Greek γένοη is not the family in the present meaning of the word, one can at least allow that it takes the place of it and that it has been conceived of in imitation of the family.

DURKHEIM: Or conversely, that the limited family of today has been conceived of in imitation of the γενος.

BLOCH: I am really frightened at the skepticism of Seignobos. If one listens to him, what would remain of history? Almost nothing. But, from another viewpoint, I think, contrary to Durkheim, that there is a profound distinction to be drawn between the methods capable of being used in history and those of the other sciences. We must study historical phenomena as they have been given to us once and for all, for, whatever we may do, we shall never succeed in repeating them. Hence the difficulty that we have in history, in formulating laws, and the impossibility of admitting, as does Durkheim, that causes are identifiable with laws. That is true in the other sciences but here, as repetition is impossible, since we cannot isolate what is essential from what is secondary, things are different.

We shall perhaps be able to enunciate laws, so long as they concern very simple and crude historical facts (such as, for example, the facts of human geography), but we must abandon the attempt as soon as we touch upon such various and complex psychological facts.

DURKHEIM: Then we must also give up formulating causal relationships.

BOUGLÉ: Like Durkheim, I think that every causal explanation, in order really to be an explanation, cannot fail to refer to laws.

It is true that historians very often believe that they are explaining certain phenomena by the causes alone, having left laws out of account. This merely means that they leave obscure and without spelling them out the laws on which their assertions rely.

Sometimes, however, they formulate laws in spite of themselves; they are thus caught in the act of being sociologists. Thus recently, in a book by Bloch, I came across this general proposition concerning the remnants of client peoples who survived in ancient Gaul: "The regime of 'protection' is imposed and predominates every time that the state shows itself to be unequal to its task, namely incapable of ensuring the security of individuals, either because it has not yet fully constituted itself or because it has already begun to break up." Examples of this kind could be multiplied. They tend to prove that one cannot explain without invoking laws.

BLOCH: This is indeed an insuperable tendency which the historian resists with difficulty, but it only shows that we should be more prudent and hedge our assertions round with more reservations than we do.

DURKHEIM: In the end I believe I am in agreement with Bloch, on condition that we distinguish between two things that are utterly different and which the historian of modern times does not distinguish between sufficiently: (1) historical events, and (2) permanent social functions. So far as events are concerned, we are presented with an indefinite mountain of facts, in whose midst the mind can only introduce with difficulty some scientific order. I admire the historians who can live comfortably amid this chaos of disordered events.

But beyond the events, there are the functions, the institutions, the ways, fixed and organized, of thinking and acting. In that domain comparisons become possible: instead of being overwhelmed by the extreme diversity of the given facts, one is soon struck by the very limited number of types, by the kind of poverty manifest when the same function is studied in different peoples or in different eras. Up to now I have only been able to carry this out for types of family, but I have noted, through the ages, a very small number of distinct types. And a type of family is in solidarity with the whole social organization. Thus it must be roughly the case for the other functions which together make up the collectivity. It is true that I have not been able to study every society and I have had to eliminate and leave many facts out of account. But it is nevertheless striking how one can coordinate and reduce to a few large but very simple forms the family institutions of a great number of peoples. Their identity is extremely remarkable and well shows up the possibility of a true historical science. For other functions doubtless the task would be more complex, but the difficulties do not appear to be insuperable. In any case the historian has the right and the duty to undertake this work, instead of giving up in despair.

SEIGNOBOS: Unfortunately there is a fundamental difficulty which makes such attempts singularly hazardous: it is that we have no method of constructing really precise categories that are comparable; we never know exactly what we are comparing. Such juxtapositions may be ingenious and suggestive, but there is nothing at all scientific about them.

LACOMBE: This is because you are too demanding or too ambitious, you are always wanting to compare large masses of facts and events with each other. We should begin by analyzing and comparing fragments. For instance, I propose to show the similar repercussions caused in different times and places by the same type of land cultivation.

SEIGNOBOS: Clearly there are simpler phenomena, for which a fairly restricted number of combinations are possible (for example, family organization). But if we take political life or languages, here there is no longer anything save indeterminateness.

BOUGLÉ: But in the study of languages they have succeeded precisely in distinguishing laws and establishing meaningful relationships.

SEIGNOBOS: They have hardly discovered more than the laws of phonetics, and even then because there was a physiological substratum which allowed the use of experimental methods, and even graphical ones.

DURKHEIM: On the contrary, many linguists believe that one might with advantage introduce a sociological viewpoint into the study of languages.

SEIGNOBOS: But that can only bring obscurity into them. What can we understand about the social mechanism of ancient collectivities? Very little, and then solely by means of analogies with our society today.

DURKHEIM: It seems to me on the other hand that we understand Australian (aboriginal) societies much better than our own.

SEIGNOBOS: We don't mean the same thing by the word "understand." For my part, it seems that we understand much better present-day societies than Australian ones. It is probably a question of imagination. I only regret that we do not succeed in studying directly the question of the unconscious.

BOUGLÉ: But you seem to persist in believing that the unconscious can be assimilated to the unknown. Why do you refuse to apply to unconscious motives the research procedures that you apply to conscious motives? The bases of your research are the same, the reasoning processes that you employ to induce the causes of actions and events are as valid for unconscious causes as for the others.

SEIGNOBOS: That's not so. When unconscious motives are in question I can find out nothing. I draw a blank.

BOUGLÉ: If you'll pardon me, our personal experience reveals to us equally well both unconscious and conscious motives. Does it not teach us that many of our actions can only be explained by causes which, at the moment the action occurs, did not occur to our consciousness at all? We are continually perceiving after the event the motives of an action which had escaped us. Thus we can just as well discover in the past cases of unconscious motivation as cases of conscious motivation.

SEIGNOBOS: Not so, because the experiences that you are talking about are not set down in the documents which relate the events and their apparent causes.

BOUGLÉ: But the unconscious causes are just as much—or just as little— to be found in the documents as the conscious causes. In both cases you don't just transcribe the document, you try to understand and reconstruct the state of mind of its author. Take Livy's history. I think that the unconscious motives which direct him are to be read just as easily as the conscious and apparent ones.

SEIGNOBOS: I haven't much faith in the possibility of reconstituting in this way the psychology of individuals or of groups.

LACOMBE: What in the world then impels you to write history?

SEIGNOBOS: To seek out relationships between series of facts and to understand the past according to the model of the present day.

LACOMBE: But behind the facts what we are always looking for is Man; agreed, this is very difficult, but the purpose is always to succeed in revealing the psychological mechanism of actions and events.

SEIGNOBOS: My purpose, very simply, is to explain, if that be possible, by what chain of well-connected events we have arrived at the present state. And in that explanation I am disposed to attribute very great importance to the motives expressed by the participants, because they have known the facts directly.

Concerning the unconscious, what I am asking is whether it can be explained by a series of inner states of individuals who act in common, or whether we must postulate the intervention of something external and superior to the individuals.

DURKHEIM: Once again, under the heading of the unconscious you are reifying an entity. I can understand that you were posing the question for all the phenomena of collective life: can they be explained by individual causes or should we allow the existence of specifically social causes? But why limit the question to unconscious phenomena?

SEIGNOBOS: Because for us they are more mysterious and because we are more inclined to concede to them causes independent of individuals.

DURKHEIM: But the fact that the events have been, or have not been, conscious phenomena is of secondary importance for the historian who is really seeking to understand and reflect. You belittle your role by hiding behind these witnesses or participants, whom you call conscious ones. So long as no methical research has been undertaken, we do not know whether such and such a phenomenon depends upon conscious and unconscious motives. So there is no criterion fixed beforehand. Such a distinction is the fruit of historical research and not a guide to it. The unconscious is often explained by the conscious, and vice versa. The unconscious is often only a lesser state of consciousness. In short, there is no particular problem posed in order to acquire knowledge of the unconscious. Really you are posing, in partial form, the great problem of sociology, that of the collective consciousness, which is too general to be tackled here.

SEIGNOBOS: I posed that question because in history we often come across inexplicable phenomena, which apparently seem to spring from unconscious causes. It is because of this phenomenon that the "historical school" and Lamprecht have postulated the influence of supraindividual realities, and I thought that it was by obeying a sentiment of the same kind that contemporary sociologists had been led to postulate a collective reality *sui generis*.

DURKHEIM: That is the mistake. I do not need to entertain hypotheses concerning the reasons which may have motivated Lamprecht. But those which have governed the contemporary sociologists to whom Seignobos is referring are completely different. And this leads me to contrast the two attitudes that you have indicated—the Voltairean attitude which confines itself to stating that there are things still unknown, and the mystical one which hypostatizes the mystery of the past—to contrast these two with a third attitude, which is the one we adopt. It consists in working methodically so as to arrive at understanding scientifically the fact, without partiality and without any imposed system.

SEIGNOBOS: But that is exactly the Voltairean attitude, the one to which I bow.

LALANDE: All in all, there can be two ways of comprehending the word "understand," that of the historian and that of the sociologist. For the historian, to understand is to represent things to oneself from the viewpoint of the psychological motivation, whose model is within ourselves at the present time. For the sociologist, on the other hand, to understand is to represent things to oneself from the viewpoint of individual cases which can be reduced to a law or at least to a general type which has already been laid down. These are two problems with no connection with each other, whose apparent contradiction derives only from the fact that they are designated by the same word, unless they are joined with other hypotheses.

DURKHEIM: In short, we do not accept as such the causes that are pointed out to us by the agents themselves. If they are true, they can be discovered directly by studying the facts themselves; if they are false, this inexact interpretation is itself a fact to be explained.

LALANDE: It seems to me that Seignobos and Durkheim are in agreement, in so far as they both admit that individuals can never be considered in isolation, before or outside society, and that they cannot even be postulated without postulating society at the same time.

DURKHEIM: Let us rest on that illusion, and let us say that Seignobos, like myself, admits that a society changes individuals.

SEIGNOBOS: Agreed, but only on condition that the society is conceived of solely as the totality of individuals.

DURKHEIM: If you prefer it, let us say that the composing of the assembled whole changes each one of the elements to be assembled together.

SEIGNOBOS: I admit that tautology.

Debate on Political Economy and Sociology (1908)*

Limousin states that political economy occupies a special place among the totality of the social sciences. It is the only one of these sciences which is at present constituted as a systematic entity, the sole one which has available a sufficient stock of observations to allow the construction of laws. It is political economy which must serve as the home and to some extent as the mother of the other sociological sciences. Even now some of its laws can be considered as regulating types of relationships other than those of economic gain. For example, the division of labor and the specialization of functions, are these not to be found in the science of marriage, the science of the family, and even in the science of religions? What is the note between priests and their flock save a form of the division of labor and the specialization of functions? The same holds good for the other sociological sciences. Other economic laws which are applicable are the law of supply and demand and the law of capital.

The speaker said that he could not end this brief exposition on sociology without saying a few words about Auguste Comte, who is held to be the founder of this science. But Auguste Comte did not create it, for it still does not yet exist. At the risk of causing a scandal, Limousin claims that Auguste Comte was not a scientist in the sense of a man who knows about natural phenomena. He who deprecated metaphysics was solely a metaphysician, a metaphysician in the same category as the mystics, as he demonstrated by the creation of a religion whose key dogma was the symbol of the "Virgin Mother." Auguste Comte was not a sociologist, although he was the inventor of this defectively formed word. He was a socialist, for his "sociocracy" is not an objectively constructed system concerning the state of present or past societies, but a Utopia in the style of those of Saint-Simon, Fourier, Pierre Leroux, Cabet, Le Play, etc. The speaker did not dispute that he [Comte] made some interesting remarks with the aim of buttressing his system. In particular, there is his basic theory, termed positivism; but if he had had the honor of formulating it, it may be said that it had been in the air since the end of the eighteenth century, since the time of Lavoisier. If Auguste Comte had not done so, someone else would have formulated it, because it was imperative to do so. Other socialists of the same era have also made discoveries: Fourier, Saint-Simon and Pierre Leroux in particular.

---

* Extract from *Bulletin de la société d'économie politique*, April 4, 1908, pp. 64–73.

174

What demonstrates that Auguste Comte did not possess a scientific mind is the singular judgment that he passes on political economy. He had not understood it at all. As regards sociology, it is all the more exact that he did not create it because the science does not yet exist; we perceive it, but we do not know it; we are called upon to construct it.

The difficulty raised by the question posed, said Durkheim, is that the facts with which political economy deals and those which are the object of the other social sciences seem at first sight to be very different in nature. Ethics and law, which are the subject matter of determinate social sciences, are essentially questions of opinion. Without bothering about knowing whether a legal or ethical system exists which is valid for all men, a metaphysical question which has no place here, it is absolutely certain that, at every moment of history, the sole moral and juridical precepts that have been really brought into practice by men are those that the public consciousness, namely public opinion, has recognized as such. Law and ethics only exist in the ideas of mankind: they are ideals. As much may be said about the religious beliefs and practices which are closely linked to them, and aesthetic phenomena, which in certain aspects are social ones, which can, and are beginning to be studied in effect from the sociological viewpoint. Thus all the sciences which correspond to these various orders of facts—the comparative sciences of ethics, law, religion and the arts—deal with ideas. On the contrary, wealth, which is the object of political economy, consists of things which are apparently essentially objective and seemingly independent of opinion. Then what connection can there be between two orders of facts so heterogeneous? The only conceivable one is that these external, objective and almost physical realities studied by the economist should be considered as the basis and the underpinning of all the rest. Hence the theory of economic materialism which makes economic life the substructure of all social life. Among the other sociological disciplines, economic science may exert a veritable hegemony.

The speaker nevertheless believed that economic facts can be considered from a different viewpoint. To a degree that he did not seek to determine, they too are a matter of opinion. The value of things, in fact, depends not only upon their objective properties, but also upon the opinion one forms of them. Doubtless this opinion is partly determined by these objective properties, but it is subject also to many other influences. Should religious opinion proscribe a particular drink—wine, for example,—or a particular kind of meat (pork), then wine and pork lose, wholly or in part, their value in exchange. In the same way it is the fluctuations in opinion and taste which give value to a particular material or a particular precious stone rather than to another, to a particular kind of furniture or style, etc. Influence is also felt in another way. Rates of pay depend upon a basic standard which corresponds to the minimum amount of resources needed for a man to live. But this standard, in every era, is fixed by public opinion. What was regarded yesterday as a sufficient minimum no longer satisfies the requirements of the moral conscience of today, simply because we are more affected than in the past by certain feelings of humanity. There are even forms of production which are tending to become general, not only because of their objective productivity, but by reason of certain moral virtues that public opinion ascribes to them: such, for example, is co-operation.

From this viewpoint, the relationships between the science of economics and the other social sciences present themselves to us in a different light. Both deal with phenomena which, at least when certain aspects are under consideration, are homogeneous, because in some respects they are all matters of opinion. Then one can conceive that moral, religious and aesthetic opinions can exert an influence upon economic opinion at least equal to that which economic opinion exerts upon them. This emerges clearly from the examples already quoted above. Political economy therefore loses that predominance which was once attributed to it, to become a social science like the others, closely linked to them in a solid relationship, without however being able to claim to direct them.

Yet, from another aspect, political economy does assume again a sort of primacy. Human opinions emerge from the midst of social groups and partly depend upon what these groups are. We know that opinion differs as between populations densely packed together and those which are dispersed, as between town and country, as between large and small towns, etc. Ideas change according to the density of the society, whether it is numerous or sparse, according to whether its communications or transport networks are numerous and rapid. But it seems certain that economic factors have a profound effect upon the way in which the population is distributed, its density, the form that human settlements take, and consequently upon the way that these factors often exert a profound influence upon the various states of opinion. It is above all in this indirect way, the speaker concluded, that economic facts act upon moral ideas.

Villey had no intention of speaking in this discussion. But he was, he stated, something of an economist and a lawyer and, in this dual capacity, he felt somewhat shocked by certain of the assertions that he had heard made.

Durkheim had said that law was a matter of opinion, that political economy and value were matters of opinion and that, for example, among Jews, pork ought to have very little value. Villey believed that Durkheim had got himself into a muddle. Opinion has a very great influence in the conception of the law and the sanctions it imposes. But it does not shape the law. It has a very great influence upon the conditions of the market, which affect value, but it does not determine value, which is determined by rigorous laws of nature.

Opinion has much influence upon the conception of the law and, for example, it is certain that some institutions have sometimes been considered to be in conformity with the law that are a clear violation of it, such as slavery. Opinion has influence upon the sanctions of the law; thus such and such an action which was prohibited in the past is allowed today, and vice versa. This is because social needs are not always the same. But to conclude from this that law is a matter of opinion, is quite simply to deny the law, to make it a pure concept of the mind, essentially fluctuating and fanciful, and this is to deliver over the fate of societies to the caprices of the pilot whom chance has given them.

Again, in the same way opinion has much influence upon market conditions. This is why pork may have been depreciated in Jewish territory, just as fish must be sold dearer on Fridays in Catholic territory. But it is always the law of supply and demand, completely independent of opinion, which regulates the price of things, just as it determines all values.

As for the question—perhaps a little theoretical—which had been posed, this was, according to the speaker, what one could reply. Social science is the science of man living in society; social life, like all life, may be analyzed according to certain rules in relation to a certain "movement"; this "movement," which consists of the unfolding of all individual activities, is the object of political economy; the rule, which consists in the limitation of individual activities, is the object of law, from which the speaker does not distinguish morality, since law is none other than morality in its application to social relationships; thus political economy and law appear to be the two essential branches of social science.

Durkheim could not make sense of the view felt and expressed by Villey. He had taken care to state that he was not dealing with the entirely metaphysical question of knowing whether morality existed, or an ideal law, inscribed in the nature of man, valid for all ages and all countries. He had spoken solely of law and morality as they existed, as they had been at any moment in history. Now it was absolutely clear that a people had never put into practice any moral and juridical precepts other than those which the public consciousness, that is to say, opinion, had recognized as such. If that opinion ceased to feel the weight of their authority, then that authority would be as if it no longer existed; it would no longer act upon the conscience; the precepts would no longer be obeyed. That is all the speaker [Durkheim] meant.

We had to be on our guard against the derogatory sense which is often given to the word "opinion." It almost seems as if it were synonymous with mindless prejudices or fanciful feelings, etc. This is to view opinion from only one of its aspects. It is to forget that opinion is also the end result of the experiences of peoples over the centuries—and that has imparted some authority to it. The speaker felt at least as much respect for a moral rule when he considered it to be the fruit of peoples' experience over the centuries as when he conceived it as the result of the dialectical constructs of the jurist and the moralist.

It is argued that opinion changes. But this is because morality changes also, and does so legitimately. Durkheim did not believe that many historians exist today who would admit that the Romans, for example, could have practiced a morality comparable to our own. The respect that we have for the human person could not have found a place in Rome without encompassing the dissolution of Roman society. Fustel de Coulanges long ago showed this to be true. The variations through which moral opinion passes are therefore not the product of mere aberrations but are founded on the changes which have occurred simultaneously in living conditions.

As for economic matters, the speaker did not state in any way that they were completely a matter of opinion, but that they too derived some *part* of reality from opinion. This would be sufficient to establish the thesis which he had advanced. His concern was solely to highlight *one aspect* of economic phenomena in which they were homogeneous with moral, juridical or religious facts, because it was on this condition that it became possible to perceive the relationships with the corresponding sciences.

The speaker ended by asserting that even less had he upheld the view that the laws of economic phenomena could be true or false just as opinion thought fit. That would simply be absurd. To say that facts are matters of opinion is not to say that there are no laws pertaining to them, for opinion itself has its laws which do not depend upon opinion.

Paul Leroy-Beaulieu, the chairman, in summing up the discussion, added a few personal remarks. He did not accept unreservedly the ideas elaborated by previous speakers. In his opinion Limousin was in theory correct: a science lacking any practical application will still remain a science which has interest for those with an inquiring mind. But doesn't the science of economics deserve great interest, given that its applications are so numerous and indisputable?

Political economy is at the present time the only social science of a really positive character. Consequently Leroy-Beaulieu would say to Durkheim that he appears to have exaggerated the influence of opinion on political economy. It is doubtless a powerful factor whose influence is to modify certain forms of the economy, but what it will never be able to transform are the great economic laws which are immutable. It is true that one cannot deny the intervention of a psychological element, for example, in the determination of value, but the latter will none the less be forever subject to the essential law of supply and demand.

Again, in the same way the law of the division of labor cannot be modified by opinion. And the division of labor will always be proportionate to the extent of the market, inevitably less developed in a limited country such as Portugal than in a greater one like Germany.

Another principle which opinion will never overtopple is the necessity for a progressive society to have capital available to it, in order at least to apply the new discoveries . . .

Leroy-Beaulieu concludes that political economy is plainly objective, at least in regard to its main laws. And these laws have the force of physical laws. Have we not seen fail all the riots of the Revolution, all the decrees establishing a maximum price and creating other hindrances to the free play of the principles of our science, in the face of the great economic law of supply and demand, the only one today, however, which is really understood by everybody?

Summing up, political economy occupies the first place among the social sciences: it alone rests upon a basis that is indestructible and positive, and its laws are immutable, whatever the variations of opinion.

The Contribution of Sociology to Psychology and Philosophy (1909)*

Some misunderstanding has often arisen regarding the way in which we conceive the relationship between sociology and psychology on the one hand, and between sociology and philosophy on the other. The explanations given above will perhaps assist in dispelling some of these misapprehensions.

Because we have been intent on distinguishing the individual from society we have sometimes been reproached with wanting to set up a sociology which, indifferent to all that relates to man, would confine itself to being the external history of institutions. The very purpose we have assigned our work demonstrates how unjustified this reproach is. If we propose to study religious phenomena, it is in the hope that the study will throw some light on the religious nature of man, and the science of morals must finally end in explaining the moral conscience. In a general manner we deem that the sociologist will not have completely accomplished his mission so long as he has not penetrated the inmost depths of individuals, in order to relate to their psychological condition the institutions of which he gives an account. To tell the truth—and this is doubtless what gave rise to the misunderstanding to which we are referring—man is less for us the point of departure than the point of arrival. We do not start by postulating a certain conception of human nature, in order to deduce a sociology from it; it is rather the case that we demand from sociology an increasing understanding of humanity. As the general traits of our mentality, in the way they are studied by the psychologist, are by hypothesis common to men of every age and land, they are likewise too abstract and indeterminate to be capable of explaining any particular social form. It is society which imparts to them that varying degree of determinateness that it requires to sustain itself. It is society which informs our minds and wills, attuning them to the institutions which express that society. Consequently it is with society that the sociologist must begin. But if for this reason, as he embarks upon his investigation, he appears to distance himself from man, it is because he intends to return to him and succeed in understanding him better. For in so far as man is a product of society, it is through society

* Extract from *Revue de métaphysique et de morale*, 17, 1909, pp. 754–8, being the third section of an article entitled "Sociologie religieuse et théorie de la connaissance," which, minus the text translated here, served as Introduction to Durkheim's *The Elementary Forms of the Religious Life* (1912).

that man can be explained. Thus far from sociology, so conceived, being a stranger to psychology, it arrives itself at a psychology, but one far more concrete and complex than that of the pure psychologists. Finally, history is for us only a tool for analyzing human nature.

Likewise, because for methodological reasons we have tried to remove sociology from the tutelage of philosophy, which could only hinder it from growing into a positive science, we have sometimes been suspected of a systematic hostility toward philosophy in general or, at the very least, of having a more or less exclusive sympathy for a narrow empiricism in which—not moreover unreasonably—was to be seen only a philosophy of minor consequence. This is to impute to us an attitude that is scarcely sociological. For the sociologist must proceed from the axiom that the questions which have been raised in the course of history can never cease to exist; they can indeed be transformed but they cannot die out. Metaphysical problems, even the boldest ones which have wracked the philosophers, must never be allowed to fall into oblivion, because this is unacceptable. Yet it is likewise undoubtedly the case that they are called upon to take on new forms. Precisely because of this we believe that sociology, more than any other science, can contribute to this renewal.

Nowadays it is universally agreed that philosophy, unless it relies upon the positive sciences, can only be a form of literature. On the other hand, as scientific studies break up and become more specialized, it is increasingly evident that the philosopher's task is an impossible one if he cannot embark upon his task of synthesis until he has mastered the encyclopedia of human knowledge. Under such conditions, the philosopher has only one resort left: to discover a science which, while sufficiently limited to be encompassed by a single mind, nevertheless occupies in relation to the totality of things a sufficiently central position to provide the basis for speculative thought which is integrated, and therefore philosophical. The sciences of the mind are alone capable of fulfilling this condition. Since for us the world exists only in so far as it is represented to us, in one sense the study of the subject includes as well the study of the object. Thus it does not appear impossible, seeing things from the viewpoint of mind, for us to take in the universe as a whole without the necessity, in so doing, of amassing an encyclopedic culture, which it is henceforth unrealistic to attempt. However, the individual consciousness possesses this capacity for synthesis only very imperfectly and is consequently unfit for this role. However wide-ranging our experience and knowledge may be, each one of us can only represent to himself an infinitesimal part of reality. It is the collective consciousness which is the true microcosm. It is in the civilization of an era—the totality made up of its religion, science, language and morality, etc.—that is realized the perfectly complete system of human representations at any given moment in time. Now civilization is eminently a social matter, being in fact the product of co-operative effort. It assumes that the succession of generations are linked to each other, and this is only possible in and through society. Indeed, it can only be sustained by groups, since every individual mind never expresses it save in an entirely fragmentary and incomplete way. None can master in its entirety the system of his time, whether it be religious, moral, juridical or scientific. Thus only on condition that he considers it from the viewpoint of the collective mind can the philosopher hope to perceive the unity of things; from this it follows that, to put it at its lowest, sociology is for him the most useful of all preparatory studies.

However, the bonds which link these two disciplines can be determined with still greater precision.

As we have seen, among our representations there are some which play a preponderant role: these are categories. They dominate thought because they sum it up; the whole of civilization is condensed in them. If the human mind is a synthetic expression of the world, the system of categories is a synthetic expression of the human mind. Thus there is no object more appropriate to philosophical thinking. Comparatively limited, and thereby amenable to investigation, it in some way includes the universality of things. Thus the study of categories appears destined increasingly to become the central concern of philosophical speculation. This indeed is what the recent disciples of Kant have realized[1] in assigning to themselves as their principal task the constitution of the system of categories and the discovery of the law which makes of them a unity. Yet, if the origin of categories is as we have attributed it, we cannot treat them according to the exclusively dialectical and ideological method at present employed. So that we can elaborate them philosophically, regardless of how this elaboration is conceived, we must first know what they are, of what they are constituted, what elements enter into their makeup, what has determined the fusion of these elements into complex representations, and what has been the role of these representations in the history of our mental constitution. These questions appear to raise no difficulty, and do not even arise, if we believe that the individual mind itself assigns categories by an act peculiar to itself; for then, to know what they are and what relationships they entertain with one another and with the whole of intellectual life subordinated to them, it is apparently sufficient for the mind to engage in a careful interrogation of itself. The law governing this dialectic is in the mind. It is therefore believed that the mind has only to grasp it intuitively, on the condition that it verifies it later, when it is applied. But if the categories are the net result of history and collective action, if their genesis is one in which each individual has only an infinitesimal share and which has even occurred almost beyond his own field of observation, we must indeed, if we seek to philosophize about things rather than words, begin by confronting these categories as if faced with unknown realities whose nature, causes and functions have to be determined before we seek to integrate them into a philosophical system. To do this a whole series of investigations must be undertaken, investigations which, as we have shown, depend upon sociology. This is how that science is destined, we believe, to provide philosophy with the indispensable foundations which it at present lacks. One may even go so far as to say that sociological reflection is called upon to expand further, in a natural progression, in the form of philosophical thinking. All the indications are that, approached from this viewpoint, the problems with which the philosopher deals will assume more than one unexpected aspect.

Note

1. But for reasons partially different from those we have set out. For these philosophers categories shape reality beforehand, while for us they sum it up. According to them they are the natural law of thought; for us they are the product of human artifice. Yet from both viewpoints they express synthetically thought and reality.

Social Morphology (1899)*

Before analyzing the works we have grouped together under the above title, we must first state the meaning of the term.

Social life rests upon a substratum determinate in both size and form. It is made up of the mass of individuals who constitute society, the manner in which they have settled upon the earth, the nature and configuration of those things of all kinds which affect collective relationships. The social substratum will differ according to whether the population is of greater or lesser size and density, whether it is concentrated in towns or scattered over rural areas, according to the way in which towns and houses are constructed, whether the space occupied by a society is more or less extensive, according to the nature of the frontiers which enclose it and the avenues of communication which cross it. On the other hand, the constitution of this substratum directly or indirectly affects all social phenomena, just as all psychological phenomena are linked either obliquely or immediately to the condition of the brain. Thus here is a whole range of problems plainly of interest to sociology which must derive from the same science, since they all refer to one and the same object. It is this science which we propose to call *social morphology*.

The studies that deal with these questions at present relate to different disciplines. Geography studies the territorial configuration of states, history retraces the evolution of rural and urban groups, while demography deals with all matters concerning the distribution of population, etc. We believe it advantageous to draw these fragmentary sciences out of their isolation, letting them establish contact with each other by assembling them under one single rubric. They will thereby become conscious of their unity. Later we shall see how a school of geographers is at present attempting to effect a somewhat analogous synthesis under the title of *political geography*. Yet we fear that this term may give rise to misunderstandings. In fact the need is not to study the forms of the earth, but the very different forms which societies assume when they are established upon the earth. Doubtless the watercourses and mountains etc. play a part as elements in the constitution of the social substratum. But they are not the sole ones, nor even the most vital ones. The use of the word geography inevitably inclines us to ascribe to them an importance which they do not possess, as we shall have

---

* "Morphologie sociale," *Année sociologique*, 2, 1899, pp. 520–1.

occasion to note. The number of individuals, the manner in which they are grouped together, the form their dwellings take—these are in no way geographical facts. Why therefore preserve a term so greatly distorted from its normal sense? For these reasons some fresh designation appears to us a necessity. The one we suggest has clearly the advantage of highlighting the unified nature of the object on which all these researches are centered, namely, the perceptible, material forms of societies—in fact, the nature of their substratum.

Moreover, social morphology does not consist of a mere science of observation, which would describe forms without accounting for them. It can and must be explanatory. It must investigate under what conditions the political territory of peoples varies, the nature and configuration of their boundaries, and the differing population densities. It must inquire how urban communities have arisen, what their laws of evolution are, how they grow, and what role they play, etc. Thus social morphology does not merely study the social substratum as it has already been formed, in order to analyze it by description. It observes it as it is evolving, in order to show how it is being formed. It is not a purely static science, but quite naturally includes the movements from which result the states it studies. Thus, like all other branches of sociology, history and comparative ethnography provide indispensable adjuncts.

Civilization in General and Types of Civilization (1902)*

In current practice the term "general sociology" is unfortunately employed with a total lack of precision. It commonly serves to designate a kind of speculation which relates, without distinction and arbitrarily, to the most varied categories of social phenomena, and which consequently touches upon all kinds of questions. In a word it is characterized by hardly anything save the extreme indeterminateness of its object. The majority of the works that we review every year under this rubric present only too frequently this character. Yet general sociology could and should be something different. While every special sociological science deals with a determinate species of social phenomena, the role of general sociology might be to reconstitute the unity of all that is dissected by analysis in this way. The problems to which it should address itself with this aim in view are in no way vague or indecisive; they can be formulated in perfectly well-defined terms and are capable of being treated methodically.

From this viewpoint, one should particularly ask how a society, which is however only a composite of relatively independent parts and differentiated organs, can nevertheless form an individuality endowed with a unity which is analogous to that of individual personalities. Very possibly one of the factors which most contributes to this result is that poorly analyzed complex which is termed the civilization appropriate to each social type and even, more especially, to each society. This is because there is in every civilization a kind of tonality *sui generis* which is to be found in all the details of collective life. This is why we have grouped here those works whose purpose is to determine the different types of civilization.

The character of peoples is another factor of the same kind. In a society, as in an individual, the character is the central and permanent nucleus which joins together the various moments of an existence and which gives succession and continuity to life. This is why we have brought together in one chapter, which is to be found immediately after the one that follows, everything which concerns collective ethnology. Moreover, it can be divined that the question of types of civilization and that of types of collective characters must be closely linked.

---

* "Civilisation en général et types de civilisation," *Année sociologique*, 5, 1902, pp. 167–8.

The Method of Sociology (1908)*

I do not need to reply to the first of the questions which you do me the honor of posing. Naturally I believe that the present movement in sociology opens up vistas for the future discovery of the laws of social evolution, for I cannot but have faith in the usefulness of the task to which, with so many others, I have devoted my life.

As for the method appropriate to be used, two words may serve to characterize it: it must be historical and objective.

Historical: The purpose of sociology is to enable us to understand present-day social institutions so that we may have some perception of what they are destined to become and what we should want them to become. Now in order to understand an institution we must first know its composition. It is a complex entity made up of various parts. These parts must first be known, so that later each one may be explained. But in order to discover them, it is not enough to consider the institution in its perfected and most recent form. Nothing gives us an indication as to the various elements of which it is made up, just as we cannot perceive with the naked eye the cells from which are formed the tissues of living matter or the molecules which make up crude substances. Some instrument of analysis is necessary in order to render them visible. It is history which plays this role. In fact any institution being considered has been formed piecemeal. The parts which constitute it have arisen in succession. Thus it is sufficient to follow its genesis over a period of time, in the course of history, in order to perceive in isolation, and naturally, the various elements from which it results. Thus in the order of social realities history plays a role analogous to that of the microscope in the order of physical realities.

It not only distinguishes these elements for us, but is the sole means of enabling us to account for them. This is because to explain them is to demonstrate what causes them and what are the reasons for their existence. But how can they be discovered save by going back to the time when these causes and reasons operated? That time lies behind us. The sole

---

* Extract from *Les documents du progrès*, 2, February 1908, pp. 131–3. Reply to an "*enquête sur la sociologie*" (questionnaire concerning sociology) in which two questions were asked: (i) Is it possible to draw conclusions, on the basis of the development so far accomplished with sociological studies, with respect to the future discovery of laws of development and causal relations in social life? (ii) By what method will sociology be able to attain that result?

means of getting to know how each of these elements arose is to wait upon their birth. But that birth occurred in the past, and can consequently only be known through the mediation of history.

Objective: By this I mean that the sociologist must take on the state of mind of the physicists, chemists and biologists when they venture into a territory hitherto unexplored, that of their scientific field. He must embark upon the study of social facts by adopting the principle that he is in complete ignorance of what they are, and that the properties characteristic of them are totally unknown to him, as are the causes upon which these latter depend. By the methodical comparison of the historical data, and by this alone, he will evolve the notions appropriate to them. It is true that such an attitude is difficult to sustain, for it goes against ingrained habits. Since we live our life in society, we possess some representation of these notions, and we are inclined to believe that with such usual representations we have seized what is essential in the things to which they relate. But these notions, because they have been developed unmethodically in order to satisfy needs that are of an exclusively practical nature, are devoid of any scientific value. They no more exactly express social things than the ordinary person's ideas of substances and their properties (light, heat, sound, etc.) exactly represent the nature of these substances, which science alone reveals to us. Thus they are so many idols, as Bacon said, from which we must free ourselves.

This very fact will cause us to perceive the inanity of simplistic explanations which would account for social facts by declaring that they derive directly from some of the most general traits of human nature. This is the method followed when we think to explain the family by the feeling aroused by blood relationship, paternal authority by the sentiments that a father naturally feels for his offspring, marriage by sexual instinct and contract by an inborn sense of justice, etc. If collective phenomena were so great a function of human nature, instead of their presenting the infinite diversity revealed to us in history, they would be in all times and places perceptibly similar to one another, for the characteristics that have gone to make up man have varied only very little. This is why I have frequently reiterated that individual psychology cannot explain social facts for us. This is because these psychological factors are much too general to be capable of accounting for what is specific in social life. Such explanations, because they are applicable to everything, in fact apply to exactly nothing.

But this conception is far from entailing some kind of materialism or another, with which I have often been reproached. Those who have leveled this reproach at me have singularly misunderstood my thinking. In social life, everything consists of representations, ideas and sentiments, and there is nowhere better to observe the powerful effectiveness of representations. Only collective representations are much more complex than individual ones: they have a nature of their own, and relate to a distinctive science. All sociology is a psychology, but a psychology *sui generis*.

I would add that in my belief this psychology is destined to give new life to many of the problems posed at the present time by purely individual psychology and even have repercussions on the theory of knowledge.

Society (1917)*

On *society*:

The great difference between animal societies and human societies is that in the former, the individual creature is governed exclusively from *within itself*, by the instincts (except for a slight degree of individual education, which itself depends upon instinct). On the other hand human societies present a new phenomenon of a special nature, which consists in the fact that certain ways of acting are imposed, or at least suggested *from outside* the individual and are added on to his own nature: such is the character of the "institutions" (in the broad sense of the word) which the existence of language makes possible, and of which language itself is an example. They take on substance as individuals succeed each other without this succession destroying their continuity; their presence is the distinctive characteristic of human societies, and the proper subject of sociology.

* Extract from *Bulletin de la Société française de philosophie*, 15, 1917, p. 57

The Psychological Character of Social Facts and Their Reality (1895)*

Bordeaux, 179, Boulevard de Talence, December 14, 1895

Dear Colleague,

Thank you very much for the kind thought you had of sending me your book. I read it with great interest, or rather re-read it, for I had followed your articles in the *Revue de Métaphysique*. Moreover, I have had the opportunity to see that it was appreciated by everybody, as it deserves. It is a study which cannot fail to bring great honor to us on the other side of the Rhine; and by showing the Germans with what care and kind feeling we are studying them, it will perhaps bring them to display more interest in what we are doing. For—and I do not know whether I am mistaken—it seems to me that Germany is committing the same error as we did before 1870 by shutting itself off from the outside world.

Thank you also for the attention you have paid to my own studies and for the great courtesy of your very interesting discussion. It is very difficult to reply to you by letter; however desirous I am to bridge the distance which separates us or appears to separate us, and although I think this to be very possible, I would not wish to assail you with arguments under the pretext of thanking you. I must however point out to you one or two points where I have not succeeded in putting across to you my ideas.

1. I have never said that sociology contains nothing that is psychological and I fully accept your formulation on p. 151, namely that it is a psychology, *but distinct from individual psychology*. I have never thought otherwise. I have defined social facts as acts and representation, but *sui generis*; I have said that the social being was a psychological individuality, but one of a new kind (p. 127). Yet once this is postulated I conclude that one has no right to treat collective psychology as an extension, an enlargement or a new illustration of individual psychology. Would this be the point at which you cease to follow me? Yet it seems to me that once the principle is postulated the consequence necessary follows.

---

* Letter to Celestin Bouglé, reprinted in *Revue française de sociologie*, 17, 2, 1976, pp. 166–7.

191

2. What is there realist about saying that *in the facts* (and not outside them) there exists a category which presents special characteristics, which consequently must be abstracted from the real to be studied separately? How is this to hypostasize them? Allow me to refer you to what I say on this subject in the note on p. 127.

    Moreover, you seem yourself to have a very strong sentiment of the specificity of social facts. Hence how are we not in agreement about the two essential points stated above and which, in the end, are only one? But these are those which I most strongly adhere to.

3. I have not heard it said that tendencies, needs, etc. are not factors of development (cf. p. 119); but to explain the changes which have this as their origin, the tendencies themselves must have changed and, for this to be, we must look outside them for the causes which have brought this about.

Please forgive these explanations. By showing you how much I wish to be understood by you, they only prove the high esteem in which I hold your book. Please do not regard them in any other light.

I am, etc.

The Nature of Society and Causal Explanation (1898)*

Bordeaux, February 6, 1898

Dear Colleague,

I have made it a rule to profit from the criticisms that may be made of my work, without replying directly to them, save when the ideas discussed in relation to myself are so foreign to me that I must disavow them in order to prevent substantive errors from gaining credence. Up to now this has only occurred once during my career. But the article that your contributor, Monsieur Tosti, devotes to me in your January issue forces me for a second time to speak out.

According to the author, I have failed to realize that "a compound is explained both by the character of its elements and by the law which governs their combining together"; and he is astounded that a logician such as myself could have been able to perpetrate such an enormity. To put an end to this astonishment I need only refer him to the following passages in my book:

1. "The intensity [of tendencies productive of suicide] can only depend on the three following kinds of causes: (1) *The nature of the individuals who make up society*; (2) the way in which they are associated together, namely the nature of the social organization; (3) the passing events which disturb the functioning of collective life without changing its anatomical constitution" (*Le suicide*, p. 363).

2. "*It is very true that society comprises no active forces other than those of individuals*"; but individuals, as they join together, form a psychological entity of a new species . . . "*No doubt the elementary properties from which results the social fact are contained in embryo within the minds of individuals. But the social fact only emerges when they have been transformed by association . . . Association is—it too—an active factor which produces special effects*" (ibid. p. 350).

---

* Letter to the Editor, *American Journal of Sociology*, 3, 1898, pp. 848–9, and *Année sociologique*, 2, pp. 348–9.

Thus I do not deny in any way that individual natures are the components of the social fact. What must be ascertained is whether as they combine together to produce the social fact, they are not transformed by the very fact of their combination. Is the synthesis purely mechanical, or chemical? This is the heart of the question; your contributor does not appear to suspect this.

Since I am also led to intervene, I should like to say a word about another objection, which, following Monsieur Bosco, he also makes. "If," he says, "you find no definite relationship between suicide and non-social factors, you have no right to conclude there is none; for the same social fact may be the product of many causes." There is nothing more certain than this. But the fact remains that, when I compare suicide to social factors, I find definite relationships in spite of this plurality of causes. Also, when I compare it to cosmic, ethnic factors, etc., I no longer find such relationships. Hence it follows that if the latter factors are operating, their effect is extremely weak, since it disappears from the overall results. On the contrary, the social causes must be extremely powerful to affect the statistics so clearly. That was all I wanted to say.

I would be very obliged if you would publish this letter in your next issue.

I am, etc.

The Psychological Conception of Society (1901)*

Dear Editor,

In the course of his recent article on "La réalité sociale," in a note which was moreover very kind to me and for which I am grateful to him, Monsieur Tarde remarks that since the foundation of the *Année sociologique*, "I have drawn much closer to the psychological conception of social facts." As I would not desire, by keeping silent, to give credence to an inexact interpretation of my thought, I would be very obliged if you would give the hospitality of the *Revue* to the few following lines.

If, by the somewhat vague expression he uses, Monsieur Tarde is referring to the theory according to which social facts may be explained immediately by the states of the individual consciousness, I must emphasize that not a single word of mine must be understood in this sense. I continue to see between *individual* psychology and sociology the same demarcation line, and the numerous facts which every year we have to record in the *Année sociologique* only serve to confirm my view in this respect.

If Monsieur Tarde simply means that for me social life is a system of representations and mental states, provided that it is clearly understood that these representations are, *sui generis*, different in nature from those which constitute the mental life of the individual and subject to their own laws which individual psychology could not foresee, then this view is indeed mine. Indeed, it has been at all times my own view. I have repeated a number of times that to place sociology outside individual psychology was simply to say that it constituted a *special psychology*, having its own subject matter and a distinctive method.

Precisely because the misunderstandings that have accumulated about this question are increasingly being dispelled, I deem it essential that they should not grow up once more. This is the reason and the excuse for this letter.

I am, etc.

---

* Letter to the Directeur, *Revue philosophique*, 52, 1901, p. 704.

The Role of General Sociology (1905)*

Dear Sir,

Thank you for sending me the observations called forth by our communications to the Sociological Society. I am glad to see, by the number and importance of the answers received, the interest the question has aroused.

I should have wished, in turn, to reply to some of my critics; but for that, the compilation of a considerable essay would be needed; and I cannot, for the moment, entertain this idea by reason of total lack of leisure.

However, many of the criticisms seem to me to rest on a misinterpretation. I was especially concerned to combat the conception—still too widely accepted—which makes sociology a branch of philosophy, in which questions are only considered in their most schematic aspect, and are attacked without specialized competence. Consequently I urged, above all, the need for a systematic specialization, and I indicated what this specialization should be. But I am far from denying that, above these particular sciences, there is room for a synthetic science, which may be called general sociology, or philosophy of the social sciences. It belongs to this science to disengage from the different specialist disciplines certain general conclusions, certain synthetic conceptions, which will stimulate and inspire the specialist, which will guide and illuminate his researches, and which will lead to ever-fresh discoveries, resulting, in turn, in further progress of philosophical thought, and so on, indefinitely.

If I have somewhat neglected this aspect of the question, it is because of the special object in view in my paper. However, I have purposed, for more than two years past, to develop this idea in an essay which would be the sequel and complement of the one summarized for the Sociological Society. Unfortunately lack of time hitherto necessitated the postponement of this project, and I do not know when it will be possible to put it into practice. But if at length I am enabled to publish this second part of my work, I shall be only too happy to lay it—as in the first case—before the Sociological Society.

I am, etc.

---

* "Letter from Professor Durkheim in reply to criticisms," to the Secretary, the Sociological Society, *Sociological Papers* for 1904 (London, Macmillan, 1905), p. 257.

Influences upon Durkheim's View of Sociology (1907)*

Paris, October 20, 1907

Dear Director,

Somewhat belatedly and by chance I have received a copy of an article which appeared in one of the recent numbers of your *Revue*, under the signature of Monsieur Simon Deploige, entitled "The genesis of Monsieur Durkheim's system."

I am grateful to your contributor for the honor he does me in occupying himself with so much care and scholarship in the reconstitution of the genesis of my ideas, as he conceives it. But without his having wished it, he has happened occasionally to use a language which is of a kind that might cause your readers to believe that I have made, in a carefully disguised form, some borrowings from German writers.

On page 352, after having reproduced an argument which I used in a paper given to the Société Française de Philosophie, Monsieur Deploige adds: "This reasoning is quite simply taken from the theory of Monsieur Wundt on moral ends"; and a long note follows designed to establish the reality of this borrowing. This demonstration was indeed useless since I had indicated myself in a note—and your contributor is not unaware of it—to whom I was indebted for this argument and from which work of Wundt's I had taken it.

Elsewhere (p. 334) he writes: "All these views . . . pass in France as being Monsieur Durkheim's own. But they are all of German origin." It would have been difficult to express it differently if one wished to make out that I had deceived my fellow-countrymen.

As for all these German works of which Monsieur Deploige speaks, it was I who had made them known in France; it was I who showed how, although they were not the work of sociologists, they could none the less serve the advancement of sociology. Indeed, I rather exaggerated than played down the importance of their contribution (cf. *Revue philosophique*, Nos. of July, August, September, 1887 and *passim*). Thus

---

* Two letters to the Directeur, *Revue néo-scolastique* (Louvain) 14, 1907, pp. 606–7 and 612–14.

197

I provided the public with all the elements needed to evaluate it. Your contributor knows this as well as I do.

I rely on your spirit of fair play to publish this letter of correction in your *Revue*.

Yours, etc.

P.S. Monsieur Deploige's article moreover contains some grave and indisputable errors. I certainly owe a great deal to the Germans, as I do to Comte and others. But the real influence that Germany has exerted upon me is very different from what he asserts.

Paris, November 8, 1907

Dear Sir,

I give below some examples of the errors contained in Monsieur Deploige's article.

1. Page 353: Your contributor asserts that an idea that I developed in a lecture given at the Ecole des Hautes Etudes was borrowed from Simmel's *Einleitung in die Moralwissenschaft*, a work, Monsieur Deploige adds, which "is hardly known in France outside Monsieur Durkheim's circle." Monsieur Deploige has made a mistake: I have never read Simmel's *Einleitung*; of this author I only know his *Arbeitsteilung* and his *Philosophie des Geldes*.

2. Several times I am depicted as having gone to Germany to follow the teachings of Wagner and Schmoller; and I am alleged to have returned from this journey completely imbued with their ideas and utterly transformed by their influence.

   Now, during the semester I spent in Germany, I neither saw nor heard Schmoller or Wagner; and I have never sought to follow their teachings, nor even to have personal contact with them, even though I did remain for some time in Berlin.

   I would add that I am only very moderately in sympathy with the work of Wagner; and as for Schmoller, among all his works I have only studied carefully and with interest the brochure entitled *Einige Grundfragen der Rechts- und Volkswirtschaftslehre*.

3. Nothing could be more untrue than to attribute to the influence of Schaeffle the conception which Monsieur Deploige terms social realism. It came to me directly from Comte, Spencer and Espinas, whom I knew long before I knew Schaeffle. Monsieur Deploige implies, it is true, that if it is to be found in Espinas, it is because he was "very well informed about German sociological literature." I do not think I am

being at all indiscreet in letting Monsieur Deploige know that Espinas only learned German very late on. In any case it is certain that he did not know of Schaeffle when he wrote his *Sociétés animales*. The note in which the German author is mentioned was added in the second edition of his book.

4. I am alleged to have borrowed from Wundt the distinction which I attempted to establish between sociology and psychology. I do not dispute that there is a tendency in this direction in Wundt, but it is also mingled with opposing tendencies. But the idea came to me from elsewhere.

   I owe it first to my mentor, Monsieur Boutroux, who at the *Ecole normale supérieure* often used to repeat to us that "every science must explain its own principles," as Aristotle states: psychology by psychological principles, biology by biological principles. Very much imbued with this idea, I applied it to sociology. I was confirmed in this method by reading Comte, since for him sociology cannot be reduced to biology (and consequently to psychology), just as biology is irreducible to the physical and chemical sciences. When I read the *Ethik* of Wundt I had been tending in that direction for a long time already.

5. On p. 343, note 1, it is stated that I found in Wundt the idea that religion is the matrix of moral and juridical ideas, etc. I read Wundt in 1887: but it was only in 1895 that I had a clear view of the capital role played by religion in social life. It was in that year that, for the first time, I found a means of tackling sociologically the study of religion. It was a revelation to me. That lecture course of 1895 marks a watershed in my thinking, so much so that all my previous research had to be started all over again so as to be harmonized with these new views. The *Ethik* of Wundt, which I had read eight years previously, played no part in this change of direction. It was due entirely to the studies of religious history which I had just embarked upon, and in particular to the works of Robertson Smith and his school.

I could quote other examples of errors or inaccuracies. It is true that I lay no claim whatsoever to some impossible originality. I am indeed convinced that my ideas have their roots in those of my predecessors; and it is precisely because of this that I have some confidence in their fruitfulness. But their origins are completely different from what Monsieur Deploige thinks. All in all, I prefer to distance myself from the socialism of the chair, which itself has no sympathy for sociology, the principle of which it denies. It is therefore paradoxical to maintain that my work has sprung from it. I certainly have a debt to Germany, but I owe much more to its historians than to its economists and—something which Monsieur Deploige does not seem to suspect—I owe at least as much to England. But this does not mean that sociology has come to us from either country, for the German jurists and economists are hardly less strangers to the sociological idea than are the English historians of religions. My aim has been precisely to introduce that idea into those disciplines from which it was absent and thereby to make them branches of sociology.

I would not dream of attributing too great an importance to the question of knowing how my thinking has been formed, but since it has been discussed in your *Revue*, I have no doubt that you will deem it useful to acquaint your readers with the errors which have occurred, errors which do not concern only details.

I am, etc.

Index

n = endnote.

abnormality, 100(n23), 116–17
  "can evolve," 66(n1)
  Garofalo, 66–67(n4)
  "signifies that a being is in an inferior
    state," 57, 66–67(n4), 117
abstraction process, 142
adults, 52, 56, 87
advanced societies/higher societies, xvii,
  xxvii, 74
  "civilized peoples," 45
  identifying the "normal," 58–59,
    67(n7–8)
  See also civilization
age, 24, 27(n2), 52, 58, 108, 116
  variations must be taken into account
    (in order to state whether a fact is
    normal or not), 56, 116
agreement, *see* method of agreement
agrégation, xxxvi
agriculture, 77(n10), 124
alchemy, 30
  search for philosopher's stone, 135,
    156(n7)
altruism, xiv, xvii, 62
American Journal of Sociology, 193n
anachronism, vii, xxiv, xxvi
"anatomical elements"
  "arranged in space," xvi
ancestors, 11, 40, 76
Anderson, B., xx
animal life, 99(n18), 125
  See also collective life
animal societies
  versus human societies, 190
animal species, xxvi, 89, 107
animals, 11, 43, 44, 76, 88
Année sociologique (1898–1913), xi,
  xxxvii–xxxviii, 6–7, 77(n10),

156(n19), 157(n28), 184n, 186n,
  193n, 195
anomie, xiv, xvii, xxix
anthropocentricity
  "blocks path to science," 15–16
anthropology/anthropologists, xxi,
  149–50
anti-Semitism, xxxix
Arabs, 89
Araucanians, 73
Arbeitsteilung (Simmel), 198
arch or Kabyle tribe, 74
aristocracy/nobility, 127, 144
Aristotle, 131, 199
Aron, R., xl
art, 35, 51, 124, 128, 149, 151
arts, 30, 77(n10), 89
Aryans, 89, 150
association, 86–87, 91, 98, 112, 126,
  139–40, 142–44, 193
  "for common purpose," xviii
  "determining condition for social
    phenomena," 91
  differences in, 86
  Simmel, 143
"associations" (Rousseau), xviii
Athens, xxxi, 64, 73, 74, 75, 108
Australia, 150
  aborigines, 74, 171
average type, 55–56, 57, 59, 60

Bachofen, J. J., 150
Bacon, F. (Viscount St. Albans), xiii,
  30–31, 48(n1), 188
  theory of idols, 39
Bancroft, H. H., 150, 157(n24)
Barbier, E., 49(n15)
Bechuanas, 73

201